( ( speak my name ) )

# (( speak my name ))

BLACK MEN ON MASCULINITY AND THE AMERICAN DREAM

EDITED BY
DON BELTON

BEACON PRESS
BOSTON

Beacon Press
25 Beacon Street
Boston, Massachusetts 02108-2892

Beacon Press books
are published under the auspices of
the Unitarian Universalist Association of Congregations.

99 98 97 96 95    8 7 6 5 4 3 2 1

Text design by John Kane
Composition by Wilsted & Taylor

Library of Congress Cataloging-in-Publication Data

Speak my name: Black men on masculinity and the American dream /
    edited with an introduction by Don Belton; with a foreword by
    August Wilson.
          p.   cm.
    Includes bibliographical references.
    ISBN 0-8070-0936-9
    1. Afro-American men.    2. Masculinity (Psychology)—United States.
    I. Belton, Don.
    E185.86.S685   1995
    155.8'496073'0081—dc20                                95-22316
                                                               CIP

Our father's thoughts come shining down.
—Traditional

This book is dedicated to the Spirit.
In the name of Papa Legba,
James Baldwin,
Jack Johnson, Kid Thompson, Countee Cullen,
Langston Hughes, Sidney Bechet, Thomas Dorsey,
John Coltrane, Romare Bearden, Ralph Ellison, Duke Ellington,
Larry Young, Melvin Dixon, Jackie Wilson, Bruce Nugent, Alvin Ailey,
Frankie Lymon, Huey Newton, David Walker, Sun Ra, Sam Cooke,
Dexter Gordon, Prophet Jones, Harold Jackman, Eddie Kendricks,
Joseph Beam, Marvin Gaye, Oscar Micheaux, Beauford Delaney,
Marlon Riggs, Richard Wright, Frederick Douglass,
Thelonious Monk, Staggerlee, Arthur H. Fauset,
Will Marion Cook, Prophet Cherry, Reverend James Cleveland,
and Reverend Doctor Gates.
In the name of mercy,
ancestors, mysteries, and friends.

Father, I stretch my hand to Thee
No other help I know . . .
—Traditional

# Contents

Contents

# Foreword

## August Wilson

The first male image that I carry is not of my father but of a family friend and neighbor, Charlie Burley, the brilliant Hall of Fame prizefighter. A combination of intelligence, the handsome yet bruised face, the swollen knuckles embodying the speed and power and grace of his rough trade, the starched white shirt, the embossed silk tie, the cashmere coat, the exquisite felt fur of the broad-brimmed quintessential hundred-dollar Stetson (the kind Staggerlee wore), and the highly polished yam-colored Florsheim shoes that completed his Friday night regalia. It was style with a capital S. But it was more than being a connoisseur of fine haberdashery; it was attitude and presentation. The men on the corner with their big hats and polished shoes carried and lent weight to a world that was beholden to their casual elegance as they mocked the condition of their life and paraded through the streets like warrior kings.

If men are warriors, then as black men we are warriors of a subject people whose history and relationship with the society in which we live has been a long and troubled one, involving, among other things, murder and mayhem. Reduced to its most fundamental truth, black men are a commodity of flesh and muscle which has lost its value in the marketplace. We are left over from history.

Out of the historical rubble of slavery, fired in the kiln of evolution and survival, black men like Charlie Burley forged and honed new disciplines and elevated their presence into an art. They were bad. If only in an abstract of style. A language of aesthetics that created its own rules and knew no limits. They styled because that is who they were. The style was not a comment. It was not how they saw themselves. It was who they were, and it was symphonic in its breadth and complexity. The style became all. It was the reason for being. And if they stumbled on their way to victory, the occasion had presented them with the possibility, however brief, that in one brilliant blaze of style and substance they might transform and forever enlarge the possibilities of what might exist. They might, by the sheer power of their presence, enlarge the universe.

It is clear that the idea we have of ourselves is drastically different from the images propagated and promoted by nineteenth-century Europe and twentieth-century America. What we lack is the ability to give the ideas and images we have of ourselves a widespread presence, to give them legitimacy and credence in the same manner in which the debasing and denigrating images that provide other Americans with a basis for their fear and dislike of us are legitimized by constant repetition through myriad avenues of broadcast and dissemination. That those images remain consistently unchallenged is one of our greatest failures as men charged with the defense of the body politic. Our ignorance of the value and the power of image as a contributing and determining factor in our condition—and most importantly in our future—is most telling in the cruel flowering of self-hate as evidenced by the suicidal bullets of misplaced rage and mock anarchy.

As men, we are charged with the defense of the race, of the ethnic tribes of our genetic marrow. We are charged with propagation and we are charged with the advancement of prosperity. But where as men do we find sustenance? In what place of our fathers, when from our father's house issues the prodigal who squanders the body's abilities? If our fathers faltered on the stairs to self-determination, we did not falter on the stairs to honor. Their courage has never been lacking. Our understanding of the processes that usurped and bludgeoned their identities, that deprived them of continuity, of their sense of history and well-being, has not been full and comprehensive. Depriving us of our language not only deprived us of a tool necessary for organizing and communicating ideas about the self and the world, it also deprived us of our understanding of our duty and the celebration of heroics.

Our duty as black men is to alter the relationship of power and responsibility. To move from the hull of a ship, so to speak, to a self-determining, self-respecting, and self-defending people. It is black men who bear the burden of the political reality of our powerlessness. To the extent that our powerlessness lessens our ability to defend and develop ourselves, that burden becomes intolerable. The heft we carry on the basketball courts and the football fields, the brawn and boldness in the boxing rings, does not translate into political heft. For too long we have been victims of political circumstance, and our failures of political will have left us standing at the levee, beholden to the roustabouts and pontificating on the virtues of poverty and victimization.

Our traverse of the continent in search of jobs and security in our homes and our persons has not met with welcome or success. We have borne the brunt of America's paranoia. Our brace of songs, our faithful hearts, and fruitful penises have enabled our survival despite the rampant hostilities we encounter. If the atlas of our geography is muted, it is not lacking the boldness of our imagination and our invention. We have traversed the soil of North America, bringing advantage to it as farmer, mule trainer, singer, shaper of wood and iron. We have picked cotton and shined shoes, we have bludgeoned the malleable parts of ourselves into new and brash identities that are shattered and bruised by the gun and the bullet. And now the only duty our young men seem ready to imagine is to their maleness with its reckless display of braggadocio, its bright intelligence, its bold and foolish embrace of hate and happenstance. If we are not our brother's keeper then we are still our brother's witness. We are co-conspirator in his story and in his future.

This is the breach into which the writers of the present volume boldly step. They bear witness. They bring testimony. They give voice and vent to our history. They recall those occasions when we did speak our names in the clandestine confines of the slave quarters where our music and manners were our own property and our names defined our character and our culture. Where our speech and remark of each other's names was a political act. They are proof that if we do not squander our inheritance, if we maintain the fervor of the acolyte and the fierce intelligence of the zealot, we can all speak our names on and on, into the last night of a universe already suspect and falling.

Finally, this book was brought to port by steady hands, an accurate compass and the furious rejection of anything resembling compromise. I salute the editor.

# Acknowledgments

I wish to thank everyone who supported the completion of this book. I am deeply grateful to *Speak My Name*'s authors, each of whom I consider a brother and a benefactor. I thank every writer who responded to the call for submissions for this anthology. Unfortunately, neither the limitations of space nor the book's thematic progression permitted me to use all the fine contributions I received. To those who provided their support and solidarity throughout this journey, I say thank you: Patrice Gaines, David Leeming, Florence Ladd, James Campbell, Glenn Ligon, Shay Youngblood, Eve Kosofsky Sedgwick, Michele Wallace, Eleanor Wilner, Charles Johnson, Gloria Wade-Gayles, Joseph Brochin, Philip Patrick, Elaine Shelly, and Patricia Bell-Scott. David Bradley, Gloria Naylor, Rashidah Ismaili, Michael Thelwell, Marita Golden, and the late Doris Jean Austin provided invaluable introductions to writers. Thank you, Deborah Chasman, Tisha Hooks, and Jonathon Aubry: I could not have done this without you.

# Introduction: Speak My Name

## Don Belton

At the 1992 Republican National Convention, presidential candidate Pat Buchanan announced there is a cultural war going on in America. Buchanan's dispatch had all the sweep and dimension of news that remains news. Indeed, America has been the site of cultural warfare for a very long time. The essential truth in Buchanan's announcement can be excavated all the way back to our nation's inception, when we were not yet even a nation but a colony.

The incredible burst of industry and imagination that created America during the seventeenth and eighteenth centuries gave birth to a nation paradoxically poised both to fulfill a potential as ancient as humanity itself and quite possibly to destroy all traces of humanity as it had previously been known.

It has now become a fairly well-accepted fact that the making of America demanded the murder of millions of Indians. Nationally, we mythologize this violence as an event occurring somewhere in the remote past, but the true legacy of our past requires our nation to re-enact those murders every day in order to perpetuate the mythic basis for America. As Americans, we, each of us as citizens, daily collect our measure of material privilege and psychic pain from this enduring violence. Still, it is perhaps our incorruptability as humans, if not our real heroism, that makes us continue to believe in the possibility of redemption. The consuming project of America went on to turn African children, women, and men into slaves, and turned those slaves into citizens, even prototypical or quintessential *Americans*.

The violence that gave birth to our nation is not especially unique in the annals of nation-making. The entire created world is either the result of warfare in heaven or the result of a riotous "big bang," depending on your preference for religious or scientific lore. According to the biblical writer Matthew, even the kingdom of heaven "allows violence, and the violent bear it away." The nature of the cultural warfare at the heart of the ongoing American experiment is the spiritual violence of a nation at war with its own soul, daily reproducing its own destruction and redemption. Though our national print, TV, and movie industries keep us entertained and terrorized with a vision of a world rent with senseless violent acts, there is actually evidence to support a belief that, on the whole, Americans live unprecedentedly long, safe, and materially rich lives. Yet, as Americans, we live in a virtual atmosphere of violence and the fear of violence.

Historically, the black male body has been scapegoated in the cultural imagination to represent the violence we fear as a nation. The irony in this, of course, is that the black male body has perhaps endured the most sustained and brutal punishment of all in the building of our nation, and all for the existential crime of being black instead of white. During the first quarter of this century, the public hanging, castration, and burning of black men was not only a regular event in the South and the Midwest but a public rite and form of civic entertainment. As Louis Armstrong sang, "What did I do to be so black and blue?" Indeed. As this century ends, black men have already been named an "endangered species" in popular and academic discussion. The national discussion about black men's lives is very often one in which the voices of black men are marginalized or silenced—one in which the only authorized voices are those of the "experts" such as journalists, sociologists, undertakers, policemen, and politicians.

In the early eighteenth century something amazing occurred, a seemingly simple thing that in reality was every bit as dramatic as the shift occurring around 10,000 B.C., when humanity went from a simpler agricultural base to the kind of civilization that could produce the Pyramids. That amazing thing was this: by the eighteenth century, within Christianity there was a new tradition in the depiction of the warrior angel Michael subduing Satan; around this time, Satan, who previously had been portrayed alternately as a dragon or as a white man twisting in chains beneath the blond Michael's feet, acquired a black face. This change coincided with the rise of America and the consolidation of the American myth of whiteness. It also parallels the white domination of Africa. Historically, there is no notion of racial whiteness before the appearance of this image of a black man chained and writhing beneath a white man's feet.

To consider, then, Buchanan's cultural war for what it is, consider this: I am a black man born into what was, in the late 1950s, Philadelphia's premier integrated neighborhood. I was a toddler lying in my mother's lap when John Kennedy's motorcade rode down our block carrying Kennedy to the presidency, trailing hope. That same neighborhood now lies stunned and vanquished, surrounded by abandoned factory buildings. I was born the third son of a man who worked himself to death, a man from whom I inherited a legacy of masculine silence about one's own pain going back seven generations. My father fought in the Second World War and daily faced both humiliation and physical torture by his white comrades in order to defend his nation. My father was not a political man, but shortly after the assassination of Martin Luther King, Jr., my father called my elementary school to have me officially excused for the day and took me to the remnant of Dr. King's Poor People's March when it passed through Philadelphia.

Despite the legacy of slavery, an institution that destroyed not only the agency of the father but also his name, I still can follow my male lineage back to a triple great-grandfather in Virginia in the early nineteenth century. What I know of this man is that he rode like a god and taught three generations of white men horsemanship and hunting, as well as the general deportment of a gentleman. I know that what dignity those white men acquired, whoever they were, they learned from the tutelage of a black man who could teach dignity because his race had lost everything and still had the heroism to recreate itself in a lost new world.

I know that it is a corrupt and meretricious lie that America is built mostly on the work and ingenuity of white men. It is also a lie that black men for the first centuries of this nation's life only picked cotton and led mules, though certainly you don't have an America without the plain labor and love of black men. I know that black men like my great-great-great-grandfather Albert Stone authored the myth of whiteness as much as did their white "masters," long before the waves of German, then Irish, then Jewish immigrants achieved the American shore to become "white" by learning to pronounce the stinging epithet "nigger."

I am one man. While I speak from a position of black and American masculinity, I am not a representative for these positions. The black man is not a monolith. There is no *the* black man. There could not be, anymore than there could be any such person as *the* white man. These are cultural myths, and yet these myths are important metaphors for power in a country still poised for either fulfilling a momentous human potential or destroying the world.

This current anthology, *Speak My Name*, grew out of my own impetus to experience a richer sense of community and communion among other black male writers and to share and apply that experience in a larger context. During the process of developing, collecting, and editing the material for this anthology I have traveled a lot. While issuing from Saint Paul, Minnesota, where I have lived and taught literature and fiction writing at a small liberal arts college, this project has also traveled with me on my first trips to Africa, Brazil, Italy, Ireland, England, France, and the Netherlands. Though I have called myself an American since I could speak, the first time I can remember being called an American *first* was in France. Africa is the only place I have been so far where being black and male is a normative experience. There, I experienced an enormous sense of relief to find that the combination of my race and gender was not enough in itself to victimize or vilify me. My work on the anthology also formed the basis of a literature course I taught, called "Black Masculinity," using race and masculinity to generate new readings of Western texts from Shakespeare's *Tempest* to Defoe's *Robinson Crusoe*. During the early stages of work on this book, my father died suddenly. The morning after I completed writing *Voodoo for Charles* for this anthology, my eldest brother shot himself to death more than a thousand miles from my writing room. I have been sustained in large measure by the fellowship that produced the book you now hold. In a way not fully understood, this book is imprinted with my life over the past few years.

When I began working on *Speak My Name*, to my best knowledge there had not been an anthology to take on the specificity and diversity of black men's lives. I edited this anthology because I personally required it in order to better understand how black men have changed since the 1960s, to better understand how those three intervening decades have *required* change of black men. At this critical hour, no one seems to know who black men are beyond a narrow mainstream representation in which it seems they can only be superathletes, superentertainers, or supercriminals. I needed to help expand and humanize that range, not only for the sake of a generation of young black men who are now making their dangerous passage into manhood, but for an entire nation and a world more intimately connected and interdependent than ever before.

*Speak My Name* is the first mainstream anthology of contemporary black men's writing. Most of the stories, essays, and personal narratives collected here were written specifically in response to my call for contributions; others are anthologized here for the first time. As for the title, within black American culture from the time of slavery, telling someone to "speak my name" has held a challenge to tell the truth about the interlocutor's deepest attributes. Names exist to counteract confusion of identity or location. The phrase also enacts a request to be held in remembrance during a time of crisis. It is a means of saying we are people with proper names and distinctive faces and familial pasts.

In structuring the book, I thought of jazz music's compositional model of theme and variation, giving my contributors a series of extended solos that develop toward visions of masculinity as a struggle for hope. Their narrative performances move through attempts to come to terms with stereotypes and vested notions of masculinity to pieces about specific relationships, to broader connections with community, and, finally, to celebration. Here is a replete ensemble of well-known authors, often in uncharacteristic voice. You will also hear some new voices along the way, illuminated by the pure pleasure of new writers reaching, hitting, and holding their notes.

*Speak My Name* does not culminate in a definitive statement about black men or America. Rather it deals with a complex set of questions from which I trust will spring dialogue and even healing. Neither is *Speak My Name* a protest. It counts the mercurial wages and gifts of laughter, love, and rage. It is an assessment of the intense beauty and dread of physical and spiritual landscapes. It is a broadcast of personal witness and triumph, and, for me personally, a true instance of grace.

# ( ( part one ) )

HOW DOES IT FEEL TO BE A PROBLEM?

# How Does It Feel to Be a Problem?

Trey Ellis

> How does it feel to be a problem?
> —W. E. B. Du Bois

Du Bois was putting words into the mouth of a white questioner. No one ever actually came out and asked him to answer them. No one has ever actually come out and asked me, either, yet I know that many are itching to. I know I would be. Black men are this nation's outlaw celebrities. It doesn't matter what other modifiers also describe our individual essences—mechanic, police officer, left-handed, Virginian, kind, gangbanger, tall—"black man" overrides them all and makes us all, equally, desperadoes. My friends and I sometimes take perverse pride in the fear the combination of our sex and skin instills in everyone else—the taxis that bolt past us as our arms wave high over our meticulously coiffed heads, the receptionists who mistake us for suit-wearing bike messengers, the cops who clutch their .45s when they see us saunter out of Häagen-Dazs. Imagine the weird power you'd feel if you were a bank teller, a postal worker, or a postmodern novelist who is able to make a cop quake with fear and call for backup. Unfortunately, these expectations can get to us after a while. Listen to black comedian Franklin

Ajaye: "I was walking down the street last night and this old white couple kept looking back at me like I was going to rob them. . . . So I did."

Don't get me wrong. I know that black men commit a disproportionate number of America's crimes. In fact, I need to know that, since murder at the hands of another black man is the leading cause of death in my age group. Ironically, black men have more right than anyone else to run and hide when other black men head our way on the sidewalk. Yet we don't (most of us, anyway), because we bother to separate the few bad from the legion of good.

American society as a whole, however tars us all with the same brush. We have become the international symbol for rape, murder, robbery, and uncontrolled libido. Our faces on the news have become synonymous with anger, ignorance, and poverty.

Increasingly, America seems to be painting us into two corners. In one, we're the monsters they've always said we were. In the other corner, we're fine but all those other black men are monsters; we are anointed honorary whites so long as we abandon every trace of our ethnicity.

Black conservatives such as Shelby Steele espouse individual liberation through assimilation. In one way, he is absolutely correct. It is irrefutable that if we African Americans abandoned our culture, stopped griping, and joined the melting pot, we would be better off. The catch is the very real limit to our ambition. If we play by Steele's rules—work hard, scrimp, save, and study—then one day one of us just might become vice president of the United States. Therein lies the rub. In this land of opportunity we can be promised riches, a degree of respect, and respectability, but we know we are still barred from the highest corridors of power. It's a crippling message. How can you expect someone to dedicate his entire life to training for the Olympics if all he can hope for is a silver medal?

Drug dealing and other criminal activities are the only pursuits that offer us unlimited possibilities. Since we are already vilified anyway, goes the twisted logic, at least the sky's the limit in that arena. I'm not making excuses for the black criminal—I despise him for poisoning and shooting more of my people than the cowardly Klan ever did. But we need to understand him as a human being if we're ever going to save him, or at least save his younger brother or his son.

When black folks mention slavery the rest of America yawns. But our country, with its history as the home of the slave, has yet to reconcile that legacy with its reputation as the land of the free. Slavery was as evil an act as ever committed by anyone on the planet. Nazis, the Khmer

Rouge—that's not the sort of company Americans like to kee
may seem like ancient history to whites, but it doesn't to blac
problems have deep roots, and until we understand the dark
history, our nation will never pull itself out of its current ra

If, in American popular culture, black signifies poor, ignorant, and angry, then white signifies upper-middle-class, educated, and moderate.
From "Ozzie & Harriet" to "Home Improvement," upper-middle-class
white households are passed off as average white families. The lives of
white folks are cleaned up and idealized. Popular culture assumes you will
attend some sort of college, own a home, and marry the mother of your
child. You are defined by the richest, handsomest, smartest, and kindest
among you. We are defined by our worst. Although seventy-five percent
of black men never have anything to do with the criminal justice system,
we are looked on as anomalies, freaks of nature, or, worse, thugs-in-
waiting.

Sadly, black people are starting to believe the bad press. If we string
two sentences together, other black folks say, "Oh my, how well-spoken
he is." If we are married to the mothers of our children, Delores Williams,
a black activist in Los Angeles, hands us a certificate and invites us to an
awards banquet. So little is expected of us that even our half-efforts are
wildly and inappropriately praised.

Finally, and curiously, some of the stereotypes that make us seem the
least human—and the most animalistic—also make us seem the most
male. We are famous around the world for our physical and sexual po-
tency. And what is more at the essence of stereotypical machismo than
bulging muscles and big dangling balls? Although we hate being America's villains, it's not always all bad—in America, villains have always
been perversely revered.

# Confessions of a Nice Negro, or Why I Shaved My Head

## Robin D. G. Kelley

It happened just the other day—two days into the new year, to be exact. I had dashed into the deserted lobby of an Ann Arbor movie theater, pulling the door behind me to escape the freezing winter winds Michigan residents have come to know so well. Behind the counter knelt a young white teenager filling the popcorn bin with bags of that awful pre-popped stuff. Hardly the enthusiastic employee; from a distance it looked like she was lost in deep thought. The generous display of body piercing suggested an X-generation flowerchild—perhaps an anthropology major into acid jazz and environmentalism, I thought. Sporting a black New York Yankees baseball cap and a black-and-beige scarf over my nose and mouth, I must have looked like I had stepped out of a John Singleton film. And because I was already late, I rushed madly toward the ticket counter.

The flower child was startled: "I don't have anything in the cash register," she blurted as she pulled the bag of popcorn in front of her for protection.

"Huh? I just want one ticket for *Little Women*, please—the two-fifteen show. My wife and daughter should already be in there." I slowly gestured to the theater door and gave her one of those innocent childlike glances I used to give my mom when I wanted to sit on her lap.

"Oh god . . . I'm so sorry. A reflex. Just one ticket? You only missed the first twenty minutes. Enjoy the show."

Enjoy the show? Barely 1995 and here we go again. Another bout with racism in a so-called liberal college town; another racial drama in which I play the prime suspect. And yet I have to confess the situation was pretty funny. Just two hours earlier I couldn't persuade Elleza, my four-year-old daughter, to put her toys away; time-out did nothing, yelling had no effect, and the evil stare made no impact whatsoever. Thoroughly frustrated, I had only one option left: "Okay, I'm gonna tell Mommy!" Of course it worked.

So those five seconds as a media-made black man felt kind of good. I know it's a product of racism. I know that the myth of black male violence has resulted in the deaths of many innocent boys and men of darker hue. I know that the power to scare is not real power. I know all that—after all, I study this stuff for a living! For the moment, though, it felt good. (Besides, the ability to scare with your body can come in handy, especially when you're trying to get a good seat in a theater or avoid long lines.)

I shouldn't admit this, but I take particular pleasure in putting fear into people on the lookout for black male criminality mainly because those moments are so rare for me. Indeed, my *inability* to employ black-maleness as a weapon is the story of my life. Why I don't possess it, or rather possess so little of it, escapes me. I grew up poor in Harlem and Afrodena (the Negro West Side of Pasadena/Altadena, California). My mom was single during my formative preadolescent years, and for a brief moment she even received a welfare check. A hard life makes a hard nigga, so I've been told.

Never an egghead or a dork, as a teenager I was pretty cool. I did the house-party circuit on Friday and Saturday nights and used to stroll down the block toting the serious Radio Raheem boombox. Why, I even invaded movie theaters in the company of ten or fifteen hooded and high-topped black bodies, colonizing the balconies and occupying two seats per person. Armed with popcorn and Raisinettes as our missiles of choice, we dared any usher to ask us to leave. Those of us who had cars (we called them hoopties or rides back in that day) spent our lunch hours and precious class time hanging out in the school parking lot, running down our Die Hards to pump up Cameo, Funkadelic, Grandmaster Flash from our car stereos. I sported dickies and Levis, picked up that gangsta stroll, and when the shag came in style I was with it—always armed with a silk scarf to ensure that my hair was laid. Granted, I vomited after drinking malt liquor for the first time and my only hit of a joint ended abruptly in an asthma attack. But I was cool.

Sure, I was cool, but nobody feared me. That I'm relatively short with dimples and curly hair, speak softly in a rather medium to high-pitched voice, and have a "girl's name" doesn't help matters. And everyone knows that light skin is less threatening to white people than blue-black or midnight brown. Besides, growing up with a soft-spoken, uncharacteristically passive West Indian mother deep into East Indian religions, a mother who sometimes walked barefoot in the streets of Harlem, a mother who insisted on proper diction and never, ever, ever used a swear word, screwed me up royally. I could never curse right. My mouth had trouble forming the words—"fuck" always came out as "fock" and "goddamn" always sounded like it's spelled, not "gotdayum," the way my Pasadena homies pronounced it in their Calabama twang. I don't even recall saying the word "bitch" unless I was quoting somebody or some authorless vernacular rhyme. For some unknown reason, that word scared me.

Moms dressed me up in the coolest mod outfits—short pant suits with matching hats, Nehru jackets, those sixties British-looking turtlenecks. Sure, she got some of that stuff from John's Bargain Store or Goodwill, but I always looked "cute." More stylish than roguish. Kinda like W. E. B. Du Bois as a toddler, or those turn-of-the-century photos of middle-class West Indian boys who grow up to become prime ministers or poets. Ghetto ethnographers back in the late sixties and early seventies would not have found me or my family very "authentic," especially if they had discovered that one of my middle names is Gibran, after the Lebanese poet Kahlil Gibran.

Everybody seemed to like me. Teachers liked me, kids liked me; I even fell in with some notorious teenage criminals at Pasadena High School because *they* liked me. I remember one memorable night in the ninth grade when I went down to the Pasadena Boys' Club to take photos of some of my partners on the basketball team. On my way home some big kids, eleventh-graders to be exact, tried to take my camera. The ringleader pulled out a knife and gently poked it against my chest. I told them it was my stepfather's camera and if I came home without it he'd kick my ass for a week. Miraculously, this launched a whole conversation about stepfathers and how messed up they are, which must have made them feel sorry for me. Within minutes we were cool; they let me go unmolested and I had made another friend.

In affairs of the heart, however, "being liked" had the opposite effect. I can only recall having had four fights in my entire life, all of which were with girls who supposedly liked me but thoroughly beat my behind. Sadly, my record in the boxing ring of puppy love is still 0–4. By the time I graduated to serious dating, being a nice guy seemed like the root of all my romantic problems. I resisted jealously, tried to be understanding, brought flowers and balloons, opened doors, wrote poems and songs, and seemed to always be on my knees for one reason or another. If you've ever watched "Love Connection" or read *Cosmopolitan*, you know the rest of the story: I practically never had sex and most of the women I dated left me in the cold for roughnecks. My last girlfriend in high school, the woman I took to my prom, the woman I once thought I'd die for, tried to show me the light: "Why do you always ask me what I want? Why don't you just *tell* me what you want me to do? Why don't you take charge and *be a man*? If you want to be a real man you can't be nice all the time!"

I always thought she was wrong; being nice has nothing to do with being a man. While I still think she's wrong, it's an established fact that our culture links manhood to terror and power, and that black men are frequently imaged as the ultimate in hypermasculinity. But the black man as the prototype of violent hypermasculinity is as much a fiction as the happy Sambo. No matter what critics and stand-up comics might say, I know from experience that not all black men—and here I'm only speaking of well-lighted or daytime situations—generate fear. Who scares and who doesn't has a lot to do with the body in question; it is dependent on factors such as age, skin color, size, clothes, hairstyle, and even the sound of one's voice. The cops who beat Rodney King and the jury who acquitted King's assailants openly admitted that the size, shape, and color of his body automatically made him a threat to the officers' safety.

On the other hand, the threatening black male body can take the most incongruous forms. Some of the hardest brothas on my block in West Pasadena kept their perms in pink rollers and hairnets. It was not unusual to see young black men in public with curlers, tank-top undershirts, sweatpants, black mid-calf dress socks, and Stacey Adams shoes, hanging out on the corner or on the basketball court. And we all knew that these brothas were not to be messed with. (The rest of the world probably knows it by now, too, since black males in curlers are occasionally featured on "Cops" and "America's Most Wanted" as notorious drug dealers or heartless pimps.)

Whatever the source of this ineffable terror, my body simply lacked it. Indeed, the older I got and the more ensconced I became in the world of academia, the less threatening I seemed. Marrying and having a child also reduced the threat factor. By the time I hit my late twenties, my wife,

Diedra, and I found ourselves in the awkward position of being everyone's favorite Negroes. I don't know how many times we've attended dinner parties where we were the only African Americans in the room. Occasionally there were others, but we seemed to have a monopoly on the dinner party invitations. This not only happened in Ann Arbor, where there is a small but substantial black population to choose from, but in the Negro mecca of Atlanta, Georgia. Our hosts always felt comfortable asking us "sensitive" questions about race that they would not dare ask other black colleagues and friends: What do African Americans think about Farrakahn? Ben Chavis? Nelson Mandela? Most of my black students are very conservative and career-oriented—why is that? How can we mend the relations between blacks and Jews? Do you celebrate Kwanzaa? Do you put anything in your hair to make it that way? What are the starting salaries for young black faculty nowadays?

Of course, these sorts of exchanges appear regularly in most black autobiographies. As soon as they're comfortable, it is not uncommon for white people to take the opportunity to find out everything they've always wanted to know about "us" (which also applies to other people of color, I'm sure) but were afraid to ask. That they feel perfectly at ease asking dumb or unanswerable questions is not simply a case of (mis)perceived racelessness. Being a "nice Negro" has a lot to do with gender, and my peculiar form of "left-feminist-funny-guy" masculinity—a little Kevin Hooks, some Bobby McFerrin, a dash of Woody Allen—is regarded as less threatening than that of most other black men.

Not that I mind the soft-sensitive masculine persona—after all, it is the genuine me, a product of my mother's heroic and revolutionary child-rearing style. But there are moments when I wish I could invoke the intimidation factor of blackmaleness on demand. If I only had that look—that Malcolm X/Mike Tyson/Ice Cube/Larry Fishburne/Bigger Thomas/Fruit of Islam look—I could keep the stupid questions at bay, make college administrators tremble, and scare editors into submission. Subconsciously, I decided that I had to do something about my image. Then, as if by magic, my wish was fulfilled.

Actually, it began as an accident involving a pair of electric clippers and sleep deprivation—a bad auto-cut gone awry. With my lowtop fade on the verge of a Sly Stone afro, I was in desperate need of a trim. Diedra didn't have the time to do it, and as it was February (Black History Month), I was on the chitlin' lecture circuit and couldn't spare forty-five minutes at a barber shop, so I elected to do it myself. Standing in a well-lighted bathroom, armed with two mirrors, I started trimming. Despite a steady hand and what I've always believed was a good eye, my hair turned out lopsided. I kept trimming and trimming to correct my error, but as my flattop sank lower, a yellow patch of scalp began to rise above the surrounding hair, like one of those big granite mounds dotting the grassy knolls of Central Park. A nice yarmulke could have covered it, but that would have been more difficult to explain than a bald spot. So, bearing in mind role models like Michael Jordan, Charles Barkley, Stanley Crouch, and Onyx (then the hip-hop group of the hour), I decided to take it all off.

I didn't think much of it at first, but the new style accomplished what years of evil stares and carefully crafted sartorial statements could not: I began to scare people. The effect was immediate and dramatic. Passing strangers avoided me and smiled less frequently. Those who did smile or make eye contact seemed to be deliberately trying to disarm me—a common strategy taught in campus rape-prevention centers. Scaring people was fun for a while, but I especially enjoyed standing in line at the supermarket with my bald head, baggy pants, high-top Reeboks, and long black hooded down coat, humming old standards like "Darn That Dream," "A Foggy Day," and "I Could Write a Book." Now *that* brought some stares. I must have been convincing, since I adore those songs and have been humming them ever since I can remember. No simple case of cultural hybridity here, just your average menace to society with a deep appreciation for Gershwin, Rodgers and Hart, Van Heusen, Cole Porter, and Jerome Kern.

Among my colleagues, my bald head became the lead subject of every conversation. "You look older, more mature." "With that new cut you come across as much more serious than usual." "You really look quite rugged and masculine with a bald head." My close friends dispensed with the euphemisms and went straight to the point: "Damn. You look scary!" The most painful comment was that I looked like a "B-Boy wannabe" and was "too old for that shit." I had to remind my friend that I'm an OBB (Original B-Boy), that I was in the eleventh grade in 1979 when the Sugar Hill Gang dropped "Rapper's Delight," and that *his* tired behind was in graduate school at the time. Besides, B-Boy was not the intent.

In the end, however, I got more questions than comments. Was I in crisis? Did I want to talk? What was I trying to say by shaving my head? What was the political point of my actions? Once the novelty passed, I began getting those "speak for the race" questions that irritated the hell out of me when I had hair. Why have *black men* begun to shave their heads in greater numbers? Why have so many black athletes decided to shave their heads? Does this new trend have some kind of phallic meaning? Against my better judgment, I found myself coming up with answers to these questions—call it an academician's reflex. I don't remember exactly what I said, but it usually began with black prizefighter Jack Johnson, America's real life "baaad nigger" of the early twentieth century, whose head was always shaved and greased, and ended with the hip-hop community's embrace of an outlaw status. Whatever it was, it made sense at the time.

The publicity photo for my recent book, *Race Rebels*, clearly generated the most controversy among my colleagues. It diverged dramatically from the photo on my first book, where I look particularly innocent, almost angelic. In that first photo I smiled just enough to make my dimples visible; my eyes gazed away from the camera in sort of a dreamy, contemplative pose; my haircut was nondescript and the natural sunlight had a kind of halo effect. The Izod shirt was the icing on the cake. By contrast, the photograph for *Race Rebels* (which Diedra set up and shot, by the way) has me looking directly into the camera, arms folded, bald head glistening from baby oil and rear window light, with a grimace that could give Snoop Doggy Dogg a run for his money. The lens made my arms appear much larger than they really are, creating a kind of Popeye effect. Soon after the book came out, I received several e-mail messages about the photo. A particularly memorable one came from a friend and fellow historian in Australia. In the course of explaining to me how he had corrected one of his students who had read an essay of mine and presumed I was a woman, he wrote: "Mind you, the photo in your book should make things clear—the angle and foreshortening of the arms, and the hairstyle make it one of the more masculine author photos I've seen recently????!!!!!!"

My publisher really milked this photo, which actually fit well with the book's title. For the American Studies Association meeting in Nashville, Tennessee, which took place the week the book came out, my publisher bought a full-page ad on the back cover of an ASA handout, with my mug staring dead at you. Everywhere I turned—in hotel elevators, hallways, lobbies, meeting rooms—I saw myself, and it was not exactly a pretty sight. The quality of the reproduction (essentially a high-contrast xerox) made me appear harder, meaner, and crazier than the original photograph.

The situation became even stranger since I had decided to abandon the skinhead look and grow my hair back. In fact, by the time of the ASA meeting I was on the road (since abandoned) toward a big Black Power Afro—a retro style that at the time seemed to be making a comeback. Worse still, I had come to participate in a round-table discussion on black hair! My paper, titled "Nap Time: Historicizing the Afro," explored the political implications of competing narratives of the Afro's origins and meaning. Overall, it was a terrific session; the room was packed and the discussion was stimulating. But inevitably the question came up: "Although this isn't directly related to his paper, I'd like to find out from Professor Kelley why he shaved his head. Professor Kelley, given the panel's topic and in light of the current ads floating about with your picture on them, can you shed some light on what is attractive to black men about baldness?" The question was posed by a very distinguished and widely read African-American literary scholar. Hardly the naif, he knew the answers as well as I did, but wanted to generate a public discussion. And he succeeded. For ten minutes the audience ran the gamut of issues revolving around race, gender, sexuality, and the politics of style. Even the issue of bald heads as phallic symbols came up. "It's probably true," I said, "but when I was cutting my hair at three-o'clock in the morning I wasn't thinking 'penis.'" Eventually the discussion drifted from black masculinity to the tremendous workloads of minority scholars, which, in all honesty, was the source of my baldness in the first place. Unlike the golden old days, when doing hair was highly ritualized and completely integrated into daily life, we're so busy mentoring and publishing and speaking and fighting that we have very little time to attend to our heads.

Beyond the session itself, that ad continued to haunt me during the entire conference. Every ten minutes, or so it seemed, someone came up to me and offered unsolicited commentary on the photo. One person slyly suggested that in order to make the picture complete I should have posed with an Uzi. When I approached a very good friend of mine, a historian who is partly my Jewish mother and partly my confidante and *always* looking out for my best interests, the first words out of her mouth were, "Robin, I hate that picture! It's the worst picture of you I've ever seen. It doesn't do you justice. Why did you let them use it?"

"It's not that bad," I replied. "Diedra likes it—she took the picture. You just don't like my bald head."

"No, that's not it. I like the bald look on some men, and you have a very nice head. The problem is the photo and the fact that I know what kind of person you are. None of your gentleness and lovability comes out in that picture. Now, don't get a swelled head when I say this, but you have a delightful face and expression that makes people feel good, even when you're talking about serious stuff. The way you smile, there's something unbelievably safe about you."

It was a painful compliment. And yet I knew deep down that she was telling the truth. I've always been unbelievably safe, not just because of my look but because of my actions. Not that I consciously try to put people at ease, to erase conflict and difference, to remain silent on sensitive issues. I can't quite put my finger on it. Perhaps it's my mother's politeness drills? Perhaps it's a manifestation of my continuing bout with shyness? Maybe it has something to do with the sense of joy I get from stimulating conversations? Or maybe it's linked to the fact that my mom refused to raise me in a manner boys are accustomed to? Most likely it is a product of cultural capital—the fact that I *can* speak the language, (re)cite the texts, exhibit the manners and mannerisms that are inherent to bourgeois academic culture. My colleagues identify with me because I can talk intelligently about their scholarship on their terms, which invariably has the effect of creating an illusion of brilliance. As Frantz Fanon said in *Black Skin, White Masks*, the mere fact that he was an articulate *black* man who read a lot rendered him a stunning specimen of erudition in the eyes of his fellow intellectuals in Paris.

Whatever the source of my ineffable lovability, I've learned that it's not entirely a bad thing. In fact, if the rest of the world could look a little deeper, beyond the hardcore exterior—the wide bodies, the carefully constructed grimaces, the performance of terror—they would find many, many brothas much nicer and smarter than myself. The problem lies in a racist culture, a highly gendered racist culture, that is so deeply enmeshed in the fabric of daily life that it's practically invisible. The very existence of the "nice Negro," like the model-minority myth pinned on Asian Americans, renders the war on those "other," hardcore niggas justifiable and even palatable. In a little-known essay on the public image of world champion boxer Joe Louis, the radical Trinidadian writer C. L. R. James put it best: "This attempt to hold up Louis as a model Negro has strong overtones of condescension and race prejudice. It implies: 'See! When a Negro knows how to conduct himself, he gets on very well and we all love him.' From there the next step is: 'If only all Negroes behaved like Joe, the race problem would be solved.'"[1]

Of course we all know this is a bunch of fiction. Behaving "like Joe"

1. C. L. R. James, "Joe Louis and Jack Johnson," *Labor Action*, 1 July 1946.

was merely a code for deference and patience, which is all the more re-markable given his vocation. Unlike his predecessor Jack Johnson—the bald-headed prize fighter who transgressed racial boundaries by sleeping with and even marrying white women, who refused to apologize for his "outrageous" behavior, who boasted of his prowess in every facet of life (he even wrapped gauze around his penis to make it appear bigger under his boxing shorts)—Joe Louis was America's hero. As James put it, he was a credit to his race, "I mean the human race."[2] (Re)presented as a humble Alabama boy, God-fearing and devoid of hatred, Louis was con-structed in the press as a raceless man whose masculinity was put to good, patriotic use. To many of his white fans, he was a man in the ring and a boy—a good boy—outside of it. To many black folks, he was a hero be-cause he had the license to kick white men's butts and yet maintain the admiration and respect of a nation. Thus, despite similarities in race, class, and vocation, and their common iconization, Louis and Johnson ex-hibited public behavior that reflected radically different masculinities.

Here, then, is a lesson we cannot ignore. There is some truth in the implication that race (or gender) conflict is partly linked to behavior and how certain behavior is perceived. If our society, for example, could dis-pense with rigid, archaic notions of appropriate masculine and feminine behavior, perhaps we might create a world that nurtures, encourages, and even rewards nice guys. If violence were not so central to American cul-ture—to the way manhood is defined, to the way in which the state keeps African-American men in check, to the way men interact with women, to the way oppressed peoples interact with one another—perhaps we might see the withering away of white fears of black men. Perhaps young black men wouldn't feel the need to adopt hardened, threatening postures merely to survive in a Doggy-Dogg world. Not that black men ought to become colored equivalents of Alan Alda. Rather, black men ought to be whomever or whatever they want to be, without unwarranted criticism or societal pressures to conform to a particular definition of manhood. They could finally dress down without suspicion, talk loudly without surveillance, and love each other without sanction. Fortunately, such a transformation would also mean the long-awaited death of the "nice Ne-gro."

Not in my lifetime. Any fool can look around and see that the situation for race and gender relations in general, and for black males in particular,

---

2. Ibid.

has taken a turn for the worse—and relief is nowhere in sight. In the meantime, I will make the most of my "nice Negro" status." When it's all said and done, there is nothing romantic or interesting about playing Bigger Thomas. Maybe I can't persuade a well-dressed white couple to give up their box seats, but at least they'll listen to me. For now. . . .

# The Night I Was Nobody

## John Edgar Wideman

On July 4th, the fireworks day, the day for picnics and patriotic speeches, I was in Clovis, New Mexico, to watch my daughter, Jamila, and her team, the Central Massachusetts Cougars, compete in the Junior Olympics Basketball national tourney. During our ten-day visit to Clovis the weather had been bizarre. Hailstones large as golf balls. Torrents of rain flooding streets hubcap deep. Running through pelting rain from their van to a gym, Jamila and several teammates cramming through a doorway had looked back just in time to see a funnel cloud touch down a few blocks away. Continuous sheet lightning had shattered the horizon, crackling for hours night and day. Spectacular, off-the-charts weather flexing its muscles, reminding people what little control they have over their lives.

Hail rat-tat-tatting against our windshield our first day in town wasn't exactly a warm welcome, but things got better fast. Clovis people were glad to see us and the mini-spike we triggered in the local economy. Hospitable, generous, our hosts lavished upon us the same kind of hands-on affection and attention to detail that had transformed an unpromising place in the middle of nowhere into a very livable community.

On top of all that, the Cougars were kicking butt, so the night of July

3rd I wanted to celebrate with a frozen margarita. I couldn't pry anybody else away from "Bubba's," the movable feast of beer, chips, and chatter the adults traveling with the Cougars improvised nightly in the King's Inn Motel parking lot, so I drove off alone to find one perfect margarita.

Inside the door of Kelley's Bar and Lounge I was flagged by a guy collecting a cover charge and told I couldn't enter wearing my Malcolm X hat. I asked why; the guy hesitated, conferred a moment with his partner, then declared that Malcolm X hats were against the dress code. For a split second I thought it might be that *no* caps were allowed in Kelley's. But the door crew and two or three others hanging around the entranceway all wore the billed caps ubiquitous in New Mexico, duplicates of mine, except theirs sported the logos of feedstores and truck stops instead of a silver *X*.

What careened through my mind in the next couple of minutes is essentially unsayable but included scenes from my own half-century of life as a black man, clips from five hundred years of black/white meetings on slave ships, auction blocks, plantations, basketball courts, in the Supreme Court's marble halls, in beds, back alleys and back rooms, kisses and lynch ropes and contracts for millions of dollars so a black face will grace a cereal box. To tease away my anger I tried joking with folks in other places. Hey, Spike Lee. That hat you gave me on the set of the Malcolm movie in Cairo ain't legal in Clovis.

But nothing about these white guys barring my way was really funny. Part of me wanted to get down and dirty. Curse the suckers. Were they prepared to do battle to keep me and my cap out? Another voice said, Be cool. Don't sully your hands. Walk away and call the cops or a lawyer. Forget these chumps. Sue the owner. Or should I win hearts and minds? Look, fellas, I understand why the *X* on my cap might offend or scare you. You probably don't know much about Malcolm. The incredible metamorphoses of his thinking, his soul. By the time he was assassinated he wasn't a racist, didn't advocate violence. He was trying to make sense of America's impossible history, free himself, free us from the crippling legacy of race hate and oppression.

While all of the above occupied my mind, my body, on its own, had assumed a gunfighter's vigilance, hands ready at sides, head cocked, weight poised, eyes tight and hard on the doorkeeper yet alert to anything stirring on the periphery. Many other eyes, all in white faces, were checking out the entranceway, recognizing the ingredients of a racial incident. Hadn't they witnessed Los Angeles going berserk on their TV screens just a couple months ago? That truck driver beaten nearly to death in the street, those packs of black hoodlums burning and looting? Invisible lines were being drawn in the air, in the sand, invisible chips bristled on shoulders.

The weather again. Our American racial weather, turbulent, unchanging in its changeability, its power to rock us and stun us and smack us from our routines and tear us apart as if none of our cities, our pieties, our promises, our dreams, ever stood a chance of holding on. The racial weather. Outside us, then suddenly, unforgettably, unforgivingly inside, reminding us of what we've only pretended to have forgotten. Our limits, our flaws. The lies and compromises we practice to avoid dealing honestly with the contradictions of race. How dependent we are on luck to survive—*when* we survive—the racial weather.

One minute you're a person, the next moment somebody starts treating you as if you're not. Often it happens just that way, just that suddenly. Particularly if you are a black man in America. Race and racism are a force larger than individuals, more powerful than law or education or government or the church, a force able to wipe these institutions away in the charged moments, minuscule or mountainous, when black and white come face to face. In Watts in 1965, or a few less-than-glorious minutes in Clovis, New Mexico, on the eve of the day that commemorates our country's freedom, our inalienable right as a nation, as citizens, to life, liberty, equality, the pursuit of happiness, those precepts and principles that still look good on paper but are often as worthless as a sheet of newspaper to protect you in a storm if you're a black man at the wrong time in the wrong place.

None of this is news, is it? Not July 3rd in Clovis, when a tiny misfire occurred, or yesterday in your town or tomorrow in mine? But haven't we made progress? Aren't things much better than they used to be? Hasn't enough been done?

•

We ask the wrong questions when we look around and see a handful of fabulously wealthy black people, a few others entering the middle classes. Far more striking than the positive changes are the abiding patterns and assumptions that have not changed. Not all black people are mired in social pathology, but the bottom rung of the ladder of opportunity (and the space *beneath* the bottom rung) is still defined by the color of the people trapped there—and many *are* still trapped there, no doubt about it, because their status was inherited, determined generation after generation by blood, by color. Once, all black people were legally excluded from full participation in the mainstream. Then fewer. Now only some. But the mechanisms of disenfranchisement that originally separated African Americans from other Americans persist, if not legally, then in the apartheid mind-set, convictions and practices of the majority. The seeds sleep but don't die. Ten who suffer from exclusion today can become ten thousand tomorrow. Racial weather can change that quickly.

How would the bouncer have responded if I'd calmly declared, "This is a free country, I can wear any hat I choose"? Would he thank me for standing up for our shared birthright? Or would he have to admit, if pushed, that American rights belong only to *some* Americans, white Americans?

We didn't get that far in our conversation. We usually don't. The girls' faces pulled me from the edge—girls of all colors, sizes, shapes, gritty kids bonding through hard clean competition. Weren't these guys who didn't like my X cap kids too? Who did they think I was? What did they think they were protecting? I backed out, backed down, climbed in my car and drove away from Kelley's. After all, I didn't want Kelley's. I wanted a frozen margarita and a mellow celebration. So I bought plenty of ice and the ingredients for a margarita and rejoined the festivities at Bubba's. Everybody there volunteered to go back with me to Kelley's, but I didn't want to spoil the victory party, taint our daughters' accomplishments, erase the high marks Clovis had earned hosting us.

But I haven't forgotten what happened in Kelley's. I write about it now because this is my country, the country where my sons and daughter are growing up, and your daughters and sons, and the crisis, the affliction, the same ole, same ole waste of life continues across the land, the nightmarish weather of racism, starbursts of misery in the dark.

The statistics of inequality don't demonstrate a "black crisis"—that perspective confuses cause and victim, solutions and responsibility. When the rain falls, it falls on us all. The bad news about black men— that they die sooner and more violently than white men, are more ravaged by unemployment and lack of opportunity, are more exposed to drugs, disease, broken families, and police brutality, more likely to go to jail than college, more cheated by the inertia and callousness of a government that represents and protects the most needy the least—this is not a "black problem," but a *national* shame affecting us all. Wrenching ourselves free from the long nightmare of racism will require collective determination, countless individual acts of will, gutsy, informed, unselfish. To imagine the terrible cost of not healing ourselves, we must first imagine how good it would feel to be healed.

# On Violence

## David Nicholson

Maybe things would have been different if instead of only being born to the culture I'd grown up in it as well. But I spent much of my childhood in Jamaica, and when my parents separated and my mother returned to America with her four children, this middle-class boy, whose dentist father and high school teacher mother had sent him to the Queen's Preparatory School in Kingston, was completely unprepared for what he found on the predatory streets and playgrounds of black Washington, D.C.

I had no sense of rhythm and I couldn't dance. I couldn't (and still can't) dribble well enough to play basketball. For years the purpose and the verbal agility of "the dozens" (which we called joneing) eluded me.

The worst, though, was the casual violence—everybody seemed to want to fight. Someone pushed someone else in line waiting to go out to the playground. Someone said something about someone else's mother. Someone *said* someone had said something about a third someone else's mother. Sex didn't matter (some girls terrified all but the most fearless boys) and neither did the pretext. If a serious enough offense had been committed, or even merely alleged, push soon came to shove as books were dropped and fists raised and the aggrieved parties—surrounded by a crowd gleefully chanting "Fight! Fight!"—circled each other with murder in their eyes.

Raised to believe gentlemen obeyed two essential commandments—they did not hit girls, and they did not hit anyone who wore glasses—I would have been fixed in an insoluble moral quandary if a glasses-wearing girl had dared me to fight. But somehow it was arranged that I would fight another boy in the fifth-grade class of Mrs. Omega P. Millen (so named, she'd told us, because her mother had forsworn more children after her birth). I don't remember how it happened, but someone probably offered the usual reasons—Furman had said something about my mother or I'd said something about his. The truth, though, was that Furman, fair-skinned and freckled, with curly, ginger-colored hair, was as much of an outsider because of his color as I was because of my accent. A fight would decide which of us belonged.

We met in an alley near school. When it was over, the spectators who'd gathered, jamming the mouth of the alley so that Furman and I had to be escorted in, must have been as disappointed as ticketholders who'd mortgaged their homes for ringside seats at the Tyson-Spinks title fight. Furman and I circled each other warily until he pushed me or I pushed him or someone in the crowd pushed us into each other. After a moment or two of wrestling on the dirty brick paving, rolling around on the trash and broken glass, I shoved Furman away and stood.

Memory plays tricks, of course, but I don't think I was afraid. Not as afraid as I would be later, when, coming home from the High's Dairy Store on Rhode Island Avenue with a quart of ice cream on Sunday, some bigger boy, backed by two or three of his cronies, demanded a nickel. If I said I didn't have one, they'd leave me to choose between two humiliations—having my pockets searched or fighting all three, one after the other. And I certainly wasn't as afraid as I would be when, as I walked home alone, four or five boys jumped me because I'd strayed into a neighborhood where outsiders had to be ready to fight just to walk down the street.

So what I remember feeling in the alley was not fear but puzzlement. The fight with Furman had seemed like a joke right up to the moment we'd squared off against one another. I hadn't taken it seriously, and now it felt like a piece of foolishness that had gone too far. No one else seemed to have enough sense to call a halt, so it was up to me. I found my glasses, put them on, and announced I wasn't going to fight. I'd done nothing to Furman. He'd done nothing to me. And, besides, one of us might get hurt.

There was a moment of silence and then a low grumbling of disappointment as the boys and girls who'd come expecting to see a fight realized there wasn't going to be one. I went home, one or two friends walking with me, assuring me that it was all right, I didn't have to fight if I didn't want to.

But I knew they were wrong. And I knew they knew it too.

It is a terrible thing to be condemned by others as a coward, but it is even worse to condemn yourself as one. For that reason, I brood about that time in the alley more often than is probably healthy, even given that I'm a writer and my stock in trade is memories and the past. Lately, however, I've been thinking about it as I read, or read about, the new violence-laden autobiographies by black men—Nathan McCall's *Makes Me Wanna Holler*, Kody Scott's *Monster*. I don't listen to rap music (the phrase has always struck me as an oxymoron), but I'm aware that the genre has become one of art-imitating-life-imitating-art as entertainers like Tupac Shakur are arrested and charged with crimes ranging from sexual assault to murder. And then, if all that wasn't enough, there were the T-shirts and sweatshirts featuring Mike Tyson's face and the ominous legend "I'll be back," and those bearing the legend "Shut Up Bitch, or I'll O.J. You."

More and more it's begun to seem, as we enter the middle of the 1990s, that violence and black men go together as well as the fingers of the hand make up the fist. What's most troubling is that not only has the media seized on America's enduring bogeyman, the bad nigger, as an object of fear and pity, but that black men (and women) have also gleefully embraced that image. It's as if a generation, soured by disappointment in the post–civil rights era, has given up all hope of achievement and decided that it's almost as good to be feared as it is to be respected.

And so where does that leave me, who long ago eschewed violence, whether from fear or cowardice or simply because I couldn't see the point of it? Feeling at forty-three much the same as I'd felt facing Furman in the alley—that I'd been given a choice that really wasn't a choice. If I fought, I'd become like the rest of the boys. If I didn't, I'd be a sissy. What I really wanted was just to be me.

•

Perhaps I'm making too much out of all this. Perhaps that afternoon in the alley was part of some perfectly normal rite of passage. Perhaps all boys test each other to find out who will fight and who will not. And perhaps by not fighting Furman or, later, any of a number of bullies and thugs, I threw away the opportunity to earn their respect. Perhaps.

All I knew then was that the rules were different from those I'd learned growing up in Jamaica, and that while almost all of the children I'd known there were also black, violence was of mystifying importance to the black boys of Washington, D.C. One reason for the difference, I see now, was poverty. My school chums in Jamaica were all middle-class, but most of us in Mrs. Millen's (and later Miss Garner's) classroom were poor enough to relish our mid-morning snack of government-issue oatmeal cookies, soft and sweet at their centers, and half-pints of warm, slightly sour milk. On winter days, windows closed and the radiators steaming, the stale air in the classroom smelled faintly of sweat and dust and urine and un-washed clothes. I remember it as the smell of poverty and of crippling apathy.

Small wonder, then, that because so many of the boys had precious little except their bodies with which to celebrate life, violence became part of that celebration. It offered them a way of feeling masculine as well as the chance to be feared, to feel important.

But I never understood the tribal nature of the violence, the random-ness and the gratuitousness of it, until I saw how they'd probably been introduced to it before they were aware of what was happening, before they were old enough to understand there might be other choices. I was driving past a public housing project one gray winter afternoon when I saw two boys facing each other on the brown lawn. Each boy howled, runny-nosed in fear, as the man towering over them directed their tiny fists at each other.

They couldn't have been much older than three.

•

Years after my abortive fight with Furman in the alley, I had a summer job downtown in the District Build-ing, working for an agency of the city government. Five of us, all high school or college students, were summer help. We spent the day sorting building plans and building permits in a narrow, dusty back room lined with filing cabinets and ceiling-high wooden shelves. Sometimes we had to deal with citizens seeking copies of plans or permits, but most of the time we were left alone to work by ourselves, only nominally supervised.

One of the other boys (I'll call him Earl) was a freshman or sophomore at Howard. Under other circumstances—if we'd met, say, in one of the integrated church coffee houses or drama groups I'd begun to frequent because they allowed me the freedom to be black and myself in ways segregated situations did not—perhaps Earl and I might have been friends. Skinny and bespectacled, we looked enough alike to be brothers. We read books and valued them. We spoke standard English. All of that, of course, set us apart from the other boys. For that reason, instead of becoming friends with Earl, I decided to hate him.

The other boys encouraged me, aiding and abetting, but they were only accomplices, because I had made up my own mind. We goaded Earl. We taunted him. Finally, one of the other boys told me Earl had dropped some of my files and picked them up without putting them back in order. Earl hadn't, of course, and I knew it. But I also knew my choice was to fight him or become identified with him. And Earl, with his suspiciously effeminate air of striving for refinement, was not someone I wanted to be identified with.

What happened was worse than if I had beaten him, worse than if he had fought back and beaten me. Earl simply refused to fight. He crumpled, stood crying, holding his glasses, begging me to leave him alone. I didn't hit him, but I joined with the others in making him do my work as well as his own while the rest of us sat drinking sodas or coffee, watching and making jokes.

I wish now I'd done something else. That I'd refused to fight Earl. That I'd suggested we join forces to resist the others. That I'd gone, on his behalf, to complain to our supervisor. But I didn't. And, sickened, I learned a lesson—it felt no better to threaten violence against someone incapable of resisting than it had been to be the one threatened and equally incapable of resistance.

•

What's missing here is the kind of Ellisonian epiphany—I am who I am, and no one else—that might have long ago allowed me to let go of all this. Instead, I've had to make do with patchwork realizations and small comforts.

One evening a few years ago I was standing on the street I grew up on, talking with a man I'd known since we were both children. He is younger than I am, so I hadn't known him well. Still, I knew him well enough to know he'd been comfortable on that street in ways I had not. So I was surprised when all of a sudden he told me he had always admired me. Puzzled but curious, I asked why, and he said it was because I hadn't stayed in the neighborhood; I'd left it to live other places and see other things.

For a moment I was speechless. I knew, of course, that there were qualities—the apparent cool and the readiness to deal that we call an ability to hang—that he possessed and I lacked. I envied him those. But it was inconceivable he might also envy me.

Hard on the heels of that realization came another. Life was a series of stages and I'd passed through one, but precisely because I'd long ago left that street I hadn't known it: violence was a function of age, even for black men (like the one I was talking to) who weren't middle-class and who lacked intellectual pretensions. A wishful capacity for it might remain one of the ways we defined ourselves, and were defined, however, the truth was that after a certain point even the bad boys were forced to realize they were no longer boys and that suddenly but almost imperceptibly they'd become one step too slow to continue in the game. It's then that, for all but the most stubborn, violence becomes a matter of ritual and voyeurism: football on Sundays, heated arguments in the barbershop, the heavyweight championship on pay-per-view.

•

During that same sojourn in the old neighborhood, I was walking to church one winter Sunday morning. I was almost there when I heard them, and then I rounded the corner and saw a man and a woman screaming at each other beside the iron fence in front of the churchyard while a little boy watched. A few late parishioners walked past, conscientiously ignoring them.

It's been long enough now so that the details are hazy. But I remember that he pushed her, and then she pushed him, and that they were screaming at each other. And I remember their faces, his young and still beardless, adorned with that practiced air of aggrievement I remembered from my childhood after one boy had sucker-punched another and gotten caught by Mrs. Millen or Miss Garner, an insolent glare that said, "Why you lookin' at me for? I ain't did shit." The girl's face would have been pretty except that it was twisted with tears and anger. The little boy stood a little away, looking at them, and what was terrifying about it was that his face showed no expression at all.

I stepped into it, right between them, begging them to calm down, circling with them, hands out to keep them apart. He was bigger than I am, and younger. He may have pushed me once, trying to reach past to get at her. She bent to pick up a brick and lunged after him. I held her back.

Finally the police came.

An hour or so later, when I was finally home, I started to shake, thinking about what I'd done, thinking about what could have happened if he'd had a gun or a knife, or if the two of them had turned on me. Mostly, though, I thought about the little boy, looking up at me from under the hood of his parka when I stooped to ask if he was all right. He'd nodded, almost diffidently, nothing in his eyes at all that I could read. And I had thought, as I patted him on the shoulder and said, "Everything's going to be okay," that I was lying, that it wasn't going to be okay at all.

Because in that moment I could see the past—and the futures—of so many of the boys I'd first encountered on the streets and playgrounds around First Street and Rhode Island Avenue. They'd all had the same look in their eyes, the same distancing of themselves from what was happening around them. In time, I thought, this boy, too, would go on to acquire the same wariness, a quality of disguised hurt, a quality of removal and disavowal. In some important way he, like them, would cease to care. It wasn't just that these boys had come to expect to be blamed when they really had done nothing, although that was part of it. No, what was really important was that they'd made it so that it didn't matter any more. Because they'd long ago discovered that the way to survive was to hide their real selves from the world. And no matter what happened, they would never, ever, let anything touch them.

I write this now for the boy I once was who almost had his love of books and poetry beaten out of him. I write it for Earl, wherever and whoever he is, as a way of asking his forgiveness for having humiliated him in a vain attempt to avenge my own humiliations. I write it for the boy whose parents fought in front of the church that winter morning, hoping he made it whole into manhood despite the odds against him. And I write it for the boys whose names I never knew or can't remember, the ones whose eyes in elementary school were deader than any child's should ever be. Now I understand, I feel the pain they could not admit. In this way perhaps I can also one day forgive them.

# Why Must a Black Writer Write About Sex?

## Dany Laferriere
### Translated by David Homel

### I Am a Black Writer

A girl came up to me in the street.

"Are you the writer?"

"Sometimes."

"Can I ask you a question?"

"Of course."

"Is the book *your* story?"

"What do you mean by that?"

"I saw you on TV the other day, and I was wondering whether all those things really happened to you."

"Yes and no."

She wasn't surprised or confused, she just wanted a straight explanation.

"Is that it?"

"I don't know what to tell you . . . No one can tell a story exactly the way it happened. You fix it up. You try to find the key emotion. You fall into the trap of nostalgia. And there's nothing further from the truth than nostalgia."

"So it really isn't your story."

"May I ask *you* a question?"

"Why would you do that?" She blushed. "I never wrote a book."

"But you read books."

"I like to read."

"Why is it so important to know if the story really happened to the author?"

She thought about that one.

"You just want to know."

"I see . . . Why?"

"I don't know," she said with a pained smile. "You feel closer to him that way."

"What if he was lying to you?"

"What do you mean?"

"What if he told you it was his story, even if it really wasn't?"

"I'd be disappointed." She laughed, a little embarrassed. "I suppose we never know the truth."

"So why bother?"

"It's just a fantasy."

She laughed.

"Are you keeping something from me?"

"Maybe, but I don't know what."

She smiled again.

"Where do you like to read?" I asked her.

"Anywhere."

"In the subway?"

"There, too."

Nothing fascinates me more than a girl reading in the subway. I don't know why, but Tolstoy wins it hands down underground. With *Anna Karenina*, naturally.

"Some people read anywhere, but not just anything," I said, without really knowing what that meant.

She gave me a penetrating look.

"I read anything."

"Which means you're the perfect reader."

A car swept by. She leapt aside to safety.

"I'm sure you don't finish every book."

"Sorry, I didn't catch that," she said, getting over her fright.

"When you start a book, do you always finish it?"

"Always."

By now she had recovered her wits.

"There's something here that doesn't add up," I told her.

"Maybe because I never remember anything." She chuckled.

"How can that be?"

"I don't remember the author's name . . ."

My heart sank.

". . . Or even the title of the book."

"I suppose that really isn't important. The book's the only thing that matters."

She sighed.

"I never remember the subject either. Sometimes I think I've never read a single book in my life."

"That's incredible! You read something, and a minute later it's gone?"

"I'm afraid so."

A long pause.

"Then why read?"

"It passes the time."

"I see . . . Does it bother you when you forget?"

"Oh, yes!"

She seemed hurt that I would ask her such a question.

"I imagine your forgetfulness causes trouble in the rest of your life."

"No. It only happens with books. Do you think I'm disturbed? Sorry—not at all. I work in an office not far from here, and believe it or not, you need a good memory in my line of work. I'm a legal secretary."

"Why did you come up to me in the street? You seem like the shy type to me."

A peal of fine laughter burst from her throat.

"I am shy, you're right. I don't know why. I guess because I saw you on TV."

"Maybe you've read one of my books . . ."

"No. At least, I don't think so."

A moment's hesitation.

"Well, maybe yes. I might have read one of your books."

"There's no way of being vain around you."

She laughed her shy laugh.

"I'm sorry."

"I'd like to ask you something."

"Yes," she breathed, turning her head to one side.

"Are you in love?"

This time her laughter was harsh.

"You're a strange one . . . But why not? You're a writer."

"A black writer," I pointed out.

"What's that mean? Is it better?"

"Unfortunately not."

"So?"

"That's the way it is."

"Is it?"

"Yes."

"Too bad."

"There are certain advantages, you know."

"For example?"

"There are fewer of us. It's easier to become the greatest living black writer."

"Then what?" she asked slyly.

"Then you die, of course."

My eye was briefly captured by a girl walking on the other side of the street. A girl with an enormously short green skirt, a veritable handkerchief, and legs that must be worth more than a brooch from Tiffany's. When I turned back to continue the conversation, the reader had gone. Where did she come from? Where was she going? What did she want from me? No sense asking those questions in America.

## America, We Are Here

Back then, I was trying to write a book and survive in America at the same time. (I'll never figure out how that ambition wormed its way into me.) One of those two pursuits had to go. Time to choose, man. But a problem arose: I wanted everything. That's the way drowning men are. I wanted a novel, girls (fascinating girls, the products of modernity, weight-loss diets, the mad longings of older men), alcohol, and laughter. My due—that's all. That which America had promised me. I know America has made a lot of promises to a very large number of people, but I was intent on making her keep her word. I was furious at her, and I don't like to be double-crossed. At the time, I'm sure you'll remember, at the beginning of the 1980s (so long ago!) the bars in any North American city were chock-full of confused, aging hippies—they were confused before they became hippies—empty-eyed Africans who always had a drum within easy striking distance—the type never changes, no matter the location or the decade—Caribbeans in search of their identity, starving white poetesses who lived off alfalfa sprouts and Hindu mythology, aggressive young black girls who knew they didn't stand a chance in this insane game of roulette because the black men were only into white women, and the white guys into money and power. Late in the evening, I wandered through these lunar landscapes where sensations had long since replaced sentiment. I took notes. I scribbled away in the washrooms of crummy bars. I carried on endless conversations until dawn with starving intellectuals, out-of-work actresses, philosophers without influence, tubercular poetesses, the bottomest of the bottom dogs. I jumped into that pool once in a while and found myself in a strange bed with a girl I didn't remember having courted. (I left the bar last light with the black-haired girl, I'm sure I did, so what's this bottle-blonde with the green fingernails doing here?) But I never took drugs. God had given me the gift of loud, powerful, happy, contagious laughter, a child's laugh that drove girls wild. They wanted to laugh so badly, and there wasn't much to laugh about back then. When I immigrated to North America, I made sure I brought that laughter in my battered metal suitcase, an ancestral legacy. We always laughed a lot around my house. My grandfather's deep laughter would shake the walls. I laughed, I drank wine, I made love with the energy of a child who's been locked inside a candy shop, and I wrote it all down. As soon as the girl scampered off to the bathroom, I would start scribbling down notes. The edge of a bed or the corner of a table was my desk. I'd note down a good line, a sensual walk, a pained smile, all the details of life. Everything fascinated me. I wrote down everything that moved, and things never stopped moving, believe me. All around me, the world (the girl, the dress on the floor, my underwear lost in the sheets, that long naked back moving towards the stereo, then Bob Marley's music), the elements of my universe turned at top speed. How could words halt the flight of time, girls wheeling away, desire burning anew? Often I would fall asleep with my head against my old Remington, asking myself those unanswerable questions. Am I the troubadour of low-rent America, always on the edge of an overdose, up against the wall, handcuffs slapped on, with two cops breathing down my neck? America discounting her life, counting her pennies, the America of immigrants, blacks and poor white girls who've lost their way? America of empty eyes and pallid dawn. In the end, I wrote that damned novel, and America was forced, at least as far as I was concerned, to come through on a few of her promises. I know she gives more to some than they need; with others, she swipes the hunk of stale bread from their clenched fists. But I made her pay at least a third of her debt. I'm naive, I know. I can see the audience smiling, but my mental system needs to believe in this victory, as tiny as it may be. A third of a victory. For others, not a penny of the debt has been paid. America owes an enormous amount to Third World youth. I'm not just talking about historical debt (slavery, the rape of natural resources, the balance of payments, etc.); there's a sexual debt, too. Everything we've been promised by magazines, posters, the movies, television. America is a happy hunting ground, that's what gets beaten into our heads every day, come and stalk the most delicious morsels (young American beauties with long legs, pink mouths, superior smiles), come and pick the wild fruit of this new Promised Land. For you, young men of the Third World, America will be a doe quivering under the buckshot of your caresses. The call went out around the world, and we heard it, even the blue men of the desert heard it. Remember the global village? They've got American TV in the middle of the Sahara. Westward, ho! It was a new gold rush. And when each new arrival showed up, he was told, "Sorry, the party's over." I can still picture the sad smile of that Bedouin, old in years but still vigorous (remember, brother, those horny old goats from the Old Testament), who had sold his camel to attend the party. I met up with all of them in a tiny bar on Park Avenue. While you're waiting for the next fiesta, the manpower counselor told us, you have to work. There's work for everyone in America (the old carrot and stick, brother). We've got you coming and going. What? Work? Our Bedouin didn't come here to work. He crossed the desert and sailed the seas because he'd been told that in America the girls were free and easy. Oh no, you didn't quite understand! What didn't we understand? All the songs and novels and films from America ever since the end of the 1950s talk about sex and sex alone, and now you're telling us we didn't understand? Didn't understand what? What were we supposed to have understood from that showy sexuality, that profusion of naked bodies, that total disclosure, that Hollywood heat? You should know we have some very sophisticated devices in the desert; we can tune in America. The resolution is exceptional, and there's no interference in the Sahara. In the evening we gather in our tents lit by the cathode screen and watch you. Watching how you do what you do is a great pleasure for us. Some pretty girl is always laughing on a beach somewhere. The next minute, a big blond guy shows up and jumps her. She slips between his fingers, and he chases her into the surf. She fights, but he holds her tight and both of them sink to the bottom. Every evening it's the same menu, with slight variations. The sea is bluer, the girl blonder, the guy more muscled. All our dreams revolve around this life of ease. That's what we want: the easy life. Those breasts and asses and teeth and laughter—after a while it started affecting our libido. What could be more natural? And now here we are in America and you dare tell us that we didn't understand? Understand what? I ask the question again. What were we supposed to have understood? You made us mad with desire. Today we stand before you, a long chain of men (in our country, adventure is the realm of men), penises erect, appetites insatiable, ready for the battle of the sexes and the races. We'll fight to the finish, America.

# Albert Murray on Stage:
# An Interview

## Louis Edwards

Albert Murray, born in 1916, is a grand surviving griot from a prodigious generation that includes writers Ralph Ellison, John A. Williams, and Ernest Gaines. He is a cultural critic (*The Omni-Americans* [1970], *The Hero and the Blues* [1973], *Stomping the Blues* [1976]) and a fiction writer (*Train Whistle Guitar* [1974], *The Spyglass Tree* [1990]). Louis Edwards is as gifted a young writer as can be drawn from a new generation of writers re-creating the story of black male witness in America. His first novel, *Ten Seconds* (1991), was hailed by critics and fellow writers alike. Edwards, born in 1962, has already won the prestigious Whiting Writer's Award and is completing a new novel. The following conversation, in part inscribing the living ritual of black, male mentorship, took place on July 13, 1994, in Murray's Harlem apartment, where he lives with his wife and daughter. [Ed.]

EDWARDS: I'd like to begin with a discussion of *The Omni-Americans*, not just because it's the beginning of your publishing history, but because it's *such* a beginning and such a way to hear your voice for the first time. So how did that book come about? Talk about the political and literary climates at the time—late sixties, early seventies—and about how the book was received.

MURRAY: Well, it was obviously a book that was stimulated by the civil rights movement. And it had to do with what I thought was basic—that is, the question of identity and who these people were and how they saw themselves in the actions that they were participating in. To me it's always a matter of context and a matter of the broadest possible human context. So I wanted to define what it meant to be an American, and how we fit into it, and I came up with the idea that we're *fundamental* to it—that you can't be an American unless you're part *us*, just as you can't be an American unless you're part *them*. I came up with the concept of a culture that as a context makes for, literally and figuratively speaking, a mulatto culture. I was thinking the whole time I was writing *The Omni-Americans* about "all-American," but I couldn't use that term because I didn't want to get confused with that term as it's used in athletics. But it means "all-American." "Omni-Americans" means "all-Americans." America is interwoven with all these different strains. The subtitle of that section of the book is "E Pluribus Unum"—one out of many. Whether you want to get all tangled up in "melting pot" or "glorious mosaic" or any of those phrases is another thing. It just means that people are interwoven, and they represent what Constance Rourke calls a composite. Then you can start defining individuals in their variations, but they're in that context and they can only define themselves in that context. They're in a position where they're the heirs of all the culture of all the ages. Because of innovations in communication and transportation, the ideas of people all over the world and people of different epochs impinge upon us, on part of our consciousness.

EDWARDS: Then the term "omni-Americans" applies not just to African-Americans, but to all Americans, and to—well, maybe not to all people, but perhaps we're discussing "omni-humanity."

MURRAY: Yes. Absolutely. We're looking for universality. We're looking for the common ground of man. And what you're doing when you separate the American from all of that, is you're talking about *idiomatic* identity. You see? And if you go from culture, instead of the impossibility of race . . . because you can't *define* race. It doesn't meet our intellectual standard with a scientific observation and definition and whatever. It won't meet it! You see, race is an ideological concept. It has to do with manipulating people, and with power, and with controlling people in a certain way. It has no reality, no basis in reality. Because, see, if you try to make a genetic definition—"has this gene, has that gene"—how many of this gene or these genes or those genes would it take to make you white or black or yellow or brown or red, if you use this crude ratio? Now how do you determine who has that many, and where's the line of demarcation? It's an *impossible* situation. So what you enter into to make sense of things are patterns and variations in culture. What you find are variations we can call idiomatic—idiomatic variations. People do the same things, have the same basic human impulses, but they come out differently. The language changes because of the environment and so forth. Now, you can get the environment, you can get the cultural elements, and from those things you can predict the behavior of people fairly well. But if you look at such racial characteristics as may be used—whether it's the shape of certain body parts, the texture of the hair, the lips, and all—you cannot get a scientific correlation between how the guy looks and how he behaves. If you find a large number of people who look like each other and behave like each other, it's because of the culture. Because there are too many other variations. If you've got guys from stovepipe black to snow blond, you're going to find all the variations in mankind, even though idiomatically they might speak the same, they might *sound* the same.

EDWARDS: The ideas that you espoused in *The Omni-Americans*, were they considered radical? I mean, there are those who would say this is wrong even today. The social scientists would still argue with you.

MURRAY: But they're segregationists. I make the point in *The Omni-Americans* that nobody is more dependent upon segregation than the social scientist.

EDWARDS: It's his work.

MURRAY: That's why I call social science as used in America a folklore of white supremacy and a *fake*lore of black pathology. Anything that black people do is abnormal. If it's good, it's still abnormal. So if you're well conditioned, like superstar basketball players, it's because there's something wrong with you. Any other time when you're discussing such matters, if you've got these things together, if you're discharging the emotional thing that your system is healthier, if you're laughing and you're making jokes and you're playing around, then you're automatically, by any other definition of psychiatry and so forth, you're happier and you're on better terms with life. But then somebody will say something is wrong with you if you're not angry enough—which is a pathological condition.

Even if you're in the face of danger, you're still in an abnormal functioning of the body because you're confronted with danger, but it's not the most desired state of human existence. You've got that balance between a perception of jeopardy and a technology for coping with it *and* a sense of the ridiculousness and a sense of the futility or the emptiness, after all, of it. Because once you get to be good enough at science, you're linked up with particles and waves! [Laughter.]

So then all you've got left are metaphors, and those metaphors had better be adequate. And they're adequate if they add up to the possibility of dynamic equilibrium which brings a sense of fulfillment and therefore happiness.

EDWARDS: Well, many of your metaphors have, I think, serious political implications and resonance, but they do not read that way. They don't read as politics. They read more as philosophy.

MURRAY: Well, it's a human thing.

EDWARDS: Back to the search for universal humanity.

MURRAY: Let me give you an analogy, a rough Murray analogy. If you went to the athletic department of a college . . . you have one guy who is a coach of the basketball team, the track team, and another guy who is a physical director. He teaches physical education, he conditions the body for all those other things. If you do well enough, if you can pass all of that, then you might be a basketball player, you might be a track guy—the application of the conditioning. In other words, if our humanities, if our metaphors, if our arts are adequate, then our ideals and aspirations will be adequate. It wouldn't be just a matter of food, clothing, and shelter. It would be a human transcendence that goes beyond that, that takes you beyond our conception of what human or plant life is. It's those ideas or those images of human possibility that make for aspiration, that make for a sense of achievement—and a sense of failure. So you've got literature right there. If you get a wrong definition of what the objectives are, if you go for material things—just go for money, or just for power—you will then cause a lot of confusion and it won't be adding toward the thing that you really want, which is that dynamic equilibrium, which is always precarious, but which makes for what we call happiness, which is very, very delicate at all times. It has to be watched at all times because it changes. But it's what we want. We know it when we get it.

EDWARDS: The requirements to bring about happiness change.

MURRAY: You've got to have a sense of actual achievement. One of the things about my writing that I want to make people conscious of is the underlying ritual that's there. That's what keeps them informed that I'm going to be applying this to politics, I'm going to be applying this to this type of administration. But you've got a vision of life which is adequate, so that it enriches your political program, your political position, or what you *want*.

Count Basie and I were working on his book, and when we got near the end we started looking through collections of pictures. At one point there—I guess just before he was leaving Kansas City to come to New York—there's a picture of him and he has a gold tooth in the front of his mouth. And when I saw this picture I said, "Hey, Count. What happened to that gold tooth?" He looked at the picture and he said, "I didn't know what to want." Isn't that terrific? "I didn't know what to want." When he got more hip, he took that thing out; he had beautiful teeth that went so well with his complexion and all.

EDWARDS: That's a great story.

MURRAY: We're talking about the political implications of what I was doing. . . . It was a matter of laying an adequate foundation, so that whatever you do on top of it would be adequate.

EDWARDS: Now, one of the most complex works that you've written would be *South to a Very Old Place*—in my opinion—which, I'll admit, I had a hard time fully comprehending. I realize that there is a very intricate pattern that is at work there. Could you discuss what you were up to? I think it might help people approach that work.

MURRAY: *The Omni-Americans* would be a discussion where I'm wearing the hat of the intellectual, where I'm trying to set up the issues and address basic questions. *South to a Very Old Place* tries to be a work of art, where the actions and the pictures have their own application. If you give people a legend, they want a picture. If you give them a picture, they want a legend. If you wear two hats, as a novelist and an intellectual, you do them both. As a college teacher, I could do them both. I wanted to be an artist. I tried my best to make *South to a Very Old Place* a work of art.

EDWARDS: It's clearly that.

MURRAY: I wanted it to be read for the pleasure of how it is written, and then all of that stuff is all loaded. You can say all kinds of things that mean all kinds of things, and it's all in focus if you get the art working for you. With the hocus-pocus you make it swing, and then you get all that other stuff. You want to make the ineffable articulate. So you're in an interesting area there, and when you get to *Train Whistle*, there's an attempt to give you the clue . . . "the also and the also" of this or that; you should get the whole. "Also and also" is the ultimate implication, the personal, the local, the worldwide implications. The also and the also: *etcetera*. It's endless.

That's like music again. I start with real fundamentals. Entropy. So when I'm writing about the blues, it's the whole philosophical system right there. What's the blues? Entropy. The tendency of all phenomena to become random, to fall apart. It's chaos. That's what so devastating about the blues. So what you've got to do is superimpose a form on that. That's why I can make jazz and the jazz musician central to my whole literary, philosophical system of American identity, because we simply are the stars of [that system], the touchstone of it. I can take a Lester Young take-off on Jefferson. I could take a Cootie Williams and Louis Armstrong thing on Lincoln. I can do all this. You can play with all that stuff and make it feel right even if you can't articulate it yet. It's that type of thing. And nobody's come up with an image of the American that I think is richer in possibility and more consistent with the assumptions underlying the social contract that we live in terms of.

EDWARDS: Are you saying or implying that the order in which you've published your work is part of an overall plan or scheme? Because from *The Omni-Americans* to *South to a Very Old Place* to *Train Whistle Guitar*— I think *The Hero and the Blues* may be in between the two latter works— the works all flow into one another. Or is that serendipity?

MURRAY: Well, in a sense. . . . When I got into the pieces that add up to *The Omni-Americans*, I realized I was writing on a theme, the theme of identity. The title of the book has to do with identity. We're the all-

Americans. We symbolize that more than anything else. It's a mulatto culture. Boom! You can just play all kinds of changes. You can write fifteen-hundred-page books on that stuff. But what I'd been doing was thinking through the whole thing and I had really written *The Hero and the Blues* first. That's what I was working on when the assignments that would become *The Omni-Americans* started coming in, so I had the context. I had the intellectual frame of reference. I was working it out, working on an aesthetic. So when I started writing these pieces, I knew I was writing a book, because it was inside a context. I wanted to deal with the richest possible context, and what came out was all I knew about literature, all this stuff on my shelves. When I was ready to open up, there I was writing a book! You know, "Thomas Mann, who said this and this . . ." I was gone! I knew where I was going on that. Then I get that *e pluribus unum*, how far back you go . . . .

If I were not so realistic and didn't have to face the tragic dimension of life—as well as life's farcical dimension—I would be very much depressed. Too many of the black intellectuals have been unable to address the first fifteen pages of *The Omni-Americans*. I enter history at the middle point in the Middle Passage. My work sets up a cultural and intellectual context in which we can define ourselves as Americans—second to none. Any African who jumped overboard en route to the New World is not my ancestor, because what we do has to do with survival in this state. You don't have a better prototype for the self-created American than Harriet Tubman, Fredrick Douglass, or Louis Armstrong picking up that horn. My work establishes the basis of our American identity. . . . And that's where the necessity of swing begins. Eternal resilience. Perpetual creativity. . . . So by the time I got into *The Omni-Americans*, I was going. It *had* to be a book. Then you feed in these other things which I was dealing with at the time—jazz, literature, style. I would just bounce them against a frame of reference. That's how *The Omni-Americans* came to be.

But when you get to *South to a Very Old Place*, that started out as an assignment for a series that Willie Morris was running at *Harper's* magazine, called "Going Home in America." Some people would go to the Midwest; some people would go to this place, that place. He asked me to do one and I decided to go south. Then I started playing with irony immediately. Go north. Go north this way, go north that way. Go north and south. Then to be sure you get it, you've got Joyce, you've got Mann, you've got all these people to help you. So you put Christopher Columbus there and say, "He went east by going west; I'm going south by going north." You're playing with all these things if you're a contemporary writer. You've got to write as if all these people exist.

EDWARDS [laughing]: That leads to another question I have. I want you to talk about some of the very significant relationships you've had with some of the great black male artists of this century.

MURRAY: What do all these guys have in common? What do Ellison, Ellington, Basie, Marsalis, and Bearden have in common? Me. [Laughter.]

EDWARDS: I know! It's interesting. I guess we can talk about some of them individually. I guess I'm most curious about your relationship with Ralph Ellison. How many years older was he?

MURRAY: Two. I'm seventy-eight, and he died at eighty. He was two years ahead of me at school. May have been more than that, but he had been there two years when I got there—Tuskegee. So we were contemporaries. I was there looking for—you know, it's like in *South to a Very Old Place*: "I'm the one determines what the value is." I would say, "Well, this is a pretty good book to read." I was doing that with upperclassmen. "This guy ain't shit. This guy is pretty good. This guy is a hustler." I was making all those judgments. But I think they stand up. I was looking for people who were serious about all this stuff, about the ancestral imperatives. Who was really shucking and who was doing the other stuff. I was looking. And he [Ellison] impressed me more than any other upperclassman. Some other guys, they looked good, they dressed well. They were taking Mr. Sprague's course in the novel. They were reading all these novels. *Clarissa Harlowe, Tom Jones*. Ellison and all these guys were reading these books. So I watched this stuff happening, and I noticed Ralph doing some other stuff. I knew he was trying to sculpt. I noticed that he would be at the other end of the library with his music paper spread out, doing copy work. And he was in the band, so he wasn't a cadet. I was a cadet. You had to be a cadet at Tuskegee. ROTC. It was like a Big Ten school, like a farm and technical school. See, Booker T. Washington wanted *everything*. [Laughter.]

EDWARDS: Which is not what you usually hear. The concept in [my] mind is something else. Something more limited.

MURRAY: Right. We had the damndest library. So the two hardest guys to read, black writers, because of all the literary background and references, are Ellison and Murray. All the other guys from Howard . . . you can read Sterling Brown and all these guys easily. But so far as the kinds of references you have to know: Ellison and Murray.

So I was watching Ralph. And then I was reading these books, and I would see his name in the books. They had that little slip in the books when you used to borrow them from the library. There was a place where you had to sign for it, and then they would stamp it. When you checked out a book, you could open the back of the book, and you could see the last time it was read and who had read it. Then I got to know his signature, and he was reading the books I was going to have to read; he had read them. So that was a real upperclassman for you. But he was always a loner-type guy, watchful-eyed, so I didn't venture to introduce myself to him. He worked in the library, a part-time student job.

The first exchange we ever had was . . . I had read Sinclair Lewis's *Arrowsmith* in a Modern Library edition, which was a flexible edition at that time. A green suede binding. I had read André Maurois's book *Ariel: The Life of Shelley*. I was reading about Byron, Shelley, and Keats and what those guys were reading. I was reading about reading and all that. I was a real college student. Everybody figured I should have gone to Yale or Harvard—to Brown, to an Ivy League school. But I was going to Tuskegee, and I was not going to let anybody at Harvard, Yale, and whatnot get a better education than was available to me there. So I was reading these books and what these guys were doing. And they'd talk about how Shelley would be reading all the time. He would fold the book and stick it in his pocket, his back pocket. So I had a flexible book, Sinclair Lewis's *Arrowsmith*, and I'd fold it up and stick it in my pocket, wherever I stopped reading. I wouldn't put a bookmark in it. Just fold it and stick it in my hip pocket, like Shelley. I was probably wearing a tam and a goatee too at that time. *Benvenuto Cellini*. I probably had seen that movie with Frederick March or something like that. All this bohemian stuff that was part of being collegiate, if you were serious. So I go to the library to turn this book in or to get it renewed, and Ralph is at the desk. And Ralph looks at the book and says, "What do you think this is? A pocket edition?" [Laughter.] That's the first exchange.

But I would see him, and I would notice him, and I would see books. . . . When I went to read T. S. Eliot, his name was there. When I went to read Robinson Jeffers, all those things, his name was in there.

In many of the books, he was the only guy. Then Hamilton and I were reading different books.

But I really didn't meet Ralph until about 1942. I knew he was in New York. I knew he had started writing. He had majored in music, but it didn't surprise me that he was writing reviews in magazines, because I knew he was a great reader and he was one of the favorites of Mr. Sprague's, who was my English teacher, too. We used to talk about Ralph. I was reading all of the magazines. I'd pick up one and say, "Hey, this guy reviewed a book by Waters Turpin called *These Low Grounds*." I can remember this. "Oh, I saw that phrase that Ellison said the other day, 'Malraux pointed out the other day that we are returning to fundamentals.'" I'd say, "Damn, boy! He's up there!" He was into the life. So when I came to New York in '42, another Tuskegian named Mike Rabb was up here on a fellowship going to Columbia, taking hospital administration because he was being moved into the position of administrative director of the Tuskegee Institute Hospital. He was staying over here at the Y. He and I were talking about other Tuskegians who were staying in New York, and he mentioned Ellison, whom he had known. He had a nickname for Ellison. he always referred to Ellison as Sousa, as in John Philip, because he was the student concert master. If you'd see the band in the stands, Ellison would be the guy conducting it. So Mike called him Sousa. So we went to see Ralph. He was living right up on the hill there where CCNY was. He was married to a nightclub singer named Rose Poindexter. When we walked into his place, the first thing I saw when he sat back in his chair, the first thing I saw was the Malraux over his shoulder. Then, having been introduced to him, I kept in touch with him on my own. It didn't take him long to find out that I was one of the few guys who read the same kinds of books. So it was automatic. Like that.

EDWARDS: So the two of you had a relationship from then on?

MURRAY: Mmm hmm. We were writing letters and so forth. You know about the stuff that I read at the funeral, the memorial?

EDWARDS: Yes. I was there. They're wonderful letters.

MURRAY: There's a whole collection of those things, which I'll show you one day.

That was '42. In '48 or '47, after I got converted to the reserves from the Air Force at the end of the war, I came to NYU to go to graduate school. And Ralph was by this time out of the merchant marines and into *Invisible Man*. I got back in touch with him. That fall when I came to grad school at NYU, he had published the first excerpt, the prologue from *Invisible Man*, in *Horizon* magazine. Then *Partisan* bought [the] "Battle Royal" [section]. But meanwhile we were in touch, you see, and I'd come up to see him. This is during the [cultural] heyday of 52nd Street.

EDWARDS: Right. So you're busy. [Laughter.]

MURRAY: You know, catching Duke at the Paramount, catching those shows. But my hangout was the 42nd Street Library, because graduate school was at night at NYU at that time. So Ralph was working on *Invisible Man* across the street from Rockefeller Center, across 49th Street, right across from Saks. Eight floors up there was a jewelry store that was run by some friends of Francis Steegmuller, author of *Flaubert and Madame Bovary* and *Maupassant: A Lion in the Path*. In the back of the jewelry store there was an office which they didn't use. Francis had used it, but he was in Europe at that time. So Ralph would get up in the morning and pack his attaché case, dress up, and go to work. Sometimes he would come down to the library and we would talk. Or we would stop at Gotham Book Mart.

EDWARDS: Were you writing at this time?

MURRAY: Yeah, I was trying to. But I was reading and figuring out what I was going to do. I had tried to write plays and stuff like that. By this time I was into Mann, Hemingway, and all that. Because it was out of Mann, out of Thomas Mann, that I got the idea that you could find a basis, an aesthetic model in your [own] idiom for literature. So when he started talking about dialectic orchestration and leitmotifs and things like that, I started thinking about riffs, breaks, and things like that. And then as I started studying, it all made for *The Hero and the Blues*—more for *The Hero and the Blues* than for *Stomping the Blues*. In *Stomping the Blues*, I just go back and clarify the whole notion of organizing literature around musical composition. If I could find the literary equivalent of Ellington, I could out-trump Melville, Twain, and Whitman.

EDWARDS: What do you see as the relationship between your work and Ellison's? *Is* there a relationship? There's certainly not, I don't think, a *simple* relationship.

MURRAY: Well, they're two different things. His is more—well, the political implications are more obvious. Whereas my aesthetic preoccupation and my sense of the total human context—although I work as hard as I can to get the local color and idiomatic particulars right, but that to me is what the writer always does. But you want the political, the social to seem incidental. You get that, and you don't even know you've got it. So he's more—I've been thinking about that. I was thinking about the differences in the sensibility. There's a certain amount of explanation of black folk stuff for white folks, which I refuse to do. See, he would do that. He would say certain things which I wouldn't say.

EDWARDS: Because of your different sensibility.

MURRAY: Yeah. It's just that you take it all, and you do it. See, you do it, and it's like "C-Jam Blues." You know, you swing it. And that's it. And then the guy himself says, "Geez, I wish I was brown-skinned." That's what you try to do.

My work doesn't ever stick to ethnicity and yet I don't want anyone ever to be thought of as a greater authority on ethnicity. They should say, "Ask him, he *knows*." Or, "He's got the voice. He's got the this, he's got the that." But the whole thing is—like Duke, you see . . . I want to say that Negroes never looked or sounded better than in Murray and Duke. With everybody else, they've got to go through a certain amount of mud. But they sump'm else, Murray and Duke. That's an *ambition*. You see what I'm saying? So the guy says, "I wanna be like that." See, I don't have any problem with teaching at an exclusive school, a white school, like Washington and Lee. When all the kids run after me it's because they're my boys. "I wanna be like him." It's that type of thing that you want to do. And you want to cut across that. Why is Stan Getz playing like that? Why are those guys running around looking like Miles? What's Gerry Mulligan *doing?* Every time he picks up his horn he wants you to feel that he was in Kansas City. He was hanging out with that. He wants to say, "I have as much authority dealing with these nuances as these guys. I don't want you to say that mine is different. I don't want you to say that I'm playing with an accent." Like the guy says, "Don't bother Stan Kenton, he thinks he's swinging." [Laughter.]

So the difference between me and Ralph Ellison is the difference between emphasis and the difference in literary strategy. But we have much of the same information and there's no conflict at all in our ultimate goals.

But I could not write *Invisible Man*. Look, look, with all the stuff and all the talk and so forth, Invisible Man is a victim. He's got the possibilities, but he's in a *hole*.

EDWARDS: But he doesn't submit. He's ultimately committed to the struggle of life.

MURRAY: He's a tragic hero with the possibility of redemption. Not really redemption, but rejuvenation, metamorphosis, all those things. But basically all the stuff that's happening to him is closer to a sense of tragedy.

EDWARDS: But a universal sense of tragedy.

MURRAY: Of course. We're not talking about disaster. We're talking about the nobility of tragedy. I'm interested in epics. It's another literary strategy altogether. I write about heroic possibility. I'm one of the few Americans to write about heroism. If you take me somewhere and the guy says, "We gotta get together because we gon' do this and them people did this to us and they did that to us, so we mad as hell," I'm going to say, "We gon' get up in the morning and we gon' do this and we gon' do that, and then we gon' *zap* the motherfuckers!" You see, that's the difference, and that's what they're not ready for. They're wallowing around being victims. I can't *stand* that! Because there is none of that in jazz. You triumph over that.

EDWARDS: Stomp it.

MURRAY: You see what I mean? And all these people know that. They go home. They play some low-down dirty blues. What did they want to do? Go out and fight white people, or go fuck? They want to get some pussy. They don't want to go out there and talk about no damn injustice and taxes and no money. The only time they talk about money is when they don't have enough money to get a gal, so she went off with another guy. So they're talking about art as fertility ritual.

EDWARDS: Which is what the blues is about.

MURRAY: You stomp the blues—that's a purification ritual. Why do you purify it? You have these two universal rituals—one to purify the environment of that which menaces human life, the other is the fertility ritual to ensure the continuation of the species. To revitalize existence. The union of lovers ensures the continuation of life. That's why we have the copulating blues. *So I can get in her pants.* [Laughter.] *If I don't get in her pants, ain't gon' be no tomorrow*—for me or nobody else! We got all these children out of wedlock because we still stomp the blues every Saturday night. This goes back not only to Storyville but also to Sophocles.

And I keep hoping against hope that I'm gonna win, you know, that people will see that our foreparents had respect for themselves, that they believed in their own humanity and integrity. They could not be torn apart. They weren't putting on a front. They were for real. In *Gone With the Wind*, when Mammy is fitting Scarlett O'Hara's corset and she tells her mistress, "You done had a baby, you ain't never gon' be no eighteen-and-a-half inches again," it's because Mammy knows what is behind the façade of the plantation mistress. *She* made Scarlett into a lady. Our foreparents knew what was behind the myth of whiteness, because they helped create it. Later, Scarlett O'Hara sees the devastation of the South, and still she keeps her dignity. Who taught her that? Aunt Jemima. Uncle Ben.

EDWARDS: Let's talk a little bit about Romare Bearden.

MURRAY: Yeah, Romy.

EDWARDS: And your relationship to him.

MURRAY: I had known about Bearden on my own, but I also knew of Bearden's work through Ralph. In fact, in [my daughter's] room there's a painting which Bearden originally gave to Ralph. Ralph gave it to me because he ran out of space, and then I was instrumental in his getting a *bigger* Bearden painting when I got him to do [his essay] on Bearden for the Albany exhibition. Then he was supposed to do another and he copped out on it and I had to do it. But by this time I was Bearden's chief literary advisor. We [Bearden and I] collaborated on most of his stuff.

EDWARDS: When you say collaborate, what do you mean?

MURRAY: He'd say, "Well, *we're* gonna do a one-man show." And then I'd say, "We oughta do something on jazz." And Bearden would say, "What should I do?" Now, we spent more time with each other than either of us spent with any other guys. Looking at paintings together, going to exhibitions. Doing things like that. So we could talk painting. We could talk music.

I met him in Paris in 1950. . . . Then, when I retired, we became buddies. We saw each other on an even more regular basis than Ellison and I did, although Ellison and I talked on the phone a lot. Romy and I would get together and we would go and look at all these paintings. That would have started in 1963, when I moved to New York and got back in touch with him. We were always doing things together—looking at paintings, buying books. And when he started making a lot of money with his painting, he would buy books. He would buy two of them, you know. And we used to meet at Books & Company, because a friend of ours had started it. We would meet over there every Saturday and we would hold court. People would find us over there. Meanwhile, I'd be setting up the outline and naming the paintings. He would say, "What should I do now?" You know contemporary painting, the major painters, right?

EDWARDS: Sure.

MURRAY: See, Romy can't stand up without Pieter de Hooch, Vermeer, the Dutch on this side—he [even] looked like a Dutchman—and Matisse on the other. To get to modern art, you can't go back through [the] Middle Passage and get there that way. Because they don't get into modern art. You go through the Musee de L'Homme. Romy and I would communicate just like that. All painting concepts and stuff like that. So he'd say, "What can I do?" And so I'd say, "What about Storyville Odalisque?" You know, Matisse. Bing! He's off. You know, you've got twelve numbers on that. So what has he got? You can see it right off. You can see the design. I would think in terms of design, but in poetic and metaphorical terms. So I would say, "Well, you've got a professor." See the piano player. You got an ornate mirror. You got a room. You've got a woman partly dressed. This guy sitting over here. So you've got the stylization of the keys. It's like Matisse's odalisques. You know, they're very busy. A long way from the cut-outs. It's boogie-woogie. It comes right out of pointillism. So you can give these things the illusion of busyness.

All these are visual statements with a literary overtone. So that, as abstract as the paintings were, they come back with a representational type of thing. But what saved it, how *we*, in a sense, saved it, was—he was moving in a direction to make it known—I came up with the concept of "The Prevalence of Ritual." He was doing a bunch of conjure women, playing around with that. This was when I came on board of collaboration. We were doing lots of other things, but then I started visiting his studio a lot, and he liked my phrases. And he was a big reader of mine. All you've got to do is look at the paintings and see how many trains there are. Trains! I saw these conjure women. And there was a bestseller a few years before that was called *The Prevalence of Witches*, and that phrase stuck with me. I gave it to him, and mine stuck—"The Prevalence of Ritual." Wham! It hit him. And that, I submit, saved his painting from genre painting. You know what I mean by that?

MURRAY: If you look at a painter like Jacob Lawrence, his painting is genre—what Negroes look like, how they live, the way their neighborhood looks. These are the peasants represented as art, like the wonderful peasant life of France. Painting critics call that genre.

EDWARDS: So how did "The Prevalence of Ritual" elevate or save Bearden from genre?

MURRAY: The stylization overshadows the report. So Romy could do a series on anything and it wouldn't be genre. See all of this jazz we did? Well, it's not just illustrating jazz. [Murray is pointing to a large Romare Bearden painting hanging in the apartment.] That's just a painting on it's own right. See, that's Duke Ellington. Look at that painting. Look at the variation. Look at these rectangles; they're different colors. Look at these rectangles on the piano legs. Look at this! Look at the glistening on the top of the piano. That's a half-moon. So you see how these figures are in there. Look how the white is played with. Now, instead of the keyboard, it's that little fence between the ringside and the others. But you've still got the same type of strokes in the painting.

EDWARDS: So it's the stylization—

MURRAY: It's swinging! That sonofabitch is *swinging*, man. But if you just get the report. . . . This is not quirky twist on a report; that's another thing. But it's the *painting* that does it. Art is a process by which raw experience is stylized into aesthetic statement. So what we have on the wall is not a report, but an aesthetic statement. When you deal with those fundamentals like that, you can keep it in focus. You can learn to appreciate what the guy's doing. You can see how he's playing with these things. This becomes not white but *light*. So the drumheads are light. They're reflecting light. So, too, with the shine on Duke's knee.

EDWARDS: What's this painting called?

MURRAY: *Duke Ellington on Stage*. Oh, I named a lot of them, and I set the context for a lot of them. Romy would call my wife and say, "Well, I've been pretty busy. Tell Al, tell Al I got to see him. I've got all these orphans over here that need names." [Laughter.] There was no sense of competition. Bearden loved writing and I loved painting. We had extremely close and shared aesthetic insights.

EDWARDS: You've written books and essays about music and literature. Do you think you'll ever write a book about art?

MURRAY: Not really. You know the Bearden piece? That's about it.

EDWARDS: You obviously have a lot to offer on the subject.

MURRAY: I might. You never know what'll happen. . . . Little articles might just happen if I find I want to say this, want to say that. Just like you want to come by and talk to me about something—

EDWARDS: Might stimulate something?

MURRAY: Mmm hmm.

# ( ( part two ) )

PLAYING HARDBALL

# Mr. Brown and the
# Sweet Science

## Randall Kenan

He stood no more than five foot eleven or perhaps even five foot ten when I first met him, though his presence made him seem seven feet tall. His face was broad, his nose—once broken in a boxing match—commanded his face, and his eyes were concentrated, fierce. He often joked that Jamaicans and Haitians and other island people often assumed him to be a kinsmen, though he was from New York, such was the darkness and ur-African nature of his features and color. He often said his hue held tones of copper: a man made of metal. He always wore his hair extremely close-cropped, and as his neck was thick and his shoulders broad, his being seemed to fill up a room—not simply by the sheer power of his body, I am convinced, but by the power and strength of his soul.

When I first met him he had given up the boxing ring itself and was now a trainer, though his physique was still that of a fighter. He told me that boxing had been called the Sweet Science, that it was an art, not mere brawling, a matter of brain more than body, a craft of intelligence and discipline. Above all, discipline. At less than five years of age I had never met a man quite like him—an athlete, an urbane, dapper gentleman. His wit was sharp, quick and humane; his learning was vast and his mind ever inquisitive.

To me his will seemed palpable, a tangible thing. Though he was gentle and genteel, he also inspired something akin to fear in those who did not know him, a dread understanding that if he were crossed in the wrong way, hell might be unleashed—his a righteous fire, that of a warrior, a shaman, a bard, and an artisan. It has been said of Pope Gregory XII that his will was so great that for him to make up his mind was for the thing to be done, that his concentration was so awesome that sparks flew up from the heels of his sandals as he paced the garden.

To me, Mr. John W. Brown is such a man. Mr. Brown.

•

I came into this world virtually fatherless and motherless. Illegitimate. Left, figuratively, on the doorstep of my paternal grandfather, a benevolent businessman, and in turn given to his sister, my great-aunt. For my first three years her husband was an early source of affection and guidance and male presence. Nearly thirty years later I still remember his image: the large face, the light coloring, the sparkling eyes, the tall carriage with the straw fedora, the expansive smile and hearty laugh.

This was in Chinquapin, North Carolina, in the late sixties and early seventies, rural to a fault, with farms and tractors and hogs and chickens and fields of corn and tobacco. The church still occupied a place of omnipresence and order in the lives of the country folk—Chinquapin being the sort of community that ideological conservatives wax idyllic over in our present age of obsession with crime and anxiety about technology.

One day during September when I was three, outside a packhouse wherein women graded cured leaves of tobacco, lying next to me, my great-uncle died.

I remember most powerfully not so much a feeling of loss, but a sense of bewilderment. The distraught and grief-stricken look on my great-aunt's face, the confusion, the sudden absence of male touch and mirth.

Bewildered I would remain, little did I know, for many, many years to come.

•

Mr. Brown loved to talk. His interests were broad, from politics to science, from history to horticulture, always centering around human nature—he was first and foremost a student of man. He knew more songs and song lyrics than I will probably ever know, and could and would sing entire songs for eras I could never know, giving me a way into seeing the thirties, forties, fifties: "Just give me flyjalapa on the side." Mr. Brown loved to laugh, and his laugh was belly-hard and soul-deep. I remember laughing so hard with him that it physically hurt me. He knew more jokes than the comedians on TV: "The other day it was so hot . . ." "How hot was it, Mr. B.?" "It was so hot I saw a man in a corn field with a mule, the corn started popping, the mule saw it, thought it was snow, and froze to death." Humor to him was a balm and a salve, a way to teach and transform the world, a way to gain distance and immediacy. Humor was weapon and medicine—with it he could do almost anything.

But behind the laughter I could almost see his brain zipping and dart-ing and crackling, taking in, analyzing. To this day I marvel at the speed of his mind—always several steps ahead, always working. Mr. Brown was the first man I knew who was composed of many parts—parts not at war, but in congress.

Make no mistake: men had been around. My grandfather, who lived in a nearby town, stopped by my great-aunt's farm several times a week, and his interest in me was genuine, but the demands of his business severely limited his time. Across the road from us lived my cousin Norman, who to me was very old when I was born, who ran his large farm with a wizard's mysterious majesty. His son, Roma, a high-school teacher—large, deep-voiced, capacious, avuncular, sometimes farmer, always deacon and trustee of the church—was certainly a frequent presence in our house. To be sure, cousins and uncles and men in this farm community were known to me, and me to them. Hard-working, often God-fearing, decent, good men. Yet for one reason or another their presence was somewhat distant; they had families of their own; their time—and rightly so—was devoted to their own sons. For many years my most important lessons were taught to me by the ever-present, seem-ingly all-encompassing, loving miracle of women. Aunts, grandmothers, cousins.

Especially my great-aunt Mary, who was a lioness and a grand vizier and a sorceress. To me she had magic powers and superhuman strength; to me she held the world together with her very fingers—and still does. I never felt neglected, in truth, or deficient; and in truth I never was. Yet beneath the surface, where changes were beginning that would later be made outwardly manifest, I had no way of knowing I had much to learn about that construct, that myth, that burden, that terrible reality of being a man, a black man in America.

•

Of course he stood out from the very beginning. Clearly he was a Yankee, which is not a disparaging term among Southern black folk, as it is among Southern white folk, but it is assuredly a mark of difference. Everything about him—his clothes, his walk, his clipped way of talking, his manners—bespoke New York City. Our good country people were at once charmed, beguiled, curious, suspicious, defensive, transfixed. Largely he was a mystery—they knew not his people, they knew not his history—for Southerners dwell within the tumult and continuity of history as do no other creatures. John W. Brown was a bright dark anomaly among them. To me he was a continuing amazement.

Early memories. At five, visiting my great-aunt's daughter in New York. Mr. Brown taking me to a gym in Harlem. The smell of sweat and the leather of boxing gloves. Watching Mr. Brown skipping rope with the speed of lightning, punching the speed bag, sparring. Visiting the Bronx zoo: the chimps, the tigers, the giraffe, seals, gorillas, polar bears, pythons. I remember most vividly the pythons. Chinatown. My first attempt to use chopsticks. Summer vacation. Waiting for Mr. Brown and my cousin to arrive down home. His vocal amazement at the remoteness and the space of the country. Everyone still chuckles at the memory of his mistaking tobacco plants for huge collard greens. His fascination with the quotidian elements of country life, those everyday miracles which a country boy finds hopelessly boring: cucumber patches, dirt roads, mockingbirds, deer, dogs, apple trees. Over time I gradually began to see his fascination with the commonplace, learning to take little for granted, gaining a new sight.

I remember one summer day him pointing out on the front page of the newspaper that Duke Ellington had died. Duke who? And my education and abiding fascination with jazz commenced. Sarah Vaughan, Count Basie, Tito Puente, and Lady Day—all suddenly became lifelong gifts. Music was no longer just music; it had a history, a form, a style, a meaning. My ears became instruments and I learned how to listen.

Nowadays we wail and gnash our teeth at our "wayward young black men," a seemingly "lost generation" given to violence, to lawlessness, to low self-esteem. I often ask, Are we truly lost? Are we truly wayward? But does anyone ever ask, Who is teaching them to listen? Who is teaching them to see?

•

I had been a dreamy kid, aloft in fantasy and make-believe. Comic books, fairy stories, tales of the amazing and especially of the fantastic were my real world. Paying little attention to the outside world, I lived for Star Trek and Spiderman and the vampires, werewolves, and bigfoots of horror novels, though I was frightened unto death of the dark.

Out on my great-aunt's farm, literally miles away from other boys my age, I made my own world in my head, peopled with elves and space aliens and wizards and whatever else I saw fit. Reality was not real, and without intervention who knows where time would have taken me? Who knows where I would have learned those lessons a young black man sorely needs to learn in order to become a man?

I did not know, as I know now, that for a young black man—struggling for some sense of himself in this world with the added pressures of his dark skin and his relegated rung on the ladder of society—the imperative is that he understand himself via his maleness, via his history, via his soul, and how that insight is of the utmost importance, the difference in some cases between life and death, for if a young African-American male does not come to terms with the myths the world holds about him and the realities of what lies in wait outside the gates of his home, then his ignorance may well rise up in the middle of the night and slay him like a thief.

•

In 1972, Mr. Brown and his wife— my cousin—and their less-than-a-year-old daughter moved down from New York to build a house in Chinquapin. They all lived with us for the year that their house was being completed. The lot on which it was to be built had been bulldozed, and in the rear of the property lurked this monstrous and forbidding mountain of earth and timber and tree stumps which had to be done away with.

Offers came from certain men in the community to dynamite the stumps; people made bids for great sums of money to take care of this onerous business. Mr. Brown was having none of it. In mid-January he struck out with a pickax, a shovel, an ax, and a few other tools, and single-handedly attacked what the family had begun to call the Pile.

This became his daily occupation, his goal—to decimate the Pile by the beginning of spring when the snakes came out, and to recover the land as the site for a garden.

Needless to say, folk in the community began to gossip behind his back about that uppity Yankee thinking he could actually take on that huge job alone and without heavy equipment, about how he'd give up in a few weeks and hire someone to do it for him. People would stop by and look, give specious advice, and go back and gossip some more. Mr. Brown would often ruefully note that for all the advice he received he never received any offers of help.

So he went on without help, except for my pitiful attempts after school and those of two other cousins on rare occasions—digging up stumps, cutting down brush, chopping wood, redistributing soil, burning debris. He once almost lost his vision when a thorn snagged his eye. He was soon back to work.

Each day after school I'd visit the site and he would show me the day's progress and give me a task. He would talk to me, debriefing me on my studies ("How did you do on that English test? Tell me what you learned about the Aztecs"), filling in gaps of history ("Ah, so you've never heard of the Black Panther Party? Well . . ."), admonishing me to take my studies and my life seriously, taking me, a ten-year-old boy with comic books and toys on the brain, seriously, seeing more of my future than I could even have imagined, recognizing about me strengths and weaknesses it would take decades for me to discover. Teaching me by example and by presence.

I say by example for in seeing in him take on the Pile alone I saw one of humankind's most awesome displays: a man sets himself a huge project, applies himself to it day by day, hour by hour, one task at a time, religiously, and by using time and discipline he accomplishes that goal. A simple lesson, in truth, but one that needs to be witnessed to be fully comprehended.

I say by presence for by being there each day, by physically being at hand and taking an active interest in my well-being and development, an unspoken bond had emerged between Mr. Brown and me which I could actually count on. Not that the women around me took no interest in me, far from it, but Mr. Brown brought another understanding, a man's understanding of how I would have to exist in the world, a knowledge of what I, as a male, a black male, would face, which a woman could not so readily foresee nor understand from personal experience.

Eventually spring came, as it is wont to do, and as Mr. Brown had decreed the Pile was a thing of the past. In its place lay a manageable piece of earth ready for tilling. He set out to plant his first garden—just as he had begun to plant a forest of ideas in my brain.

Oddly enough, folk in the community were not so quick to refer to Mr. Brown as that crazy Yankee after that.

•

Mr. Brown believed that a sound body promotes a sound mind. He would cajole me to come running with him early in the morning (he spat upon the word "jog"). I never matched his number of miles or his endurance, but he pushed me to go my limit.

I would watch boxing matches with him on television and he demystified the sport for me, teaching me the difference between a jab and an uppercut, between when a fighter was fighting smart and when a fighter was fighting dumb, sending orders through the television screen.

Once he tried to teach me to box. In his garage he put me through the paces, the muscle-wrenching exercises, the breathing exercises, the skipping rope. Only when we sparred did it become apparent that I had no aptitude—or desire—to hit or be hit. I remember beginning to sob, at eleven or twelve, as much as from embarrassment as from the sting of a few light raps to the noggin. Mr. Brown simply stopped and helped me off with my gloves—the Golden Gloves he had been awarded as a youth—the tears slipping down my cheeks. He said to me that day, as he looked me square in the face with no hint of either judgment or disappointment, "Remember, tears are not a sign of weakness."

Though I never put on a pair of boxing gloves again in my life, I never felt like a weakling.

•

When Mr. Brown said he was going to join the Chinquapin Volunteer Fire Squad, I didn't give it much thought. When he said later that he was going to join the rescue squad, my interest was piqued.

Being a small, unincorporated community, all of Chinquapin's services were strictly volunteer. Mr. Brown thought it only reasonable that if he, being a homeowner, was going to depend upon the goodness of his fellow neighbors for the safety of his home, then he should participate in the process for them. He also noted how few black men in the community actually belonged to the fire and rescue squads and who took active roles, and he felt—especially since many of the community's so-called leaders were not members—that this negligence sent out not only a message of hypocrisy, but also a generally negative message about the response of African-American males to their own responsibilities.

He quickly became an officer in the fire squad, took a course at the local community college to become a certified emergency medical technician, and joined the rescue squad.

Those nights he was on call, sleeping over at the station, he sometimes allowed me to stay over with him—on non-school nights, of course. For a kid who had to go to bed after the eleven o'clock news, the prospect of sitting up all night at the fire station in the company of men waiting to "come to the rescue" was a predictably heart-pumping experience. Imagine the glee of an already too-fertile imagination at being One of the Men for a night, at the exciting prospect of being in the Action, as if awaiting a call from the Batphone! Often on Friday nights someone would be out back roasting a hog for the weekly Saturday barbecue sale to benefit the Fire and Rescue volunteers, and Mr. Brown and I would bring a chicken which we would season and place on the coals. To date that's the best chicken I can ever remember having—so succulent, so tender—me munching that good and hot chicken over tales of Mr. Brown's exploits as a youth in New York not as rough-and-tumble as it would become, but tougher and angrier than a country boy could truly imagine. Wide-eared, I gobbled up the stories with the chicken, not realizing that in truth Mr. Brown was feeding me cautionary tales as well, tales of survival and ingenuity, tales of growing up.

There were fires and rescues during "my watch," and though I was not allowed to go out, later I would be there, wide-eyed and expectant, to hear the sad tales of demise or the happy tales of success, and I would see how Mr. Brown, either stoic in reflection or jubilant in victory, would examine the event—the squad's work, his work, the mistakes, the cause for the accident—in effect teaching me some of life's harshest and most practical of lessons, giving me a firm sense of reality: Beware, be aware, be wise.

On two distinct occasions, I remember Mr. Brown and his partner being called to fatal accidents involving classmates of mine. Any illusions about my own immortality were duly snuffed out. Though I did not actually see the car wreck or the shooting accident, I saw the blood in the ambulance afterward and no greater cautionary message exists—especially if you know where the blood came from. We spoke of death, Mr. Brown and I, of how it came when it came and of how we should be, could only be, prepared. Such intense lessons about reality are indeed rare, and only years later am I beginning to see the depth and the clarity of those moments, and how at such an early age I came to an appreciation of the brevity and frailty of our lives upon this earth.

Being there with Mr. Brown, though great fun, also affixed in my head the idea of a black man sharing in responsibility and involving himself in altruistic causes. Any time I hear disparaging nonsense about the selfishness and irresponsibility and inconsistency of African American men, I remember Mr. Brown and think, No, I know a hero. He is a black man.

•

Mr. Brown taught me how to squeeze water from a knife, how to separate my thumb from my hand and make it glide across my palm—illusions. He also taught me how to tell the difference between illusion and reality.

It was my twelfth birthday. Mr. Brown asked me if I would like all the hamburgers and french fries and hot dogs I could eat. My eyes grew big. My mouth watered. Sure! He took me down to the local Tastee Freeze, where I greedily ordered something like four hamburgers, four hot dogs, several orders of fries, a coke. O what gustatory bliss! Imagine a newly twelve-year-old boy with carte blanche to eat unlimited amounts of junk food. Mr. Brown sat next to me calmly with a devilish grin planted on his face which I was too absorbed to note, egging me on. "Have another, why don't you? Oh, you can eat another. Sure. Come on. Knock yourself out. It's your birthday! Another hot dog, please. You want another hamburger? Give him two more. There you go . . ."

I have no recollection of how much I actually ate that day, but needless to say I vividly remember the ensuing night and day—the first day of my school career that I was forced to stay home with profound stomach pains. Mr. Brown came by to visit. "Would you like another hamburger?"

I got the message. Literally years passed by before I could look at a hamburger or a hot dog without feeling sick to my stomach. I had never been a greedy child, but to this day the brilliance of that lesson is not lost on me, the crystalline wisdom of teaching a young boy a lifelong lesson about gluttony he'd never forget, a lesson no amount of preaching and punishing could accomplish. Diabolical, to be sure, but frightfully wise nonetheless. And effective.

•

Life lessons don't come easily, nor the wisdom to concoct them. Mr. Brown in many ways remained a mystery to me throughout my growing up, even as we grew closer. Much of the mystery was intertwined with how he came to be so wise, so resolute, so independent, and at base so kind and so loving—as when I saw his fierce love for his wife and two daughters. He would tell tales of working for the City of New York and of his earliest jobs, of the difficulties and the determination involved in his own "making it," of how his discipline and caginess were born out of necessity. He would tell me I had one thing he did not have—him, someone to teach me the lessons he had had to figure out on his own. So when he lectured me on the evils of drugs and alcohol and crime and violence, these conversations never felt like lectures but like messages from some other side, guideposts left by a wanderer who had safely made a journey.

•

Many lessons, much wisdom. Even after I went away to college he continued to teach me by word and by example—when he told me to follow my heart and head in writing, when he supported my move to New York and bolstered my courage and calmed my fears, when he himself began a new career as a special education teacher and basketball coach for "challenged" youngsters and demonstrated how mirth and honesty and genuine concern can turn people around. When I would come home to visit he would talk for hours about these kids and their problems and about how, beneath the surface, they just needed someone to take time with them, to be real with them and dole out a little glee, understanding, and caring.

Undoubtedly the most painful lesson came in the late eighties, when Mr. Brown had reached his late fifties and out of the blue was stricken with a rare blood disease. His health, his energy waned. He was hospitalized. I was called home from New York.

I remember the scene in the hospital: the fear and anguish of his two daughters and his wife, and of my great-aunt, his mother-in-law, who had become, over the years, his best buddy. And Mr. Brown himself, hitched up to all manner of blipping, blurping, blinking machines—the jungle of IV tubes, the respirator down his throat. I remember standing by and feeling absolutely helpless. Helpless for him, helpless for my family, helpless for me. Remembering all those lessons, remembering his admonition. Beware, be aware, be prepared. I wasn't. He was pronounced dead. But he didn't stay dead.

His recovery was full, though he lost a thumb, and I do believe he even gained something in the process—something grand and not easily uttered. I could see it in his eyes, hear it in his voice. Especially in those quiet moments when I would catch him peering into the evening sun. Certainly I and my family gained something, something more than time, more than hope. I attributed his resurrection to his indomitable will, to those sparks that flew from his heels when he thought and walked. He simply said it just wasn't his time, that God had further use for him on this plane. In any case, seeing him literally on his deathbed and coming back to life, going back to gardening and fishing, taught me something more. As before, implicitly and explicitly he had shown me a lesson that Batman and the Lone Ranger and Rambo never could, for in seeing him battle with death and the imponderable mystery, in seeing him contemplate his mortality and his loved ones, I never once saw him lose his dignity or his courage or his grand humor or his unshakeable sense of self and what was most important and valuable to him. Here was a new profile in courage and will and strength, something undreamt of in fantasies of musclebound warriors and gun-toting action heroes.

What is courage? I had seen it firsthand. The only times I saw him cry were when he was faced with the outpouring of concern and love from his former students and friends—a note of prayer scribbled on a greeting card by a nine-year-old or a visit from members of the basketball team he had coached made him mist up, made his voice crack, and he'd pause, look at his wife, and shake his head in a sign like gratitude, like acceptance, like affirmation of these demonstrations that he was held not only in high esteem but in love and affection.

Though there was a cornucopia of lessons, the most abiding lesson learned from Mr. Brown is this: Yes, one man can make a supreme difference. Do not merely try—do. If you fail—and you might—no one can fault you, especially and most importantly, not you yourself.

We are none of us mistakes, but rather the simple and complex merging and parting of events and genetics, the coincidences and absences and doubts which surround and make up the human heart. The mysteries that we are—so naked to ourselves, but seen only through a glass darkly even by our closest friends and kin, if at all—are but the sum of these life particles. Or, to paraphrase the poet Tennyson, I am a part of all the people and places I have met. None are more important to my being who I am than Mr. Brown.

Such words as "father" and "mentor" pale next to the devotion and gratitude I feel toward this one man, a man made of dust and water, just like the rest of us, no more or less, another mortal being, simply. But in this life, in this country, in this black America, I count myself as one of the more fortunate among black men. I had Mr. Brown, who taught me the Sweet Science of Life.

(from *Colored People*)

# Playing Hardball

## Henry Louis Gates, Jr.

Daddy worked all the time, every day but Sunday. Two jobs—twice a day, in and out, eat and work, work and eat. Evenings, we watched television together, all of us, I'd done my homework and Daddy had devoured the newspaper or a book. He was always reading, it seemed, especially detective stories. He was a charter subscriber to *Alfred Hitchcock's Magazine* and loved detective movies on TV.

My brother Rocky was the one he was close to. Rocky worshiped sports, while I worshiped Rocky. I chased after him like a lapdog. I wanted to be just like him. But the five years between us loomed like Kilimanjaro. We were always out of phase. And he felt crowded by my adoring gaze.

Rocky and I didn't exactly start off on the right foot. When I was born, my parents moved my brother to Big Mom's house, to live with her and Little Jim, who was our first cousin and Nemo's son and the firstborn male of our generation in the Coleman family. It was not an uncommon arrangement to shift an older child to his or her grandparents', because of crowding. Since we had only three rooms, plus a tiny room with a toilet, my parents thought the move was for the best. And Big Mom's house was only a couple hundred yards straight up the hill. Still, it's difficult to gauge the trauma of that displacement, all these years later. Five years of bliss, ended by my big head popping out.

But Rocky was compensated: he was Daddy's boy. Like the rest of Piedmont, they were baseball fanatics. They knew who had done what and when, how much everyone had hit, in what inning, who had scored the most runs in 1922, who the most rbi's. They could sit in front of a TV for hours at a time, watching inning after tedious inning of baseball, baseball, baseball. Or sit at Forbes Field in Pittsburgh through a doubleheader without getting tired or longing to go home. One night when I was seven, we saw Sandy Koufax of the Dodgers pitch one game, then his teammate Don Drysdale pitch another. It was the most boring night of my life, though later I came to realize what a feat I had witnessed—two of baseball's greatest pitchers back-to-back.

I enjoyed *going* to the games in Pittsburgh because even then I loved to travel. One of Daddy's friends would drive me. I was fascinated with geography. And since I was even more fascinated with food, a keen and abiding interest of mine, I liked the games for that reason too. We would stop to eat at Howard Johnson's, going and coming. And there'd be hot dogs and sodas at the games, as well as popcorn and candy, to pass the eternity of successive innings in the July heat. Howard Johnson's was a five-star restaurant in Piedmont.

I used to get up early to have breakfast with Daddy, eating from his plate. I'll still spear a heavily peppered fried potato or a bit of egg off his plate today. My food didn't taste as good as his. Still doesn't. I used to drink coffee, too, in order to be just like Daddy. Coffee will make you black, he'd tell me, with the intention of putting me off. From the beginning I used a lot of pepper, because he did, and he did because his father did. I remember reading James Agee's *A Death in the Family* and being moved by a description of the extra pepper that the father's wife puts on his eggs the very morning that he is killed in the car. "Why are you frying eggs *this* time of day?" Mama asked me that evening. "Have you seen the pepper, Mama?" I replied.

An unathletic child with too great an interest in food—no wonder I was fat, and therefore compelled to wear "husky" clothes.

My Skippy's not *fat*, Mama would lie. He's husky.

But I *was* fat, and felt fatter every time Mama repeated her lie. My mama loved me like life itself. Maybe she didn't see me as fat. But I was. And whoever thought of the euphemism "husky" should be shot. I was short and round—not obese, mind you, but *fat*. Still, I was clean and energetic, and most of the time I was cheerful. And I liked to play with other kids, not so much because I enjoyed the things we did together but because I could watch them be happy.

But sports created a bond between Rocky and my father that excluded me, and though my father had no known athletic talent himself, my own unathletc bearing compounded my problems. For not only was I overweight, I had been born with flat feet and wore "corrective shoes." They were the bane of my existence, those shoes. While Rocky would be wearing long, pointy-toed, cool leather "gentlemen," I'd be shod in blunt-ended, round toed, fat-footed shoes that nobody but your mother could love.

And Mama *did* love those shoes. Elegant, she'd say. They're Stride-Rite. Stride-*wrong*, I'd think. Mama, I want some nice shoes, I'd beg, like Rocky's.

Still, I guess they did what they were meant to do, because I have good arches now. Even today I look at the imprint of my wet foot at a swimming pool, just to make certain that my foot is still arched. I don't ever again want to wear those dull brown or black corrective shoes.

What made it all the more poignant was that Rocky—tall, lean, and handsome, blessed with my father's metabolism—was a true athlete. He would be the first Negro captain of the basketball team in high school and receive "the watch" at graduation. (He was the first colored to do that, too.)

Maybe Mama thought I was husky, but Daddy knew better, and he made no secret of it. Two-Ton Tony Galento, he and Rocky would say, or they'd call me Chicken Flinsterwall or Fletcher Bissett, after Milton Berle's and Jack Benny's characters in a made-for-TV movie about two complete cowards. I hated Daddy for doing that and yielded him as unconquerable terrain to my brother, clinging desperately to my mother for protection.

Ironically, I had Daddy's athletic ability, or lack thereof, just as I have his body. (We were the same size ring, gloves, shoes, shirt, suits, and hat.) And, like him, I love to hear a good story. But during my first twelve or so years we were alienated from each other. I despised sports because I was overweight and scared to death. Especially of baseball—hardball, we called it. Yet I felt I had no choice but to try out for Little League. Everyone my age did Little League, after all. They made me a Giant, decided I was a catcher because I was "stout, like Roy Campanella," dressed me in a chest protector and a mask, and squatted me behind a batter.

It's hard to catch a baseball with your eyes closed. Each time a ball came over the plate, I thanked the Good Lord that the batter hadn't confused my nappy head with the baseball that had popped its way into my mitt. My one time at bat was an experience in blindness; miraculously, I wasn't hit in the head. With a 3 and 2 count, I got a ball, so I walked. They put in a runner for me. Everybody patted me on the back like I had just won the World Series. And everybody said nice things about my "eye." Yeah, I thought. My tightly closed eye.

Afterward, Pop and I stopped at the Cut-Rate to get a caramel ice cream cone, then began the long walk up the hill to Pearl Street. I was exhausted, so we walked easy. He was biding his time, taking smaller steps than usual so that I could keep up. "You know that you don't have to play baseball, don't you, boy?" All of a sudden I knew how Moses had felt on Mount Sinai. His voice was a bolt out of the blue. Oh, I want to play, I responded in a squeaky voice. "But you know that you don't *have* to play. I never was a good player. Always afraid of the ball. Uncoordinated, too. I can't even run straight." We laughed. "I became the manager of the team," he said. That caramel ice cream sure tasted good. I held Daddy's hand almost all the way home.

In my one time at bat I had got on base. I had confronted the dragon and he was mine. I had, I had . . . been absurdly lucky . . . and I couldn't *wait* to give them back their baseball suit. It was about that time that Daddy stopped teasing me about being fat. That day he knew me, and he seemed to care.

Yes, Pop and I had some hard times. He thought that I didn't love him and I thought he didn't love me. At times we both were right. "I didn't think you wanted me around," he told me much later. "I thought that I embarrassed you." He did embarrass me, but not like you might think, not the usual way parents embarrass children in front of their friends, for example. He had a habit of correcting me in front of strangers or white people, especially if they were settling an argument between me and Pop by something they had just said, by a question they had answered. See, I *told* you so, he'd say loudly, embarrassing the hell out of me with a deliberateness that puzzled and vexed me. I hated him when he did that.

And despite my efforts to keep up, he and my brother had somehow made me feel as if I were an android, something not quite a person. I used to dream about going away to military school, and wrote to our congressman, Harley Staggers, for a list of names. I used to devour *McKeever and the Colonel* on Sunday nights and dream about the freedom of starting over at a high-powered, regimented school away from home. Daddy and Rocky would make heavy-handed jokes about queers and sissies. I wasn't their direct target, but I guess it was another form of masculine camaraderie that marked me as less manly than my brother.

And while I didn't fantasize about boys, I did love the companionship of boys and men, loved hearing them talk and watching their rituals, loved the warmth that their company could bring. I even loved being with the Coleman boys at one of their shrimp or squirrel feeds, when they would play cards. Generally, though, I just enjoyed being on the edge of the circle, watching and listening and laughing, basking in the warmth, memorizing the stories, trying to strip away illusions, getting at what was really coming down.

# On the Distinction of "Jr."

## Houston A. Baker, Jr.

I am eleven years old, giddy with the joy of fire and awed by the seeming invulnerability of my father. He is removing dead coals from the glowing bed of the furnace. He is risking the peril of flames. We are sharing, I think, the heroism of taking care of the family. We are together. He is intense, sweating slightly across the brow. He still wears the shirt and tie from another long day's work. For some reason I am prompted to move with the pure spirit of being. I begin dancing around the furnace room with light abandon. My voice slides up the scale to a high falsetto. I am possessed by some primitive god of fire; I feel joyful and secure. I am supremely happy, high-voiced, fluid.

Then I am suddenly flattened against a limestone wall, bolts of lightning and bright stars flashing in my head. I have been hard and viciously slapped in the mouth as a thunderous voice shouts, "Damnit! Houston, Jr.! Stop acting like a sissy!" (sissy, *n*. 1. an effeminate boy or man; a milksop 2. a timid or cowardly person 3 [informal]. sister). Having heard my falsetto chant, my father had turned from the furnace with the quick instinct of an exorcist. He had hit me with the fury of a man seeing a ghost. The smell of woodsmoke is what I recall as I ran up the basement stairs and out into the Louisville night, astonished at how much I had angered my sacred and invulnerable father, whose moods of manhood were as predictable as the San Andreas Fault.

My name contains the sign of ownership and descent appropriate to the bourgeoisie. I am not a "second" or "II." I am a "junior" (junior, *adj.* 1. younger: used to distinguish the son from the father of the same name, and written, *Jr.* after the full name). The inheritance that passes to me from "Sr."—the man at the furnace—remains a mystery seasoned by small details.

He was born in Louisville, Kentucky, to a mother whose entire life was spent as a domestic for white families. His great-grandmother had escaped, or so the story was told, from a Mississippi slaveholder. She made her way to Kentucky with her owner in hot pursuit. His father, my paternal grandfather, was so light-complexioned that he might easily have been mistaken for the white slaveholder from whom my great-great-grandmother escaped. Harry was my paternal grandfather's name, and his greatest talent, or so I was led to believe, was fishing.

The cryptic unreadability of my father's life appears before me with the strange attraction and repulsion of a keloid. (keloid, *n.* a mass of hyperplastic, fibrous connective tissue, usually at the site of a scar). I want to turn away from his wounds, the scars, the disorder that I believe ripped his consciousness and shredded his boyhood days. But I cannot turn away. With each new revelation or additional detail supplied by my mother, who is in her mid-eighties, or by my older brother, in his mid-fifties, my attention is more firmly riveted. My head and gaze are fixed like Winston's in Orwell's *1984.* I see the pain coming, but am never certain where it will fall.

Prostitutes were a successful and shame-free business for my father's grandmother. From my father's boyhood perspective, his grandmother's "girls" must have seemed like uncanny citizens of a bizarre extended family. I vaguely remember his telling me one day, in a faraway voice, that his first sexual encounter was with one of his grandmother's girls, who in effect "raped" him.

So much is difficult to turn away from in what I perceive to be the scarring of my father's life. There is his mother urging him to stay forever her own "good Negro Christian boy," yet regaling, tempting, titillating him with tales of the glory of white success. Tales of the spartanly clean windows, shining cars, and infinite spaces of white opportunity in America. His boozy father, hunkered down in an old leather chair with the radio playing schmaltzy popular songs, dozing in the middle of some urgent question his son was trying to ask. Reverend Shepherd, a white Anglo-Saxon messiah of a boxing coach, urging those black Presbyterian boys of Grace Church to self-extermination for the glory of God and the good health of a "Negro race" that white American insurance companies would not even consider as clients.

Houston, Sr.'s answer to the aching incoherence of his boyhood was summed up in an exhortation that he barked at my brothers and me whenever we came close to tears or were on the brink of a child's response to pain. This exhortation—an admonishment that was his Rosetta stone for surviving chaos—was "Be a man!" There was nothing, mind you, ethnic or racial in this injunction. Just "Be a man!"

Since I remember no stories from my father's lips about being comforted by the arms of his mother or told fuzzy bedtime stories by Harry, I have to assume Houston, Sr., was like the children of the Dickens character Mrs. Jelleby, who just "tumbled up." This process translates in Afro-American terms as "jes' grew."

Houston, Sr., was left on his own to formulate commandments for his life. There were no tender revelations from his parents or burning-bush epiphanies from the mountaintop. "Be a man!" was therefore his resonant admission that only the most tightly self-controlled and unbelievably balanced postures could ensure a journey from *can't* to *can* in America. There was no time or space for sentimentality, tears, flabby biceps, fear, or illness in the stark image of American conquest my father set before himself. His notion of success was as deadpan and puritanical as the resolutions scripted by F. Scott Fitzgerald's Great Gatsby. Houston Sr.'s manhood code was every bit as full as Gatsby's of cowboy morality, gutsy goodwill, and trembling guilt about treating one's parents better. Mental control was like sexual control in my father's vision; it was a kind of *coitus interruptus* expressed in maxims like "illness and pain are all in the mind," "a woman should never make a man lose control," "race has nothing to do with merit in the United States," "the successful man keeps himself mentally, physically, and spiritually fit." Manhood was a fearless, controlled, purposeful, responsible achievement. And its stoutest testimony was a redoubtably athletic body combined with a basso profundo for speaking one's name—especially to white folks. "Hello," he would growl in his deepest bass, "my name is **Baker—Houston A. Baker!**" I often step back and watch, and hear myself in the presence of whites—especially those who overpopulate the American academy—growling like my father: "Hello, I'm **Houston A. Baker, Jr.!**"

If Houston, Sr., had a notion of heaven, I suspect he saw it as a

brightly modern building where his own well-lit and comfortably furnished office was situated right next to the executive suite of Booker T.
Washington. Washington's manly singleness of purpose and institutional
achievements were taught to my father. He absorbed them into his very
bones while putting himself through West Virginia State College under
the mentorship of the great John W. Davis. Houston, Sr., and Booker T.,
building a world of American manhood, service, progress, and control;
Houston, Sr., and Booker T., in their lives of service becoming swarthy
replicas of ideal white businessmen like Carnegie or Vanderbilt the Elder.

And, like Booker T.'s paradise at Tuskegee, Houston, Sr.'s ideal heaven
would surely have housed wives tending children who if they were male
would be vigorously instructed to "Be a man!" When not tending children, these wives would be satellites of manly Negro enterprise, raising
funds and devoting themselves to the institutional growth of a world de-
signed by and pleasing principally to men. In my father's heaven there
would certainly be no confusion between love and sex, race and achievement, adults and children, men and not-men.

•

With the household furnace billow-
ing smoke and ash on that evening long ago, my father must have suffered
the fright of his life when he heard my falsetto and turned to see my lithe
dance, accentuated by the whitewashed walls and the glow of the fire.
Houston, Sr., could only, I think, have grasped this scene as a perverse
return of his arduously repressed boyhood. His boyhood had been
marked by a Louisville East End of commercial sexuality and muscular
Christianity. The West End had been colored by a mother's ambivalent
love for her light-skinned prodigy. He struck out in a flash against what
he must have heard and seen as my demonic possession by the haunting
fiends of unmanliness. What, after all, could God be thinking if he had
somehow bequeathed to Houston, Sr., a sissy instead of a son? And so
he hit me very hard. Walking in the woodsmoke air that autumn evening
(actually just around the block and through the back alley, since I didn't
dare stay out too long), I could not get a handle on what precisely I had
done to make Houston, Sr., so angry.

Many years after the event, I learned the term "homophobia" and la-
belled my father's actions accordingly. As I think now about that moment
long ago, I realize that my father was indeed afraid, yet his fear was not
nearly so simple or clearly-defined as an aversion to physical, emotional,

intense and romantic love between men. There is a strong part of me that knows my father was fascinated by and even attracted at a level of deep admiration to what he believed, with great earnestness, to be the intellectual superiority and discipline of what he called the homosexual lifestyle. I think what terrified him on that evening years ago was not homosexuality as he ideally conceived it. Rather, he was afraid on that autumn evening that I was fast approaching adolescence and had not found what he deemed to be the controlling voice of American manhood. Clearly, then, it was time for Houston, Sr.—he knew this with both fierce dismay and instinctive terror—to busy himself with the disciplining of Jr.

The tragic emotional shortcoming of that evening was that my father did not realize that the letters at the end of my name were not meant to confirm his ownership or responsibility with respect to my name. "Jr."— as its formal definition makes abundantly clear—is meant to distinguish a younger self from the woundings of "Sr." It is sad that my father failed to realize that it was precisely those feelings of assurance, security, and protection which he had bestowed on me that overwhelmed me, that made me want somehow to dance for him.

It has required many hours of painful thought since that violent moment in which my father branded me a sissy to extract and shape for myself a reasonable definition of my life in relation to my father's. For decades I have sought patterns to fulfill a Jr.'s life. Mercifully, I have found some. They include much that my father was forced to ignore, deny, reject, or misunderstand. He could never, for example, have given approving voice to the informal definition of "sissy" that is sisterhood. Tragically, he never envisioned a successful man's life as one measured and defined by its intimate, if always incomplete, understanding and sharing of a woman's joys, dangers, voice, and solacing touch—shaped definitively, that is to say, by sisterhood.

Unlike the "Sr." produced by ordeals I have yet fully to comprehend, it is impossible for me to imagine "Jr." without a strong woman's touch. I am now the middle-aged father of a quite remarkable son. And at this moment I imagine that with God's grace I shall be able to live up to the standard of distinction the concluding marks of my name are meant to signify. If I do achieve such distinction, perhaps in some far-off fall twilight my son will dance for me. Speaking through rhythmic motion and with the very voice of possession, he will pronounce his own name in the world.

( ( speak my name ) )

# A Mighty Good Man

## Dennis A. Williams

He was Confectioner's, the old candy-and-drug store where I bought my first copy of *Fantastic Four* while he had a beer next door. And Proctor Park, where I learned to chase a frisbee while the women dished potato salad and other people's business. And the transistor radio that brought the Yankees to life while we barbecued chicken in the back yard. And the best toy on Christmas, and a ride on the ferris wheel. He was my past and also my future: he never told me about women and never had children, but he showed me how to be a husband and a father. It's not his fault that I'm not as good at either as he was; without him I might never have bothered at all.

Orphaned at a young age, Willis Hall was raised by an older sister and her husband in the Italian-accented, semi-industrial confines of Utica, on the Mohawk River in upstate New York. He grew to be an easy-going, gentle man, tall and handsome in the 1940s style that never left him, with a pencil-thin mustache and stocking-cap wavy hair. One summer, while he worked as a hotel waiter, a local hairdresser introduced him to a girl from North Carolina who was working in the service of a white family. Milia—he called her Mally—was a bold beauty, as outspoken as he was reserved, and maybe that was what got his attention: she was the rest of him and brought out the best of him. He knew it right away, but she went back home a few times before he won her heart. And then, in the first year of their marriage, he was called to three years' service in World War II.

After he came home he never left her again, not until the day he died in his sleep five months after he'd asked her to help him up and drive him to the store so he could buy her a Valentine's Day card, unable to bear the thought of missing the occasion. That was four months after she had somehow wangled a ride to join him in the hospital during the East Coast's worst storm in decades (the doctors sent her home before she was snowed in for several days, which would have been fine with her). He died only, in fact, after she had finally told him, as he lay asleep in the hospital bed in their home, that it was all right for him to go. They'd hung on as long as they could, for fifty-two years. A few days later, he ran his last errand—he went on ahead to hold a table for them on the other side.

While Willis was away at war, Milia befriended a precocious teenager who had moved up from Mississippi with her mother, the niece of the husband of Willis's sister. Milia and the teenager decided to simplify the relationship by calling themselves cousins, and fifty years later it was she—my mother—whom Willis asked to stay with Milia when he made his final trip. By the time I was able to untangle the actual familial relationships (I was well into adulthood), they hardly mattered. It was enough to know that I belonged to Willis—that we all belonged to one another—in a way that biology could never account for. Willis and Milia never had children of their own. With her family still in North Carolina and his scattered, our family—my mother, grandmother, older brother, and I—living fifty miles away in Syracuse, became next of kin. For some reason it was I, the second child, who was named their godson, even though it was understood that they were the surrogate parents for both of us. That was a particular blessing because they were the only married parents I had; my mother and father had separated when I was a year old and later divorced.

Significantly, Willis knew my father and never attempted to take his place. It would have been easy to do. My father lived farther away and communicated regularly but saw me less often. He was a sometimes mysterious and fearsome figure, a writer and bachelor living a strange life in the Oz of Manhattan. Though never mean and often generous, he presumably felt compelled to assert his authority in order to make up for lost time and to mold my brother and me, as was his obligation. In many ways, being with my father was work; being with Willis was uncomplicated fun. He always seemed willing to let us do whatever we wanted to do, but that never turned out to be anything bad. I can only now begin to appreciate how much effort and genius that requires—to guide without commands, to correct without rebuke, to set limits without saying no. I took this apparently effortless form of implicit parenting for granted. I knew always how much my brother and I meant to Willis, but I didn't know and shouldn't have known how much he might have wanted to claim us. Unlike the women in my life—my mother, grandmother, and godmother—Willis never said a word or made a gesture to criticize my father or diminish his authority, though arguably he would have had the most to gain from doing so. Instead, he became his own special kind of father figure. He drew his authority from kindness and earned my love by loving me as if I were his own while never pretending that I was.

Willis was something of a square, though he never seemed so to me because the residual hipness of his adult world clung to him in his casually natty appearance, the rarely played (when I was around, anyway) Joe Williams and Dinah Washington records in the living room, the passing references to this club and that pool hall. When he did party, it seemed more out of a desire to escort Milia and my young mother on a fun outing. That, of course, was the telling difference. I knew even then without being told that to be truly hip, to be that kind of manly man, one had to enjoy a life without women. Willis was the opposite kind of ladies' man, the kind considered by women to be "a good man." He had no friends with whom he would rather keep company than his wife. He was also a man of the church, and in that peculiarly female atmosphere, only the pastor gets to be "the real man," the sultan of the harem. All the others, the deacons and trustees and ushers and Sunday school teachers, admired as they are as civic-minded role models, in the end are doing women's work. Willis filled the role cheerfully. At his funeral, I learned that he had been known as the Minister of Kindness among his congregation, a description that fit his relationship with the rest of the world as well, and one that demonstrated his dignity and pleasure in being uncool.

For my childish purposes, however, he was just as cool as he needed to be. He played tonk and crazy eights with my brother and me, bought us suction-cup bow-and-arrow sets and didn't mind when we lost all the arrows on the roof, took us up to the park to launch frisbees and water-powered rockets. It didn't take much out of him, because he supervised our more active play without actually taking part, often getting us going and then laying back to dig it. My brother, not the most lively of characters, would eventually join him, perhaps stretching out under a shade tree in the park, while I dashed around like a puppy, retrieving a variety of projectiles, and the womenfolk chided them both for running me ragged. I can't say I didn't mind; at some point I usually began to feel ganged-up on and taken advantage of. But any frustration or anger I felt was always directed at my brother, who was getting his own brand of manhood training by aligning himself with the big guy at my expense.

Though he was a big man, six-foot and farm-solid, Willis believed in taking it easy. He worked hard, but I never saw him in that role, and in fact my only personal confirmation that he was a working man at all was the lunchbox on the kitchen counter that Milia would pack for him on Sunday nights, after we had gone. (She worked as well, as a nursing-home dietician; two-earner families were the norm among working-class black folks of my acquaintance, and so the notion of a working wife as threatening to one's manhood has always seemed silly to me.) For me, Willis was entirely a creature of leisure—weekends, holidays, vacations—and primarily the sort now scorned as "couch potatoes." He watched baseball and football on TV and drank beer; he drove to outings and tended the barbecue at gatherings, and ran domestic errands with us in tow. He did what needed to be done with unfailing good spirits that made any request, especially from Milia, seem urgent. But he didn't go looking for action. One of my earliest memories of him is washing the car, a two-tone green '57 Chevy, and maybe I remember that precisely because he wasn't the sort who was always waxing or crawling underneath. When automated car washes became more available, he had no qualms about giving up that duty, either.

My father, on the other hand, preferred to move. With him we were always doing—and learning. A much-anticipated vacation in New York might turn into a camping trip in the then wilds of Easthampton, with target shooting and no toilets. Even now, I never know when I'll have to hold a ladder or some power tool before I get to sit down and hold a scotch. That's not all bad; it has become a part of our ritual. Such activity, however, always carries expectations. It's not just getting it done or even doing it together, but also about the responsibility to get it done right, and the pending judgement of dissatisfaction if (when) I've screwed it up (still). Even at rest, my father was always teaching, cramming us with lessons that often had the short-term effect of taking the fun out of things he invariably judged racist, corrupt, or just plain stupid.

Being with Willis was relaxing in more ways than one. His laid-back demeanor helped cool my brother and me out without replacing our youthful activity with chores. When there was work to be done we joined him because we wanted to—the fellas hanging together—and helped when we could without any performance pressure. When he accompanied me on my one and only Cub Scout camping trip, I knew he was there only for me and wouldn't care if I couldn't catch a fish. But most of the time it was okay just to sit around, play cards, look at TV, and talk that noncommital man-talk, occasionally filling gaps in the silence that buffered us from the girl-talk in the next room. And in doing so my brother and I absorbed a different lesson than the ones my father so diligently conveyed: that we were equals, and could act like (literally mimic) a grown man without seeming to audition for the part; that this was our birthright, who we already were though yet to become; that we didn't have to put a bullet through a beer can, start a proper fire, or pass a current events quiz to belong.

As a father, I've never quite gotten the knack of Willis's more benign approach, which may have something to do with the difference between being a father and being a father figure. I still can't dependably make a decent fire, but I'm always conscious of showing my children how to do things properly. (Somehow I still feel I'm the one with the performance pressure, though.) The quizzes I'm good at; I constantly find myself delivering mini-lectures to a daughter and son who have far fewer qualms than I ever had about rolling their eyes in impatience and changing the subject—or even warning me that I'm starting to sound like Grandpa, which I take as a compliment. Yet as much as I know that these things are a father's duty, my lazy afternoons with Willis remind me always that there must be more. And so I catch myself and stop teaching and preaching and try to let them share my space uncritically, to offer the easy companionship—the security of being—that I finally settled into with my father and that Willis could afford to give me all along.

Like the occasional sip of Utica Club or Genesee beer. It seemed to me that he drank a lot of it, but he didn't; it was just one of those man-things I didn't see often in a house run by women. At our place, he drank from tall, slender glasses, otherwise unused, embossed with a spiral of dalmatians pursuing a bright red fox. (Highballs, on the other hand, were a unisex, special occasion treat; in either case, I was left with ginger ale.) Being more a regular guy than my father, Willis also became the primary target of traditional man's gifts: cigarette lighters (though he rarely smoked), cheap cologne, shaving supplies. I had no idea about what things men really used or wanted, other than what the drugstores told me on Father's Day and Christmas. Willis was no help, of course, because he never wanted anything from us except to be around.

Timing was everything. While they came to our house for Christmas—Santa and Mrs. Claus in a Chevrolet—we always went to Utica on the weekend nearest my birthday, which is usually also Father's Day. I have always related the two in my mind, and the transference has been remarkably completed; the celebration of my status takes precedence over the marking of my birth, and I want nothing more—really—than to be with my children.

When I was six, my mother took me on a train trip to St. Louis, a grand adventure for which I still don't know why I was selected. We returned home on a Sunday afternoon, and I was thoroughly prepared to rub my brother's face in the triumph of my special status as our mother's chosen escort. But he wasn't home. Willis and Milia, with their unfailing sense of justice, had appeared to whisk him off to the local amusement park. They brought him back hours later full of junk food and thrills, and my deflated—no, outraged—reaction only confirmed that they had done their duty and evened the scales. Of course they would have done the same for me, as I knew perfectly well. They were *my* godparents but *our* guardian angels.

One September Saturday when I was eleven, Willis and Milia came to spend the weekend. As usual, "the boys" hung out together, which meant toys and comics, games and TV, while "the girls" went shopping. The difference this time was that both groups were mobile, because my mother had bought our first car a few months before. But that mobility brought a new risk, and late in the afternoon, after we had finished our rounds, Willis answered the phone and learned that there had been an accident. All my mothers—my mother, grandmother, and godmother— were in the hospital, and for a short, scary time I was forced to confront the possibility that the boys might be all that was left of the family. The thought was scary only because of the potential loss, not because I was concerned for an instant about what would become of me. I knew we were in the right place, and in the right hands. In retrospect, I'm sure that had the worst happened, my brother and I would have gone to live with our father; Willis would have insisted, no matter how much he may have wanted, in that moment especially, to embrace us as his sole and rightful heirs.

As it turned out, the panic, at least the worst of it, was momentary. My grandmother, whose head had shattered the windshield, was hurt the worst but not badly. Willis was perfectly calm throughout, as he conveyed the news, took us to the hospital, and waited with us through several hours until everybody came home in one piece. It was a typically bravura performance, without fear or bluster or any hint of the over-emotionalism that might have undone us. Just as he would do thirty years later, when he sought to hold off death as he hadn't been able to hold off Uncle Sam, he simply asserted that everything was going to be okay. In fact, it didn't occur to me *until* thirty years later, when I realized how desperately he wanted not to be separated from Milia, how fearfully great the prospect of his own loss must have been for him then.

By rights, my experiences with Willis should have left me eager to re-create them with a son of my own. But that was not the case. I always wanted a daughter. Maybe I just never believed that Willis's kindly ap-proach could really work with anyone whose maleness hadn't already been dampened by relentless matriarchy. Luckily, because my wife fa-vored boys as much as I did girls, I had no qualms about entering par-enthood. When our daughter was born, my wife's first words, delivered without any obvious bitterness, were, You got what you wanted. She never gave up hope for a boy, although it was fully seven years later before I was able to believe that I was ready for a male child. When our son ar-rived, it wasn't long before all the matriarchs pronounced him, with equal parts admiration and dread, "a real boy." He was physical and intuitive, completely and stereotypically unlike our willful and obsessively orga-nized daughter, who commanded more attention and energy simply by being there than our son did by literally climbing walls. The pronounce-ment of the women triggered all my deepest insecurities. If "real boyness" was a good thing, why hadn't they sought to promote it in me? If it was a bad thing, was I being implicitly challenged to train him as if he were a German shepherd? And how was I supposed to do that when I had been, in a sense, so effectively neutered as a boy-child myself that I had hardly ever pulled at the leash?

My father offered one model, which remains useful. One move in par-ticular ranks in memory with anything I ever saw from any commanding figure, from Jim Brown to Patrick Ewing. Sitting on the floor of our apart-ment with my brother, helping him set up an electric train, my father once became extremely annoyed. In a single movement he snatched my brother up by the collar, unfastened and withdrew his belt, and delivered a series of lashes with the speed of Ali's jabs. I was thoroughly impressed and intimidated—no way was I ever going to mess with *this* guy. My grandmother, who was home at the time, was apparently impressed as well. For all her sideways criticism of the man who had left her daughter, she did nothing to intervene. I suspect now that she was gratified in the way women are when a man takes charge of a situation they *want* him to take charge of. It was the sort of performance my wife may have in mind when she tells me I need to do something about *my* son.

But Dad was a visitor. Kicking ass becomes much less complicated when you know you're leaving town the next day. Watching his day-to-day dealing with my younger brother by a second marriage yielded few comparable moments of righteous clarity. Alternately tough and conspiratorial, he often seemed just as confused and frustrated as everybody else.

It took me a long time to figure it out, but Willis was the answer. At least half the answer, because it was impossible to know for certain how he would have acted if he had had to deal with me *all* the time. Somehow, though, I suspect he could never have resorted to even the kind of physical punishment usually applied to children in general and to boys in particular. Firm when necessary, he never became angry enough to raise a hand. It probably helped that he was a master at the secret warning that is far more common than the wait-till-your-father-gets-home cliché. Your mother wouldn't like that, he would say, or, Milia might get upset if you do that. That he himself might disapprove—that I might let *him* down—was too horrible a prospect to contemplate, and therein lay his power.

It doesn't always work, but it helps. It would be wrong to suggest that my mother and grandmother ever gave me anything but unconditional love. Willis, however, added the irreplaceable ingredient of friendship, a luxury the women never felt, justifiably, that they could provide. For most men, including myself, it is nearly impossible to pull off this man-to-boy solidarity without at the same time conveying a sense of disrespect for the woman involved—it usually comes across as, I don't know why she's so pissed off and in fact I think she's crazy, but you know she's going to go off on you and make my life miserable, too, so just do what she wants and forget about it. Willis's absolute devotion to my godmother made it work, because his deflection of anger never translated into the notion that Milia was unjust or unreasonable. How could she be? He adored her, and he himself would never do anything to make her unhappy. As a result, his warnings reaffirmed rather than undermined her authority, developed within me a healthy respect for her, and had the benefit (in addition to getting me to do right) of teaching me how to love a woman.

I haven't lived up to his standard. Who could? However, as I grew into his kind of ladies' man, often wondering whether my eagerness to please others, especially women, was the perverse accomplishment of some matriarchal conspiracy, his example fortified me. It's easy enough to know that a man's greatest pleasure should come from the happiness of the woman he loves, but it's hard not to feel like the world's last fool when trying to live by that rule. Nearing the end of a second decade of marriage (not even halfway to Willis's record), I become increasingly conscious of his unselfconscious legacy.

But it is with my children, my son in particular, that I feel his influence most strongly. Playing ball in the back yard with him, making a run to the comics shop, or watching the Knicks on TV, I am eerily aware of the parallels—and of my desire for such moments to mean as much to him as they once did to me. Not long ago, as we were walking somewhere, my son tried to position himself so that his shadow could disappear completely into mine. It was an innocent, spontaneous gesture, typical of his fascination with natural phenomena. And it filled me with awe. Instinctively, I began to puff myself up, to make myself big enough to contain him, to assure myself that I was equal to the task. It worked. He felt satisfied, I felt blessed.

The last time I saw Willis I carried with me a secret. A few days before, I had discovered what I believed to be a tumor and I was convinced it was malignant. It later turned out to be neither, but the hypochondria served a purpose. Instead of coming to Willis with the mournful pity of a scheduled (and unacknowledged) farewell, I came for a final lesson in dignity and strength, more amazed than ever that he could be so fearlessly tranquil in the face of losing what he loved so fiercely—not life itself, but his life with Milia.

As it happened, my actual birthday fell on Father's Day that year, and I knew I had to be there with him. Reality intervened; Milia suggested we come two weeks earlier, because at that point you could never be sure. He was dressed and sitting up for the occasion, though confined to his bedroom. "Getting stronger every day," he said as he had before, although by then he must have known it wasn't true. Having finally found a physical activity worthy of his mightiest efforts, he had spent much of his bulk wrestling death to a standstill long after the doctors had expected him to succumb.

We sat together for a while pretending it wasn't the bedroom, and watched the New York Mets play the Houston Astros, and traded knowing comments about how dreadful an exercise that was. I was ready for him to falter, to show a hint of despair so that I could comfort him for a change. I had steeled myself to be ready to do that for him. He never needed it, or if he did he never let me know, just as he had never let Milia know. It wasn't in him. Milia brought him a plate of lunch on a tray, which he barely touched—said he wasn't hungry but that the food, as usual, was good. My son joined us for a bit before urging me to play a game of nerf-catch in the back yard. I was reluctant to go, but Milia said Willis needed a nap anyway. So we went and played, while my wife and daughter followed the script by becoming the girls who chatted with Milia in the kitchen. Everything was as it was. Finally, we brought the kids upstairs to say good-bye (for now, ostensibly), and I embraced him. And we went home.

I had imagined that at that point I would have been consumed by grief. Instead, despite my imagined tumor and his all-too-real one, I felt wonderful. Because I had left Willis knowing with absolute certainty two things I had not known before. One was that the only reason I had to fear dying was that I would leave my wife and children alone, and as long as I realized that—and lived as if I believed it—I could face death, paradoxically, with no fear at all.

The next day my doctor exposed my tumor as a fantasy. A month later Willis was dead. I tried to be sad, but he had left me nothing to be sad about, except in the most self-pitying way, which he himself would have found pointless. I felt proud of him, not so much for his yearlong struggle with death as for his seventy-eight-year conquest of life, which proved that good men *aren't* hard to find. What's hard for us is accepting that it's okay to be one—to purge ourselves of ego and to find satisfaction, even joy, in a generosity that invites the scorn of those who will always see weakness in unselfish strength. Our friends will think we have grown soft. Our children will seize upon any indecision or resentment as evidence that our indulgence is artificial. And even our women will suspect our motives. The only way to achieve that heightened level of manhood and retain the barest measure of respect is to let go the notion of manhood itself almost entirely, at least as it's commonly understood, as a role that obliges us to bury part of ourselves prematurely, just because. Willis avoided that trap by finding his manhood in his humanity. And in the example of his living he left me a map so that I might do the same—if I'm man enough to try.

# Shades

## William Henry Lewis

I was fourteen that summer. August brought a heat I had never known, and during the dreamlike drought of those days I saw my father for the first time in my life.

The tulip poplars faded to yellow before September came that year. There had been no rain for weeks and the people's faces along Eleventh Street wore a longing for something cool and wet, something distant, like the promise of a balmy October. Talk of weather was of the heat and the dry taste in their mouths, and they were frustrated at having to notice something other than the weather in their daily pleasantries. Sometimes, in the haven of afternoon porch shade or in the still and cooler places of late night, they drank and laughed, content because they had managed to make it through the day.

What I noticed was the way the skin of my neighbors glistened as they toiled in their back yards, trying to save their gardens or working a few more miles into their cars. My own skin surprised me each morning in the mirror, becoming darker and darker, my hair lightening, dispelling my assumption that it had always been a curly black, the whole of me a new and stranger blend of browns from day after day of basketball on asphalt courts or racing the other boys down the street after the Icee truck each afternoon.

I came to believe that it was the heat that made things happen. It was a summer of empty sidewalks, people I knew drifting in and out of the alleyways where trees gave more shade, the dirt there cooler to walk on than any paved surface. Strangers would walk through the neighborhood seemingly lost, the dust and the sun's glare making that place look like somewhere else they were trying to go. Sitting on our porch, I watched people I'd never seen before walk by seemingly drawn to those rippling pools of heat glistening above the asphalt, as if something must be happening just beyond where that warmth quivered down the street. And at night I'd look out from the porch of our house a few blocks off Eleventh and scan the neighborhood, wanting to see some change, something besides the nearby rumble of freight trains and the monotony of heat, something refreshing and new. In heat like that, everyone sat on their porches looking out into the night and hoping for something better to come up with the sun.

It was during such a summer, my mother told me, that my father got home from the third shift at the bottling plant, woke her with his naked body already on top of her, entered her before she was able to say no, sweat on her through moments of whiskey breath and indolent thrusting, came without saying a word, and walked back out of our house forever. He never uttered a word, she said, for it was not his way to speak much when it was hot. My mother was a wise woman and spoke almost as beautifully as she sang. She told me he'd left with the rumble of the trains. She told me this with a smooth, distant voice, as if it were the story of someone else, and it was strange to me that she might have wanted to cry at something like that but didn't, as if there were no need anymore.

She said she lay still after he left, certain only of his sweat, the workshirt he'd left behind, and her body calming itself from the silent insistence of his thrusts. She lay still for at least an hour, aware of two things: feeling the semen her body wouldn't hold slowly leaving her and dripping onto the sheets, and knowing that some part of what her body did hold would fight and form itself into what became me nine months later.

I was ten years old when she told me this. After she sat me down and said, This is how you came to me, I knew that I would never feel like I was ten for the rest of that year. She told me what it was to love someone, what it was to make love to someone, and what it took to make someone. Sometimes, she said, all three don't happen at once. When she said that I didn't quite know what it meant, but I felt her need to tell me. She seemed determined not to hold it from me. It seemed as if somehow she was pushing me ahead of my growing. And I felt uncomfortable with it, the way second-hand shoes are at first comfortless. Soon the pain wasn't as great, just hard to place.

After that she filled my home life with lessons, stories, and observations that had a tone of insistence in them, each one told in a way that dared me to let it drift from my mind. By the end of my eleventh year I learned of her sister Alva, who cut two of her husband's fingers off, one for each of his mistresses. At twelve, I had no misunderstanding of why, someday soon, for nothing more than a few dollars, I might be stabbed by one of the same boys that I played basketball with at the rec center. At thirteen I came to know that my cousin Dexter hadn't become sick and been hospitalized in St. Louis, but had gotten a young white girl pregnant and was rumored to be someone's yardman in Hyde Park. And when I was fourteen, through the tree-withering heat of August, during the Watertown Blues Festival, in throngs of sweaty, wide-smiling people, my mother pointed out to me my father.

For the annual festival they closed off Eleventh Street from the downtown square all the way up to where the freight railway cuts through the city, where our neighborhood ends and the land rises up to the surrounding hills dotted with houses the wealthy built to avoid flooding and neighbors with low incomes. Amidst the summer heat were the sizzle of barbecue at every corner, steamy blues from performance stages erected in the many empty lots up and down the street, and of course the scores of people, crammed together, wearing the lightest clothing they could without looking loose. By early evening the street would be completely filled with people and the blues would have dominion over the crowd.

The sad, slow blues songs my mother loved the most. The Watertown Festival was her favorite social event of the year. She had a tight-skinned sort of pride through most days of the year, countered by the softer, bare-shouldered self of the blues festival, where she wore yellow or orange-red outfits and deep, brownish-red lipstick against the chestnut shine of her cheeks. More men took the time to risk getting to know her and every year it was a different man; the summer suitors from past years learned quickly that although she wore that lipstick and although an orange-red skirt never looked better on another pair of hips, never again would she have a man leave his workshirt hanging on her bedpost. With that kind of poise she swayed through the crowds of people, smiling at many, hugging some, and stopping at times to dance with no one in particular.

When I was younger than fourteen, I had no choice but to go. Early in the afternoon she'd make me shower and put on a fresh cotton shirt. You need to hear the blues, boy, a body needs something to tell itself what's good and what's not. At fourteen, my mother approached me differently. She simply came out to the yard where I was watering her garden and said, You going? and waited for me to turn to her and say yes. I didn't know if I liked the blues or not.

We started at the top of Eleventh Street and worked our way downtown over the few hours of the festival. We passed neighbors and friends from church, my mother's boss from Belk's Dry Goods, and Reverend Riggins, who was drinking beer from a paper cup instead of a can. Midway down Eleventh, in front of Macky's Mellow Tone Grill, I bumped into my cousin Wilbert, who had sneaked a tall-boy of Miller High-Life from a cooler somewhere up the street. A zydeco band was warming up for Etta James. We stood as still as we could in the intense heat and shared sips of that beer while we watched my mother—with her own beer—swaying with a man twice her age to the zip and smack of the washboard.

Etta James had already captured the crowd when Wilbert brought back a large plate of ribs and another beer. My mother came over to share our ribs and Wilbert was silent after deftly dropping the can of beer behind his back. I stood there listening, taking in the heat, the music, the hint of beer on my mother's breath. The crowd had a pulse to it, still moving up and down the street but stopping to hear the growl of Etta James's voice. The sense of closeness was almost too much. My mother was swaying back and forth on her heels, giving a little dip to her pelvis every so often and mouthing the words to the songs. At any given moment, one or two men would be looking at her, she seemingly oblivious and lost in the music.

But she too must have felt the closeness of the people. She was looking away from the stage, focusing on a commotion of laughter in front of Macky's, where voices were hooting above the music. She took hold of my shoulders and turned me towards the bar. In a circle of loud men, all holding beer, all howling in laughter—some shirtless and others in work clothes—stood a large man in a worn gray suit, tugging his tie jokingly like a noose, pushing the men into new waves of laughter each moment. His hair was nappy, like he had just risen from bed. But he smiled as if that was never his main concern anyway, and he held a presence in that circle of people which made me think he had worn that suit for just such an appearance. My mother held my shoulders tightly for a moment, not tense or angry or anxious, just firm, and then let go.

"There's your father," she said, and turned away, drifting back into the music and dancing people. Watching her glide towards the stage, I felt obligated not to follow. When I could see her no longer I looked back to the circle of men and the man that my mother had pointed out. From the way he was laughing he looked like a man who didn't care who he might have bothered with his noise. Certainly his friends didn't seem to mind. Their group commanded a large space of sidewalk in front of the bar. People made looping detours into the crowd instead of walking straight through that wide open circle of drunken activity. The men stamped their feet, hit each other in the arms, and howled as if this afternoon was their own party. I turned to tell Wilbert, but he had gone. I watched the man who was my father slapping his friends' hands, bent over in laughter, sweat soaking his shirt under that suit.

He was a very passionate-looking man, full in his voice, expressively confident in his gestures, and as I watched him I was thinking of that night fourteen years ago and the lazy thrust of his that my mother told me had no passion in it at all. I wondered where he must have been all those years and realized how shocked I was to see the real man to fill the image my mother had made. She had made him up for me, but never whole, never fully graspable. I was thinking of his silence, the voice I'd never heard. And wanting nothing else at that moment but to be closer, I walked towards that circle of men. I walked as if I were headed into Macky's Mellow Tone and they stopped laughing as I split their gathering. The smell of liquor, cheap cologne, and musky sweat hit my nostrils and I was immediately aware not only that I had no reason for going or chance of getting into Macky's, but also that I was passing through a circle of strange people. I stopped a few feet from the entrance and focused on the quilted fake leather covering the door's surface. It was red, faded fabric and I looked at that for what seemed a long time because I was afraid to turn back into the laughter. The men had started talking again, slowly working themselves back into their own good time. But they weren't laughing at me. I turned to face them and they seemed to have forgotten that I was there.

I looked up at my father, who was turned slightly away from me. His mouth was open and primed to laugh, but no sound was coming out. His teeth were large and I could see where sometime before he had lost two of them. Watching him from the street, I had only seen his mouth move and had to imagine what he was saying. Now, so close to him, close enough to smell him, to touch him, I could hear nothing. But I could feel the closeness of the crowd, those unfamiliar men, my father. Then he looked down at me. His mouth closed and suddenly he wasn't grinning.

He reached out his hand and I straightened up as my mother might have told me to do. I arced my hand out to slide across his palm, but he pulled his hand back, smiling, a jokester, like he was too slick for my eagerness.

He reached into his suit jacket and pulled out a pair of sunglasses. Watertown is a small town, and when he put those glasses on he looked like he had come from somewhere else. I knew I hadn't seen him before that day. I wondered when in the past few days he must have drifted into town. On what wave of early morning heat had he arrived?

I looked at myself in the reflection of the mirrored lenses and thought, So this is me.

"Them's slick basketball sneakers you got," he said. "You a bad brother on the court?"

I could only see the edge of one eye behind those glasses, but I decided that he was interested.

"Yeah, I am! I'm gonna be like George Gervin, you just watch." And I was sure we'd go inside to Macky's and talk after that. We'd talk about basketball in its entirety and then he'd ask me if I was doing well in school and I'd say, Not too hot, and he'd get on me about that as if he'd always been keeping tabs on me. Then we would toast to something big, something we could share in the loving of it, like Bill Russell's fingerroll lay-up or the pulled pork sandwich at Ray's Round Belly Ribs or the fact that I had grown two inches that year, even though he wouldn't have known that. We might pause for a moment, both of us quiet, both of us knowing what that silence was about, and he'd look real serious and anxious at the same time, a man like him having too hard a face to explain anything that had happened or hadn't happened. But he'd by trying. He'd say, Hey, brother, cut me the slack, you know how it goes . . . And I might say, It's cool, or I might say nothing at all but know that sometime later on we would spend hours shooting hoop together up at the rec center and when I'd beaten him two out of three at twenty-one, he'd hug me like he'd always known what it was like to love me.

My father took off his sunglasses and looked down at me for a long, silent moment. He was a large man with a square jaw and a wide, shiny forehead, but his skin looked soft, a gentle light brown. My mother must have believed in his eyes. They were gray-blue, calm and yet fierce, like the eyes of kinfolk down in Baton Rouge. His mouth was slightly open; he was going to speak and I noticed that his teeth were yellow when I saw him face to face. He wouldn't stop smiling. A thought struck me right then that he might not know who I was.

One of his friends grabbed at his jacket. "Let's roll, bro. Tyree's leavin'!"

He jerked free and threw that man a look that made me stiffen.

The man read his face and then laughed nervously. "Be cool, nigger, break bad someplace else. We got ladies waitin'."

"I'm cool, brother. I'm cool . . ." My father looked back at me. In the mix of the music and the crowd, which I'd almost forgotten about, I could barely hear him. "I'm cold solid." He crouched down, wiped his sunglasses on a shirttail and put them in my pocket. His crouch was close. Close enough for me to smell the liquor on his breath. For him to hug me. Close enough for me to know that he wouldn't. But I didn't turn away. I told myself I didn't care that he was not perfect.

He rose without saying anything else, turned from me, and walked to the corner of Eleventh Street and the alleyway, where his friends were waiting. They were insistent on him hurrying, and once they were sure he was going to join them they turned down the alley. I didn't cry, although I wouldn't have been embarrassed if I had. I watched them leave and the only thing I felt was a wish that my father, on this one day, had never known those men. He started to follow them, but before he left he stopped to look over the scene there on Eleventh Street. He looked way up the street, to where the crowd thinned out and then beyond that, maybe to where the city was split by the train tracks running on a loose curve around our neighborhood to the river, or maybe not as far as that, to just a few blocks before the tracks and two streets off Eleventh, where sometime earlier than fourteen years ago he might have heard the train's early morning rumble when he stepped from our back porch.

# A Turn for the Worse

## Bruce Morrow

[My father] is kind and gentle, and has worked hard for me so that I am able to write these words. We are not friends: he is my father, and I am his son. We are silent when alone together . . . Our love for each other, though great, may never be spoken. It is the often unspoken love that Black men give to other Black men in a world where we are forced to cup our hands over our mouths or suffer under the lash of imprisonment, unemployment, or even death. But these words, which fail, are precisely the words that are life-giving and continuing. They must be given voice. What legacy is to be found in our silence?
—Joseph Beam, "Brother to Brother: Words from the Heart"

Things have taken a turn for the worse. My mother, upon returning from my brother's house outside Atlanta for a one-week Christmas vacation, has found a crack addict in her own home again. Things have taken a turn for the worse, my mother said. She was so happy that I'd called, and I might as well know that Rufus was back on his drugs again. After a short pause she said she was tired, she'd just finished bringing the laundry up from the basement and that was the reason she was out of breath, from climbing those stairs, and now she had to go get Rufus's rent-a-car out of the pound. He'd gone and given it away, she said, just let somebody have it. After an absence of four days he'd arrived home on foot. I asked her why he had rented a car in the first place, what had happened to his car. He gave that away, too, she said, or someone took it. I don't know, she said, and tried to catch her breath, to think it through again, to make sure it all made sense. Maybe somebody did steal it. That's what he told her when he got home: someone had stolen his car and he was scared, and she *had* to take him to the police station to report it. I told my mother—half joking, half speaking my mind—that she should report him, too.

Since she found out last summer that my stepfather of twenty-six years is a pipehead my mother has tried everything she can think of to help him. But things only get worse. She's tried pleading, then crying, yelling and crying, begging while crying. She's tried outpatient care, inpatient care, God's care—all to no avail. I say now is the time for my mother to change the locks on the doors, pack up his things, and set herself free. Get rid of him. Kick him out and keep him out. Don't let him back in ever again.

And yes, I know. I know these aren't easy things for my mother to do. I know it's easier said than done. I know something, anything, everything could go wrong. *I know. I know.* But something has to be done. These things have to be said. He might end up taking my mother down with him, that's what scares me. He already goes away for days and days without calling. He's now given away his car and a rent-a-car for drugs. What's he going to do—give the house away, turn the basement or the garage into a little drug den? When's he going to start stealing (if he hasn't already) from my mother's wallet? Her jewelry box? Her bank account? Has he already taken things from the house? Has he given his body away for drugs? Has someone given him sex so he can buy *them* drugs? Does he know about safe sex? It's too close, too close, even if I live in New York and they live in Ohio, and all I can do is call every day and make sure everything is all right.

These aren't easy things for me to say. Rufus, my stepfather, is the only father I know. He married my mother, an unwed mother of two, when she was twenty-six and he thirty. I was four, my brother three. And, like the scar on my face, an upside down check-mark above and to the right of my lips, he has been in my life ever since. (Mind you, he didn't give me that scar; his whippings never left permanent marks. The two incidents, the corner of a schoolbook slicing my face open and Rufus marrying my mother, just happened at about the same time.) My brother and I never called him Father or Daddy and he never adopted us. We have different last names but he's my father nonetheless. When someone asks me about my father, it's him that I talk about, him that I think of. When I fill out official papers, forms and applications, I fill in the blank "Father's Name" with his.

•

He's got brown, brown skin that always seems to have a brilliance, like a piece of hardwood furniture waxed and polished to a high, satiny glow. He's got a square face, a firm face with dark eyes you hardly see because what you really notice, even after that first look, is his forehead covered in brown shiny skin curving over the top of his balding head. The hair he does have is short, curly, and black and is usually hidden under a baseball cap, the kind truckers like to wear, the kind made of foamlike material with ventilating mesh sections on the sides and the brand names of auto parts written on the front—Champion, Firestone, Motorcraft, Delco.

He's a big man, not tall, but thick like a tree trunk, wide through the chest, broad across the shoulders from years of hard work. The thickness of his neck and arms always makes it hard for my mother to find shirts that fit him without being too long in the sleeves. When they first married, Rufus could flex his melon-sized biceps and lift me on one side and my brother on the other. Like a large crane or an amusement park ride at Geagua Lake, he'd lift us up off the ground and swing us around until we fell to the floor dizzy with delight and laughter and asked him to do it again. He always said funny things like "What's up, Zeek?" or "Slide me some skin" or "Holy mackerel, Andy" or "Save the bones for Henry Jones 'cause Henry Jones don't eat no meat." After everyone finished dinner he'd take the bones off of all the plates and stack them on his; he'd put a whole bone in his mouth, lick it clean, then break it in half and suck out the marrow. "That's right," he'd say when he was finished and there were nothing but chewed up shards of bones on his plate, "Henry Jones don't eat no meat."

He always boasted about the foods he liked to eat, how much he liked to eat, the way he liked to eat. Crispy fried frog legs. Buckets of chitlins with hot sauce. Plates of greens, turnips, and mustards and collards, with cornbread to soak up the puddles of green juice—"lickah," as he called it. He ate second and third plates of dinner, with loaves of bread and six-packs of beer—all in one sitting. He liked good scotch (Chivas, Johnny Walker, Glenlivet). He liked good cognac (Courvosier V.S.O.P.), good gin (Tanqueray, Bombay), any kind of whiskey, bourbon, but never rum. He liked Budweiser, Old English 800 Malt Liquor, Rolling Rock, and some Red Bud every once in a while.

He was never drunk, sloppy, or out of control, as I remember it. I didn't consider him an alcoholic or a person with a drinking problem. He just liked to consume mass quantities out of pure braggadocio; he had to have the best and most of everything he wanted in life. Ever since I moved to New York City almost ten years ago, Rufus's ongoing joke with me has been, "When you gonna send that?" which means, When you gonna send me that gold Rolex with diamonds around the dial? He's asked this question so often he doesn't even have to say "Rolex" anymore—or even "watch." Whenever I call or visit for Christmas he asks about "that." "That" is all he has to say. "So, Bruce, when you gonna send me *that*?"

Rufus is like that. He repeats things, says the same things over and over again. "Save the bones for Henry Jones 'cause Henry Jones don't eat no meat." He tells the same jokes, the same stories over and over again. Like how when he was growing up in West Memphis, Arkansas, he had to lift washing machines and bathtubs all by himself and put them on his father's pickup truck; poor, black and undereducated (he didn't finish high school), Rufus had to contribute to his family's income by working lots of odd jobs. "That's right," he would say, "that's right, I had to fix those machines and lift them too." And it seemed he'd get madder and madder every time he said it. "That's right," he'd say as he pulled his belt off.

He never punched us or hit us with his big thick hands, scarred and callused from working the night shift in an aluminum stamping plant for years and years. He always used the closest belt, the one around his waist; or he'd use a switch, a strong green vine he'd found in the yard and kept in the basement just in case; or he'd use an extension cord, a telephone wire, the old rubber fanbelt he'd just taken out of his good car. He would beat us until the welts ran together on our arms and it looked like we were stained the color of mashed grapes, fruit pulp ready for making wine. He turned like that, without notice, with little or no provocation. That's the way Rufus was. You never questioned his authority or you wouldn't hear the end of it—or you'd wish hearing was all there was.

He was an American success, of a certain kind, who'd risen above his humble beginnings to the middle class. He had a high-paying blue-collar job, a loving family, and a suburban house. He was a doer, always fixing things, changing the oil in his bronze-colored showboat of a Buick, waxing his car to a satiny finish with Turtle Wax car polish, painting the front porch and the trim on the house (the rest of the house was aluminum-sided), cleaning the gutters, cutting the grass, trying to get rid of the tree in the front yard because he thought it was ruining the grass. To have the perfect yard, a suburban American dream, he resodded twice, rolled the ground flat then planted a special blend of grass seeds that were supposed to grow well in dark, damp areas with lots of gnarly tree roots. He cut branches off of trees that blocked the sunlight and dropped too many leaves in the yard and the gutter.

He finally decided that the tree in the front yard had to go if his lawn was ever going to look as good as our neighbor's across the street, so he tried killing it by pouring acid down a hole he'd bored deep into the trunk. But that tree wouldn't die, didn't die until he had it cut down by a well-paid team of professionals equipped with heavy-duty saws, hooks, pulleys, and hydraulic lifting cranes. We watched from the front porch as the men, in regulation red plaid lumberjack shirts, yellow hardhats, tan utility belts, faded blue dungarees, and greased brown hiking boots, started from the top, sixty feet high, and worked their way down to the withered tree trunk, taking every precaution necessary to avoid any damage to our fine house or that of our neighbors.

Now, my mother says, Rufus won't even fix himself a sandwich. He hardly ever eats. He doesn't sleep or rest much, either. He's just wasting away. He's almost scrawny, she says. But I can't imagine it. A two-hundred-thirty-pound, five-foot-ten-inch man who had his shirts custom made or special ordered from a "big-and-tall" men's fashion catalogue. How much does he weigh now? I can't imagine him not making sure the driveway's shoveled when needed and the garbage is bagged for pickup every week and his hair's cut short and neat every month even though he wears a baseball cap most of the time. I can't imagine my stepfather a crack addict, a dope fiend, a pipehead. My mother says he's down to a thirty-two-inch waist. His skin doesn't shine anymore, it's gray, my mother tells me. He works a few days a week, afraid someone's going to ask for a urine sample, or, worse, a blood sample. Ain't no way around that one, my mother says, ain't no Chinese tea gonna clean you out *that* good. All he want's the pay, get some money and call in sick the rest of the week. He gives his whole check away so he can smoke for days and days straight. He doesn't do much else. He doesn't come home, my mother says, he doesn't worry about where he sleeps or where he shits. He lifts his pipe to his mouth, puts the pipe to his lips, lights, relights, and lights again. I imagine all around him tiny lights flickering in the dark. He's a firefly caught in a mayonnaise jar. He's a crackhead caught in a crack house burning his fingers trying to light his "shit." But he don't drop it, not even after inhaling it all into his lungs, not even after holding it, clutching it oh so near and dear to him. He holds onto his pipe while everything else dwindles away.

.

I walk home from the subway with my head held low and my shoulders hunched over to fight the cold. It's been the worst winter I've ever experienced in New York. The temperature hasn't gone above freezing in weeks. All I want to do is get home, stay home, be home. I want to go visit my mother but I can't afford it. Maybe I could talk some sense into Rufus, stay there with him, watch him, make sure he doesn't slip or fall. I could shovel the driveway, throw salt down, organize my parent's bills, protect them.

Until recently I'd never worried about my parents facing "the problems of today"—drugs, crime, AIDS. I thought of them simply growing old together, retiring, getting pensions and social security, getting high cholesterol, arthritis. Cancer and Alzheimer's were my biggest worries. Not drugs. I never thought about drugs—crack—really affecting my life. Those nightmare stories of "the chronic" were just that, stories, cautionary tales. For me the drug problem in America was the problem of others—the poor, the undereducated, the underachievers, the overachievers. Or at least that's the way the drug problem in America is portrayed. It's them over there, the blacks who've taken over and destroyed our cities, the minorities who've never finished high school, the ones on welfare; or it's those white corporate megalomaniacs, or those white suburban teenagers turned into bad seeds.

(On my way home this frigid cold winter night, I see many black and Latino male youths just hanging out on street corners, and I see at least five cars filled with white male youths driving through the narrow side streets of Washington Heights, then heading back to Jersey. I don't know for sure that drug transactions are occurring all around me, but it's definitely suspect.)

When I was in high school I used to pinch from the brown paper grocery bag of weed that Rufus kept in the back of his closet. I'd take a whole handful, sell some at school, and smoke the rest with friends. I did it to spite him. I always made sure I didn't take too much at one time. But he knew. He'd ask me for a cigarette and then ask if I had anything else, something stronger. I'd laugh knowingly but never answer.

Like all our other missed conversations, our chances to get to know one another, we never talked about getting high. We never shared a joint. I took and he accepted. It was our secret.

•

I've spoken to Rufus twice since I found out he was a drug abuser, an addict, a crackhead. The first time I spoke to him was to return the Christmas greeting he left on my answering machine. His voice sounded giddy and light when I listened to his message, and for a moment, for a bit of a quick second, I thought he was as high as a kite. He laughed—giggled—as he wished me a merry Christmas. I knew he was alone in Cleveland and my mother away in Atlanta visiting my brother. It didn't sound like a good idea to me for him to be left alone on a holiday two weeks after getting out of rehab, but as my mother told me, "He's going to do what he wants to do. He's going to do drugs if I'm there or if I'm not there. It's up to him. I can't be responsible for him doing drugs. You want to go watch him?" I didn't. But I was more than happy to get a Christmas message from Rufus and I refused to consider for any amount of time that he was fucked up and filled with more than holiday cheer.

I called him back the day after Christmas and we had a nice conversation. He immediately asked, "When you gonna send me that?" He asked it six or seven times in our ten-minute conversation. "I guess it's in the mail," he joked, and I asked him about the record amount of snow in Cleveland and if it really looked like the picture in the *Times*. "Yeah, I had to dig my way out the house," he said. "Over two feet of snow and it's still snowing." He said he'd spent Christmas with his daughter (the stepsister I didn't meet until I was in college), her husband, and their two children. He said it was real nice and I made up some lame excuse about getting off the phone and going to bed early. I just didn't have much to say to Rufus and I didn't want to reveal my suspicions about his state. He'd been out of his four-week rehab for less than two weeks.

The next time I spoke to Rufus was a surprise. I hadn't expected him to answer the phone when I called home. He's seldom home when I call. He used to always be at work. And now that my mother was sure Rufus had spent over a thousand dollars between Christmas and New Year's and had also given his car away, I was so surprised he was home that I hung up the phone. A drug addict had answered the phone; I'd called long distance and a crackhead in Cleveland Heights, Ohio, had answered. I figured I'd better wait awhile so he wouldn't suspect me of hanging up on him. I called back ten minutes later.

"Hello," he said in his normal, sleepy voice.

"Hey Rufus," I said, "so you decided to come back." I couldn't stop myself from saying what was on my mind.

"Yeah, I'm back. I know, I guess I didn't make it long."

"Well, why'd you come back? You should have just stayed away." I couldn't stop myself. I had to just ask and get it out of the way.

"What, Bruce? Just who do you think you are?"

I hadn't expected him to react, but he was already as angry and mad as I was. My mother had told me it was no use arguing with him because it didn't faze him, it just added fuel to his anger. I thought I could be smarter than that. But I wasn't.

"Just who do you think you are telling me I shouldn't come here? I live here, you don't."

"Well, then, why'd you go away for so many days? Why don't you just go live there?" I asked, raising my voice to match his. I couldn't help myself.

"Who do you think you are?" he asked again and again. "I'm not ready. I guess I'm not ready to stop. And I can't stop until *I* want to." He had learned twelve-step-speak during his rehab. "That's right. Until *I* want to. I don't need you telling me what I should and shouldn't be doing. Shit, this is my house. Where else am I going to go?"

"You can just go back where you've been. Smoking crack. Doing drugs. Just go back there."

"Well, I can't quit until I want to. I can't do it 'cause you say so. I can't do it 'cause your momma say so. I need to quit when I'm ready, that's the only time. Where the hell do you get off telling me not to come to my own house, my home?"

I didn't think that was what I had said, but he did. I couldn't say a word. I didn't want to get him mad—at me, at my brother, at my mother. He just kept right on anyway.

"This is *my* house," he said, "and I can be here if I want to. Who are you to judge me? I ain't judging you. That's right. I ain't judging the way you living."

That pretty much knocked me over. I'd played right into it. I sat down and stopped listening to what he was saying. I thought, Here I am arguing with Rufus, with my stepfather, with this man who'll do anything to justify his big mistake, even make some crazed equation about my life with my lover of five years to his smoking crack. I refused to let it play out that way.

"How *am* I living, Rufus?" I asked. "You're the drug addict. I'm gay, and maybe you think that's illegal, but it's not. You're the one addicted to crack. You're the crackhead. You should be in jail. I'm not doing anything illegal. I'm not doing illegal drugs."

"Why you want to judge me that way, Bruce?" he asked in a hurt voice. "I ain't never said anything about the way you live over there. I ain't."

"Rufus, you don't seem to understand. You're the drug addict."

"Why you calling here telling me I got to go back, I got to go? This is my home. I ain't moving no fucking place. That's right. Who do you think you are? Who do you think you're talking to? Why are you saying these things?"

"Because I care about you."

"Well, why didn't you say that sooner? Why didn't you say that a long time ago?"

I didn't have an answer for that. I couldn't speak of love. My anger had blurred my vision.

"I called to talk to my mother," I said. I wanted out of this conversation. "Where is she? Where's my mother?"

"She's not here."

"Well, I'll call back."

"You better," he said, knowing he was victorious. The stakes were love, unspoken, understood love between a father and a son, and if I couldn't put up I better shut up.

"You must be out of your mind," he said after a brief pause. "This is my home and I'm not leaving."

And that was exactly what I was afraid of. I still am. That's what I fear the most—my mother being held hostage in her own home by her husband of twenty-six years.

My mother walked in the house right then and he gave her the phone. She told me she was all right, that she had to take it a step at a time, she got too scared if she thought it all had to be over with at once. I agreed, but it sounded like something a facilitator would say at an AlAnon meeting. Why couldn't she just give him the boot, kick him out and be over and done with it? I wanted it to be that simple but I knew it wouldn't be. Rufus had just proved that. I didn't know shit. There was no room in his life for my reality as a gay man content and happy in a long-term relationship, just like there was no room in my life for a drug abuser. I just wanted him to ask me, "So when you going to send me that? I hope you put that Rolex in the mail first-class." Why didn't he ask?

I've always thought the reason Rufus wanted me to get him a gold Rolex was because he thought things like gold watches and designer clothing were cheaper in New York, or he thought everyone in New York had expensive things, lived the high life, so why didn't I send him a nice watch? But now that I'm writing about this running joke with Rufus, I'm beginning to think there's even more implied and embedded in that question. Maybe in his roundabout way Rufus was also asking me when I'm going to make it big in New York, be the success "that" he knows I'm going to be, and send him "that" gold Rolex with diamonds around the dial. He knows I'm going to be a success. He's encouraging me in that secret code we speak, that secret we share. Our love for one another.

When I was young and determined to get away from this man who is my father, I thought of nothing but getting away. I was scared of him then and I hid in my room reading, watching TV, listening to the radio, and planning my escape. I didn't know I was going to New York, I didn't know I was going to become a writer, but I knew I was going to get away, to make it. Now I want him back.

# ( ( part three ) )

GO HOME TO YOUR WIFE

# Go Home to Your Wife

## Cecil Brown

"Speakin' of marriage," Uncle Elmo announced. He took a swig from the mason jar and smacked his lips while he screwed the lid back on the jar tightly, as if he was never going to drink another drop from it, then placed the jar along beside his boot. "If I'm a happily married man today—and I am!—I owe it to my sistuh Amanda!"

"Sho' you do!" Essau Nealey, the old man sitting next to him chanted. "That's right! Uh-huh!"

Uncle Elmo took the mason jar up again, unscrewed the lid, took another swig, screwed the lid back again tightly and placed it in the exact same spot near his clay-crusted boot.

"Yup, you sho' right about that!" Gordon Tuggles, sitting across from them, agreed. "That woman's always got her nose in somebody else's business!" The other man, Isham Hinson, pulled on his long red beard and chuckled to himself.

"Just to give ya some idea of how she gets into people's business, I was in love with a gal and Amanda knowed it before I did!" He glared at us incredulously. "That's right! She did!" Uncle Elmo said. "Now of course that was many years ago. That man sittin' right there," he said, pointing a finger at me, "wasn't nothin' but a baby then. Now look at 'im. He's a man now." The men looked at me as if I had suddenly grown from a baby to full maturity in a few seconds.

"Now, the way she figured out I was in love," he went on, "was she had cooked this big meal—an' my sistuh could really cook up some grub—and that man right there"—he pointed again at me—"looked down at my plate and said, 'Elmo ain't ate nothin' yet.' And my sistuh seed this and said, 'He ain't ate nothin' yet 'cause he's in love!' See, in them days when folks fell in love they lost they appetite for food. And me bein' a young feller that liked to eat, when my sistuh seed that I hadn't touch my food, figured I was in love. And she was right. I was in love with this gal and didn't even know it. That's why I said Amanda was so nosey that she would know somethin' about you before you knowed it about yo'self."

I sat there and tried to remember that particular incident, but I couldn't. It had been many years since I had left home, and even these old faces staring at me were only vague in memory. I had come home to the wedding of a childhood friend. The wedding was to take place at Lee's Chapel church, and this was the night before, the night when all the men got together with the bridegroom for a bachelor party.

We had gathered at my Aunt Amanda's house, probably because she, with the biggest brick house in the town, had the most available space, but also because she had the biggest heart in town and whenever there was a social function everybody assumed it would take place at her house. This living room we sat in was the very one I was forbidden to enter when I was growing up in her house as a child.

When I was about four or five I came to live with this aunt because my father was "in trouble" and couldn't support his wife and two children. I was too young to know what this "trouble" meant, but Aunt Amanda raised us like her own children, and it was because of her that I had a happy childhood, went to the university, and became a normal human being.

Each year she would pile my brother and me into her big Buick and take us to visit my father, who lived in a huge gray building at the foot of the green Shannadoh Valley mountains, and on each visit my father would take me on a walk alone and call me his "little man," and tell me to be a good boy, to obey his sister, and that when he came home we would have us a "real good time." I was exceedingly proud of these private talks and loved my father very much.

When I was twelve my father came out of prison, and of course by this time I knew much more about his trouble. I also knew a great deal about how hard his sister had worked to bring up my brother and me to be un-scathed by my father's tragedy. I knew how hard she had worked to save money to pay for his lawyers—how she, working beside men, had cut down timber, had farmed the land, had dug roots out of the ground, had picked cotton, had cooked for white people to get the money to bring us up with.

When my father was reunited with our mother, Aunt Amanda, with-out a murmuring word, simply handed us over to our parents even though she had grown to love us, had sent us off to our first days at school, had comforted us at night when we were afraid of the dark, had told us our first ghost stories, had ironed our clothes and packed our lunchboxes. I'd often felt the desire to put something down on paper about her, but it wasn't until I heard my Uncle Elmo tell the story about how she had in-fluenced his life that I began to gather an idea about how to do it.

It was at this bachelor party that my uncle told this story about his sister, the indefatigable woman who'd raised us. Picture, then, a group of ten Southern men, some of them still in their teens, others in their sixties, but all of them the products of a small town. The older men, with names like Essau Nealey, Isham Hinson, George Russia, and Gordon Tuggles, sit around my Uncle Elmo swapping lies, just as they have been doing for the past forty years, with their legs crossed at the knee, their long, wrin-kled hands in easy reach of a mason jar of clear-colored corn whiskey.

The younger men are dressed in gabardine slacks of bright blues and reds. The older men are still in their overalls, which are frayed and thread-bare; huge boots are laced to their feet. The story they are going to hear the older men have heard many times before. It is a story in which they themselves have played a major part, and yet they each follow its unfolding with the interest of someone hearing it for the first time. They will laugh or grimace to the expression of it according to their own in-dividual remembrances, and will nod at each other occasionally as if they arc reacting to the same impressions.

My Uncle Elmo is a long, thin black man, with a thin face and small, inscrutable eyes that seem to glow with an inner light. He speaks in a voice which is neither old nor young but young when he is speaking of his youth and old when he means to draw a conclusion from his youthful experiences. He is wearing a plaid sports jacket over his overalls, a jacket he wears on special occasions to suggest that he has "dressed up." We are sitting in Aunt Amanda's living room, on plastic-covered sofas (the sofas were new when I was a child and the plastic covers have turned yellow in their duty to protect the material beneath). Also in the room are a piano, a table upon which a gold-gilt edition of the King James Bible lies, and a statue of Jesus Christ that stands on a whatnot table in the corner.

My Uncle Elmo has a curious way of telling the story. Sometimes he looks off into the distance, training his eyes on the corner of the room and addressing the statue, and then suddenly, without notice, he looks right into the eyes of his auditors. When he speaks of the sound of an animal, he makes the sound by slapping his open hand against his leg. It's strange for me to witness this master storyteller because I still remember him when he was a young man who was always at odds with the family because he spent most of his time hanging around the alley, drinking and living a life without aim. The story he is telling, however, is about the time he fell in love, got married, and became an upstanding member of the community—and how it all came about because of the peculiar character of his sister.

•

"My sistuh said, 'He ain't ate nothin' 'cause he in love with Kathleen Smith.' And at the mention of the gal's name my heart come jes' a-jumpin', see—'cause she was right! 'Him and that gal bein' courtin' each other on the sly,' she says, and she was right! You know what we called courtin' back in them days. You took a gal out for some ice cream a couple times and she smiled at you and you *grinned* at her and you was courtin'. Now this Kathleen was a light brown-skinned gal, and had this here little tiny waist and a pair of great big hips, and the purtiest smile in the world. And when Amanda let the cat out the bag, I realized I was in love and so I come jest to talkin' about how much I liked Kathleen.

"Next thing I knowed, Lofton—that's my sistuh's husband, y'all know 'im—asked me, said, 'Boy, when you gettin' married?' jest like that. Now I was puzzled 'cause I jes' done found out I was in love, so how am I gonna know when I'm gonna get married? So I says, 'I donno,' and my sistuh says, 'Do you want to marry Kathleen?' And I didn't even think about it, I says, 'Yes.' And my sistuh says, 'When you gonna tell Kathleen?' and I says, 'Right now,' and jumps up from the table, see. But 'fore I can get out the door, Amanda says to me, 'When you gets married, where you gonna live?' and I says, 'I donno,' and she says to me, 'When you gets married you can have Pappa's house.'

"Now Pappa hadn't been dead more'n a year and I always liked Pappa's house, but he left the house to Amanda, see? But she says to me, 'Mamma and Pappa would want you to have that house,' and so she give me the house.

"So I run over to Kathleen's house to ask her if she'll marry me and she said she would and so we gets married right down the road here in Lee's Chapel, where that boy over there gonna get married tomorra, see. And everybody come to the weddin', and I mean everybody—even a few white people come. Now we move into Pappa's house with all the gifts my sistuh and our friends give to us. A new frigidaire, dishes and spoons, and blankets for the bed, and jes' about everything you can imagine. And so we're jes' as happy as a newly married couple could be, see.

"Now here comes the mean part of the story, and the reason why I'm tellin' it in the first place. Marriage is a mean business for a young man if he don't watch his step. Now I tell you why I say this. A lot of married men start tipping out on they wives, see. They look at these young gals and next thing they know, they done forgot about the vow of faithfulness they make to God and their wives. See my point? So one of these married men—I ain't callin' no names—said to me, 'Now that you married, you oughta be gettin' some of the benefits of married life!' said 'Yeah, these young gals in this town loves married men,' said, 'These young gals like the married men 'cause they know what to do.' Yeah, they kept sayin' things like this to me, see, but I would go on about my business, not payin' them any attention 'cause I was happy with what I had at home, see.

"Now I had me a good job at Reiglewood Paper Company, mixin' chemicals, makin' good money, and buyin' my young wife anything her heart desires. And when I come home she be waitin' for me in a new negli-jay and we put on some of this here rock 'n' roll music, not none of this here loud rock 'n' roll but the slow kind, see, and we pull down them shades just when the sun goin' down and turn on this red light we had and we'd have ourselves a good time! So what these wicked married men would tell me in one ear would go out the other ear.

"But you know if you keep hearin' wickedness, one day you gonna start thinkin' wicked too. So I start noticing the way these young gals would be so free with me, see. But I wouldn't give 'em no real opportunity to tempt me. Now I don't know how she knew it, but my sistuh Amanda come by the house one day when Kathleen was out in the garden and she said to me, she said, 'Elmo, you married a good woman.' And I said, 'That's right.' And she said, 'Now I'm yo' sistuh and I wants you to remember—if you get any more wicked thoughts about these young gals, come talk to me about it.'

I said to myself, She must be readin' my mind. Then she goes on, 'If you can't stop listenin' to these married men, I'll have the pastor talk to you. Would you like for me to have the pastor talk to you on Sunday?' I told her I didn't mind talkin' to the pastor, jest to pacify her, see. But you know what? Come next Sunday, I had clean forgot all about it. Here come Reverend Ezell Banister saying he want to have a little chat with me, so I says okay and we walks over to the sycamore tree, jest me and him, see.

"Now as y'all know, this Ezell Banister is a curious fellow. He's thin as a rail despite the fact that all week he eats chicken and cakes at the houses of the women while their husbands are workin'. Before he was a preacher he was livin' up in Harlem shinnin' shoes, I heard. And he got this part down the middle of his head, which is sign of either a con artist or a number runner. I still ain't made up my mind about that feller! Anyway, he come home a'askin' me a whole lot of questions about my wife, see. But I figure since he's a man of God, I'd go along wit him. He ask me, 'Brother Elmo, have you been tempted by women other than yo' wife?' I didn't want to have this talk with him any longer, now that's a fact! And I'm thinkin' Amanda done gone too far now! So I tells him, 'Naw, Reverend, I ain't tempted,' and he shake his head, like he do, and says, 'Uh-huh,' like he don't believe me.

"Now, by this time I'm pretty disgusted by the whole thing and can't wait to get away. 'Now you know you oughtta do somethin' for the Lord,' he says, 'to get this wickedness out of yo' heart!' And then he tells me I should go chop wood for Lucille Green. Y'all know she'd been sick for a long time, bless her soul—she's dead now. So I says okay, I'll do it, mostly just to get away from 'im. I go home and I tells this to Kathleen, and she says it's a good thing to do.

"So later on that week I go by the old woman's house, down in the alley. Lucille lived right in the middle of a busy neighborhood, and so I goes on out the back to the woodpile, chop up some wood and take it in the back door. A young gal is in the kitchen but I didn't see it was Rosina, the gal that Lucille's daughter Rose had. She was then nearly seventeen years old.

"'Hello,' she says, 'how you doin', Elmo?' I says, 'Ain't you Rose's chile?' She says, 'Yeah, that's right,' and I says, 'Well, you certainly have grown up some!' Now she's followin' me with her eyes and a big grin on her pretty little face, see. I dumped the wood in back of the stove, in the woodbox, said, 'How's yo' grandma?' 'She's asleep,' she says, smilin' again, and give out a sort of chuckle that had a dark mysterious meanin' to it. 'She won't be up for a long while.' 'In that case, I'll be goin'. You tell her I chopped the wood for her. An' I hope she gets better. We miss her over at the church.'

"Rosina ran around me quick and stood with her back at the door. 'Don't go so soon, Elmo,' she said, 'I want somebody to talk to!' 'Somebody to talk to? Talk to yo' friends!' I told her. 'I don't have any,' she said. 'At school,' I said. 'That's just the problem,' she said, moaning with her head downcasted, 'I done finished school. When Gramma gets better, I can go up to Philly and get a job. But right now I ain't got nobody to talk to. Most of my friends done left.'

"I felt a little sorry for her, 'cause she was right. These kids nowadays, soon as they get out of high school they shoot up North. This poor girl had to sit home with her grandma. I stood there thinkin' about loneliness.

" 'What's yo' sign?' she asked me all of a sudden. I guess I'd been standing there starin' at her like a fool. 'What astrological sign were you born under?'

"When I told her my birthday she said I was a double sagittaris and I felt like sayin' that my wife was waitin' for me, which, incidently was the truth, but like a fool I didn't say a word. And why I didn't, I'll never know. Anyway, Rosina asked me if I'd help her with somethin'. I says 'What?' and she says she bought a new dress and she wanted to get my opinion on how it looked, and I says, 'Okay,' and the next thing I know I'm in her bedroom watchin' her put on this dress and take it off. And let me tell you now, she was a very attractive girl under those clothes!

" 'How you like this dress?' Rosina asked me, pullin' that dress up over her brown thighs. She gave me another invitin' smile. She was a curious girl, this Rosina. 'I like it fine,' I told her, and got up from the chair. I couldn't help but think all this had been arranged by my sistuh and that slick-headed preacher. They thought I'd be tempted by Rosina to go after her stuff, but I felt good I hadn't been tempted.

"I turned towards the door an' Rosina ran after me like a hungry dog bein' cheated out of a piece of juicy meat. 'Elmo, don't go!' she moaned. I just let her go on. She pressed her hot body up against my leg and put her arms around my waist and buried her head in my chest.

" 'I love married men,' she told me, and that's when I knowed she musta been put up to this by my sistuh. They were tryin' to tempt me! To see if I'd betray my wife! 'You're wicked, chile!' I told her, an' I pushed her away from me and hurried out the door.

"I got on in my truck and drove down to the swamp. Took my new shotgun with me an' walked along the edge of the cornfield. It was gettin' dark now and the jackrabbits were out nibblin' on that green corn. I kilt two and headed on to the house. Now, all the time I'm feelin' pretty good about the business with Rosina, see. I'm figurin' real proud 'cause I didn't fall into my sistuh's trap.

"I seed a kerosene lamp in the window and I knowed Kathleen done lighted it, waitin' up for me. When I get in the door I smells turnip greens and I sees Kathleen sittin' at the dinner table with the plates turned down, but she's lookin' down in the mouth. 'I kilt a couple rabbits,' I says and take 'em in the kitchen, but she don't say nothin'. I don't say nothin' but I know somethin' is wrong. I sit down at the table and pretty soon she looks up at me and her face is wet. She been crying, see.

"'Where you been?' she asked me, looking like she about to cry again.

"'Honey, you know I had to go cut wood for Miz Lucille Green, then I went down into the swamp to try out my new gun.' I had jest bought that new pump gun not more'n a week before and I hadn't had time to try it out.

"'Naw you ain't! You been with that Rosina!' she blurted out and started just a'cryin' like crazy. Now who could've told her that but my sistuh? I did my best to tell her it wasn't true, but I knowed I was already lyin'. She wouldn't listen and we had our first fight. In bed she turned her back to me and wouldn't say a word to me even the next mornin'. Doubt had already cast his shadow between me and my wife, see.

"I went on to work next day feelin' pretty disgusted with my sistuh. When I got off, I drove right over to her house. I took my gun with me, meanin' to show Lofton how it worked. When I come into the livin' room I hear the piano just a'goin'. Amanda had bought her a piano and at fifty-three she decided to learn to play it. She couldn't play but two songs after workin' at it a whole year and one of those was 'Nearer My God to Thee,' and that was what she was playin' when I walked in. I sat the gun down in the corner, and she finally turned to me and closed the lid to the piano.

"'Amanda, I don't like the way you been puttin' your nose into my business,' I said right off. Her smile showed me the gold in her back teeth. 'If the shoe fit,' she said pushin' her heavy weight off the piano stool, 'wear it.' And she headed towards the kitchen, 'I don't like to see you abuse Kathleen like that.'

"'What you talkin' about? You and that damn preacher got me to go over to that woman's house in the first place! I love my wife, and I ain't interested in that damn Rosina! I'da never been over to that woman's house if you hadn't got that man to have me chop her wood.'

"'You was tempted and don't you deny it! I know you men,' she said, and started stirrin' a pot of rice on the stove. 'I wasn't tempted!' I yelled back. 'That's the whole point. I was gettin' along good with my wife. Why did you have to go spoil it?! Ain't nothin' between me and Rosina.'

"'Just like Pappa.'

"'What you mean by that?!' I asked her. But I already knowed what she was gettin' at. She always believed Pappa had been mean to Mamma, that he had women while she was still livin'.

"'You men ain't no damn good. All you want to do is whoremonger with these young gals. And you married a good woman, but look how you treatin' her. Layin' up with that trashy thing, Rosina. Kathleen is a saint, and if you keep on with that Rosina you gonna lose her!'

"'Well, *you* ain't no saint!' When I said that, Amanda turned on me like a tiger. It's hard to get her angry but I know how to do it, boy. By the way I said what I said she knowed what I was talkin' about. See, I know things about my sistuh that nobody in this town knows. But I'm not a tattletale like she is. Everybody has some secret they don't want nobody to know that she had a child, but being an unwedded mother, she gave it to the lady next door an' the boy grew up without hardly ever layin' eyes on her. I was at her house one day when the boy came by to see her. He was a man then, twenty years old or so, had on an Army uniform. Lucky Amanda's husband wasn't there, 'cause she's always been embarrassed by that boy's comin' into the world the way he did. She gave him some money and told him never to come see her again. I believe it's the shame about this boy that made her so generous to children.

"She stood there, holdin' the spoon at me. 'After all I done for you, boy, you gonna talk to me like that?!' She was barkin' at me.

"'Just stay out of my damn business,' I told her, 'and whatever I do with Rosina is my own business.'

"'You better go on to your wife, Elmo,' she said an' she swung that spoon at me. I went through the livin' room, but she picked up the broom and came behind me with it. 'Stay out of my damn business,' I yelled, 'or I'll tell Lofton somethin' he don't even know about you!'

"When I got to the front porch, I turned around and I saw her standin' under the front porch light, holdin' the broom at her side and cryin' like a baby. I never seen my sistuh cry before. I got in the truck and started down the road. It really made me feel bad that I'd said what I said to her like that. I didn't mean to hurt her feelings, but she really got on my nerves. Stickin' her nose into other people's business.

"When I got to the highway I realized I left my gun at her house. I started to turn the truck around and go back for it, but I decided against the idea. With her havin' hurt feelin's I didn't feel like facin' her. Not now,

I thought, maybe later. Maybe I'll go by Rosina's house. Why not? My sistuh thinks I'm sleepin' with her anyway! But I really had no interest in goin' to bed with that gal. I figured I'd get her to make me some coffee or I'd jest sit there and talk with her. Get this confusion off my mind.

"When I walked in Rosina's house I asked about her grandma. She winked at me and said her grandma was asleep, jest like before. I followed her to the kitchen. Well, I thought, since Amanda knows everythin' about my life, I wonder if she knows *when* I'm gonna sleep with Rosina. Can she find out I'm gonna sleep with her *now*? I made up my mind to go all the way with Rosina if she tempted me again. Let Amanda go tell my wife *that*! After all the temptation I had to put up with, nobody believed me, an' was I to blame if I did it? No, 'course not. An' who put me up to do it? The damn preacher himself and my nosy sistuh!

"While Rosina fixed me somethin' to eat, all I could hear ringin' in my head was my damn sistuh's voice—'Go home to your wife, go home to your wife'—and it really got me goin', I tell you!

"As soon's I finished eatin' the cabbage and pig tails she fixed for me, Rosina took me by the hand and led me to her bedroom. We sat down on the bed. 'Is there somethin' wrong, Sweet Daddy,' she asked me. I liked it when she called me Sweet Daddy. See, that evilness was already workin' its magic in my heart. 'Amanda told me I should go home to my wife,' I told her.

"'Go home to your wife?! That's an old idea. Sweet Daddy, if you go home to your wife, you'll miss this present I have for you.' She stood up and walked over to the middle of the room and started untyin' the knot that held her dress together. I sat there watchin' as that knot came a'loose in long, slender brown fingers. When she finished the dress fell open.

"'I loves you, Rosina,' I heard myself sayin'. She slipped part of the dress over her shoulder. Before, when she undressed for me she was just showin' off. Now she was for real.

"'What you say, Sweet Daddy?'

"I told her again. 'As much as your wife?' she asked me. She dropped the dress from the other shoulder.

"'More than my wife,' I muttered. My tongue done got swollen up in my mouth from seein' her buck naked and shameless before me.

"'Prove it, Sweet Daddy,' she said, and she came and sat on the bed near me. I reached for her, but she pulled back. 'What you mean?' I axed her.

"'Take off your clothes, too,' she said. Now, just to show you how the devil can slip into ya' heart without you knowin' it, I jumped up—done forgot about my wife, see—and got outta my clothes. I stood there buck naked. I started for the bed where she was, but she held me off with her hand.

"'Cool down, Pappa,' she said, 'or you gonna blow yo' stack.' Anyway, we was jest gettin' in bed when I heard a loud explosion. Jumpin' up, I ran to the window.

"*Kaaapow! Yaaawrr! Kaaapow! Yaaawrr!*

"'What in the name of God is that?!' I exclaimed to Rosina. She lept up. 'An earthquake!' the poor gal cried out, an' before we could move another inch a second one come. The windows of the bedroom shook. I could hear the voices of the neighbors risin' like an ocean of concern. The sound of windows goin' up and people yellin' out.

"'What the hell's goin' on out there?!' I grabbed for my pants but couldn't find 'em. Instead, I pulled the sheet around me just as another explosion went off.

"*Kaaapow!* I rushed to the window where Rosina was, but all we seen was George Russian's big black head stickin' out the window next door. I didn't want him to see me, naturally, so I stuck my head back in quickly. Whatever was goin' on out there I wasn't goin' to go out because somebody would see me. And that was the thing I couldn't afford.

"Rosina was already in the kitchen, peepin' out the back window.

"*Kaaapow! Kaaapow!* Rosina pushed me down. 'Everybody's out there! Don't let 'em see you!' she warned me, and she took me by the hand quick. But I managed to pull away from her and take a peep myself.

"From the window all I seen was Esau Nealey standin' on his back porch in his overalls. Isham Hinson was also standin' on his porch. Then I looked to the left and saw George Tuggles and his wife standin' on *their* porch. They all lookin' down at somebody or somethin' I couldn't see.

"'What is it?' I ask Rosina. I could tell from the look on her face—a guilty look—she's seen what I ain't.

"'What you gotta do,' she said, quiet, 'is go out the front door.'

"'Me? Go out the front door? With all those people, the whole damn town practically out there? You crazy!'

"She shook her head. 'No, you got to—quick,' she said and grabbed my arm.

"'I ain't goin' nowhere!' I screamed in a whisper.

"*Kaaapow! Kaaapow!* The explosion went off again. Rosina said, 'Come on. You better go now!'

"Again I resisted. If it was an earthquake I'd a rather die in the rubbish than let these people catch me. 'Why should I go out there?' I asked her.

"'I'll show you why,' she said, an' she took me to the kitchen window again. She pulled back the curtain. Standin' there in the yard under a chinnyberry tree was my sistuh Amanda, holdin' my automatic shotgun, which she was pointin' up in the air. And while I watched she let off a shot.

"'*Kaaapow! Kaaapow!*' the gun went, and then my sistuh yelled out, 'Go home to your wife!'

"I thrusted the curtain back and turned to Rosina. 'Jesus almighty! How can I get outta here?'

"'I told you. Out the front!'

"I suddenly remembered I'd parked my truck in front of George Russian's house, so I could pretend I was vistitin' him. Now all I had to do was make it to the truck. If everybody was in the back, I figured I had a good chance.

"'My pants! Where's my pants?' I searched the room, but I couldn't find 'em. 'Here, take this,' Rosina said, and put somethin' in my hand. I didn't care, long as it covered my nakedness. She led me to the front door and I went out with the cloth she gave me to cover myself. Outside I didn't see a soul.

"Great! Then I came down the steps. Dan Creek pulled up in his Ford pickup. Now Dan Creek is a white boy and he don't live in the alley but sometimes he comes down here to buy liquor. 'Why, Elmo,' he's grinnin' out the window, 'What the hell you doin' standin' there with a dress on?'

"'Eh? What? Dress?' I look down at myself and realize Rosina done handed me one of her old dresses and I'm holdin' it up against my chest for protectin' against my nakedness.

"'Oh, this jest a joke . . . Eh? 'scuse me, Dan, but I must be goin'. See ya later!' I turned and started off jest as natural as I could, see. But jest as I turned, somebody called my name. 'Elmo! Elmo!' I looked up and saw Leon Lord leanin' off the bannister of his porch. 'Whatcha been doin'? Getting a little bit of tail? Ha, ha, ha.' And I seen everybody who been starin' out their windows in the backyard was now gatherin' around me in the *front* yard. Gordon Tuggles started laughin' with Leon Lord, and Esau Nealey joined in wit 'em. Then Isham Hinson, pullin' on his beard, grinned wit 'em. Mary Pierce came around the house with Amanda, still holdin' my shotgun.

"She fired another shot, '*Kaaapow yaawr!* Go home to your wife!'

"'Please,' I heard myself sayin', 'please don't tell my wife! Please don't tell my wife!'

"They laughed together and some of 'em took up the chant from my sistuh. 'Go home to your wife,' Mary Pierce jeered at me, 'You whore-monger!'

"I started to my truck, but I kept sayin' to 'em, 'Jest don't tell my wife! Jest don't tell my wife! Thank you!'

"When I pulled Rosina's dress up to my neck they all laughed. My sistuh laughed harder'n anybody. I ran to the truck and jumped in. Just when I'd got in gear I turned and seen Rosina on the porch, laughin' with the rest of 'em, and my heart jest about sunk to the bottom of my feet.

"When I drove up into the yard, I saw the kerosene lamp burning its yellow glow. I figured Kathleen would leave me for sure then. The best I could do, I thought, was to tell her the truth and then pack my bags and get up North, maybe to Harlem. Then I realize there's somethin' sittin' beside me in the truck seat. I saw somebody'd put a bundle of clothes in the seat next to me. I threw the dress off and put on my work clothes and went on in the house.

"Kathleen was sittin' at the dinner table. And when she saw me she jumped up and ran into my arms.

"'Elmo, I'm sorry I ever doubted you,' she said, coverin' my face with kisses. 'I'll never doubt you again. Amanda came over this mornin' and told me I was wrong to suspect you. She told me you loved me and wasn't studin' that Rosina. Amanda's right! Forgive me, baby?'

"I realized then I was safe.

"'Rosina? Honey, you gotta be jokin,' I told her, holdin' her tight in my arms. 'I never thought about that gal once! I love you and I'll always be faithful to you.'

"'Supper's on the table,' she told me and then led me to the dinner table.

"This is a curious town. I've lived with my wife for the last ten years and not one person's ever mentioned this incident to Kathleen. If they did, she never let me know about it. But sometimes one of these fellows, like old George Russia, will tease me about it. We maybe huntin' in the woods or just playin' checkers and somebody'll say, 'Go home to your wife,' and we have a good laugh, and then it's over with.

"Now, as far as my sistuh goes, I understand why she has her nose in everybody's business. If she don't have her nose in yo' business, how can she know when you need help? She helped me see how close I came to losin' my love for my wife. And Rosina? Well, I never talked to her about that 'cause not long afterwards Amanda helped her get the money for a bus ticket to the North, but my own suspicion is she was in on the whole thing from the start. Like I said before, she was a strange gal.

"I told you this story to show you how I come to be a happily married man and how I live with a clear conscience with my Kathleen all these years because of my busybody sistuh. An' even now, whenever I get the urge to do somethin' like that again, I hear my sistuh's voice sayin', 'Go home to your wife!' I tells all the young fellers gettin' married they oughtta have a sistuh like Amanda."

# My Mother and Mitch

## Clarence Major

He was just somebody who had dialed the wrong number. This is how it started and I wasn't concerned about it. Not at first. I don't even remember if I was there when he first called, but I do, all these many years later, remember my mother on the phone speaking to him in her best quiet voice, trying to sound as ladylike as she knew how.

She had these different voices for talking to different people on different occasions. I could tell by my mother's proper voice that this man was somebody she wanted to make a good impression on, a man she thought she might like to know. This was back when my mother was still a young woman, divorced but still young enough to believe that she was not completely finished with men. She was a skeptic from the beginning, I knew that even then. But some part of her thought the right man might come along some day.

I don't know exactly what it was about him that attracted her, though. People are too mysterious to know that well. I know that now and I must have been smart enough not to wonder too hard about it back then.

Since I remember hearing her tell him her name, she must not have given it out right off the bat when he first called. She was a city woman with a child and had developed a certain alertness to danger. One thing you didn't do was give your name to a stranger on the phone. You never knew who to trust in a city like Chicago. The place was full of crazy people and criminals.

She said, "My name is *Mrs.* Jayne Anderson." I can still hear her laying the emphasis on the "Mrs." although she had been separated from my father for twelve years by 1951, when this man dialed her number by accident.

Mitch Kibbs was the name he gave her. I guess he must have told her who he was the very first time, just after he apologized for calling her by mistake. I can't remember who he was trying to call. He must have told her and she must have told me, but it's gone now. I think they must have talked a pretty good while that first time. The first thing that I remember about him was that he lived with his sister who was older than he. The next thing was that he was very old. He must have been fifty, and to me at fifteen that was deep into age. If my mother was old at thirty, fifty was ancient. Then the other thing about him was that he was white.

They'd talked five or six times, I think, before he came out and said he was white, but she knew it before he told her. I think he made this claim only after he started suspecting he might not be talking to another white person. But the thing was he didn't know for sure she was black. I was at home lying on the couch pretending to read a magazine when I heard her say, "I am a colored lady." Those were her words exactly. She placed her emphasis on the word "lady."

I had never known my mother to date any white men. She would hang up from talking with him and she and I would sit at the kitchen table and she'd tell me what he'd said. They were telling each other the bits and pieces of their lives, listening to each other, feeling their way as they talked. She spoke slowly, remembering all the details. I watched her scowl and the way her eyes narrowed as she puzzled over his confessions as she told me in her own words about him. She was especially puzzled about his reaction to her confession about being colored.

That night she looked across to me with that fearful look that was hers alone and said, "Tommy, I doubt if he will ever call back. Not after tonight. He didn't know. You know that."

Feeling grown up because she was treating me that way, I said, "I wouldn't be so sure."

But he called back soon after that.

I was curious about her interest in this particular old white man, so I always listened carefully. I was a little bit scared, too, because I suspected he might be some kind of maniac or pervert. I had no good reason to fear such a thing except that I thought it strange that anybody could spend as much time as he and my mother did talking on the phone without any desire for human contact. She had never had a telephone relationship before and at that time all I knew about telephone relationships was that they were insane and conducted by people who probably needed to be put away. This meant that I also had the sad feeling that my mother was a bit crazy too. But more important than these fearful fantasies, I thought I was witnessing a change in my mother. It seemed important and I didn't want to misunderstand it or miss the point of it. I tried to look on the bright side, which was what my mother always said I should try to do.

He certainly didn't sound dangerous. Two or three times I myself answered the phone when he called and he always said, "Hello, Tommy, this is Mitch. May I speak to your mother?" and I always said, "Sure, just a minute." He never asked me how I was doing or anything like that and I never had anything special to say to him.

•

After he'd been calling for over a month I sort of lost interest in hearing about their talk. But she went right on telling me what he said. I was a polite boy, so I listened despite the fact that I had decided that Mitch Kibbs and his ancient sister, Temple Erikson, were crazy but harmless. My poor mother was lonely, that was all. I had it all figured out. He wasn't an ax murderer who was going to sneak up on her one evening when she was coming home from her job at the factory and split her open from the top down. (We were always hearing about things like this, so I knew it wasn't impossible.)

My interest would pick up occasionally. I was especially interested in what happened the first time my mother herself made the call to his house. She told me that Temple Erikson answered the phone. Mother and I were eating dinner when she started talking about Temple Erikson.

"She's a little off in the head."

I didn't say anything, but it confirmed my suspicion. What surprised me was my mother's ability to recognize it. "What'd she say?"

"She rattled on about the Wild West and the Indians and having to hide in a barrel or something like that. Said the Indians were shooting arrows at them and she was just a little girl who hid in a barrel."

I thought about this. "Maybe she lived out West when she was young. You know? She must be a hundred by now. That would make her the right age."

"Oh, come on, now. What she said was she married when she was fourteen, married this Erikson fellow. As near as I could figure out he must have been a leather tanner but seems he also hunted fur and sold it to make a living. She never had a child."

"None of that sounds crazy." I was disappointed.

"She was talking crazy, though."

"How so?"

"She thinks the Indians are coming back to attack the house any day now. She says things like Erikson was still living, like he was just off there in the next room, taking a nap. One of the first things Mitch told me was his sister and he moved in together after her husband died, and that was twenty years ago."

"How did the husband die?"

"Huh?"

"How did he die?"

She finished chewing her peas first. "Kicked in the head by a horse. Bled to death."

I burst out laughing because the image was so bright in my mind and I couldn't help myself. My pretty mother had a sense of humor even when she didn't mean to show it.

She chewed her peas in a ladylike manner. This was long before she lost her teeth. Sitting there across the table from her, I knew I loved her and needed her and I knew she loved and needed me. I was not yet fearing that she needed me too much. She had a lot of anger in her, too. Men had hurt her bad. And one day I was going to be a man.

When I laughed my mother said, "You shouldn't laugh at misfortune, Tommy." But she had this silly grin on her face and it caused me to crack up again. I just couldn't stop. I think now I must have been a bit hysterical from the anxiety I had been living with all those weeks while she was telling me about the telephone conversations that I wanted to hear about only part of the time.

It was dark outside, and I got up when I finished my dinner and went to the window and looked down on the street lights glowing on the wet pavement. I said, "I bet he's out there right now, hiding in the shadows, watching our window."

"Who?" Her eyes grew large. She was easily frightened. I knew this and I was being devilish and deliberately trying to scare her.

"You know, Mister Kibbs."

She looked relieved. "No he's not. He's not like that. He's a little strange but not a pervert."

"How do you know?"

By the look she gave me I knew now that I had thrown doubt into her and she wasn't handling it well. She didn't try to answer me. She finished her small, dry pork chop and the last of her bright green peas and reached over and took up my plate and sat it inside of her own.

She took the dishes to the sink, turned on the hot and cold water so that warm water gushed out of the single faucet, causing the pipe to clang, and started washing the dishes. "You have a vivid imagination," was all she said.

I grabbed the dishcloth and started drying the first plate she placed in the rack. "Even so, you don't know this man. You never even seen him. Aren't you curious about what he looks like?"

"I know what he looks like."

"How?"

"He sent me a picture of himself, and one of Temple."

I gave her a look. She had been holding out on me. I knew he was crazy now. Was he so ugly she hadn't wanted me to see the picture? I ask if I could see it.

She dried her hands on the cloth I was holding, then took her cigarettes out of her dress pocket and knocked one from the pack and stuck it between her thin pale lips. I watched her light it and fan the smoke and squint her eyes. She said, "You have to promise not to laugh."

That did it. I started laughing again and couldn't stop. Then she started laughing too, because I was bent double, standing there at the sink, with this image of some old guy who looked like the Creeper in my mind. But I knew she couldn't read my mind, so she had to be laughing at me laughing. She was still young enough to be silly with me like a kid.

Then she brought out two pictures, one of him and the other one of his sister. She put them down side by side on the table. "Make sure your hands are dry."

I took off my glasses and bent down to the one of the man first, so I could see up close as I stood there wiping my hands on the dishcloth. It was one of those studio pictures where somebody had posed him in a three-quarter view. He had his unruly hair and eyebrows pasted down and you could tell he was fresh out of the bath and his white shirt was starched hard. He was holding his scrubbed face with effort toward where the photographer told him to look, which was too much in the direction of the best light. He was frowning with discomfort beneath the forced smile. There was something else. It was something like defeat or simple tiredness in his pose and you could see it best in the heavy lids of his large blank eyes. He looked out of that face with what remained of his self-confidence and trust in the world. His shaggy presence said that it was all worthwhile and maybe even, in some ways he would not ever understand, also important. I understood all of that even then but would never have been able to put my reading of him into words like these.

Then I looked at the woman. She was an old hawk. Her skin was badly wrinkled, like the skin of ancient Indians I'd seen in photographs and the Westerns. There was something like a smile coming out of her face, but it had come out sort of sideways and made her look silly. But the main thing about her was that she looked very mean. On second thought, to give her the benefit of the doubt, I can say that it might have been just plain hardness from having had a hard life. She was wearing a black iron-stiff dress buttoned up to her dickey, which was ironically dainty and tight around her goose neck.

All I said was, "They're *so* old." I don't know what else I thought as I looked up at my mother, who was leaning over my shoulder looking at the pictures too, as though she'd never seen them before, as though she was trying to see them through my eyes.

"You're just young, Tommy. Everybody's old to you. They're not so old. He looks lonely to me."

I looked at him again and thought I saw what she meant.

•

I put the dishes away and she took the photographs back and we didn't talk any more that night about Mitch and Temple. We watched our black-and-white television screen, which showed us Red Skelton acting like a fool.

Before it was over I fell asleep on the couch and my mother woke me when she turned off the television. "You should go to bed."

I stood up and stretched. "I have a science paper to write."

"Get up early and write it," she said, putting out her cigarette.

•

"He wants me to meet him some-place," my mother said.

She had just finished talking with him and was standing by the telephone. It was close to dinnertime. I'd been home from school since three-thirty and she'd been in from work by then for a good hour. She'd just hung up from the shortest conversation she'd ever had with him.

I'd wondered why they never wanted to meet, then I stopped wondering and felt glad they hadn't. Now I was afraid, afraid for her, for myself, for the poor old man in the picture. Why did we have to go through with this crazy thing?

"I told him I needed to talk with you about it first," she said. "I told him I'd call him back."

I was standing there in front of her, looking at her. She was a scared little girl with wild eyes dancing in her head, unable to make up her own mind. I sensed her fear. I resented her for the mess she had gotten herself into. I also resented her for needing my consent. I knew she wanted me to say, Go, go to him, meet him somewhere. I could tell. She was too curious not to want to go. I suddenly thought that he might be a millionaire and that she would marry the old coot and he'd die and leave her his fortune. But there was the sister. She was in the way. And from the looks of her she would pass herself off as one of the living for at least another hundred years or so. So I gave up that fantasy.

"Well, why don't you tell him you'll meet him at the hamburger cafe on Wentworth? We can eat dinner there."

"We?"

"Sure. I'll just sit at the counter like I don't know you. But I gotta be there to protect you."

"I see."

"Then you can walk in alone. I'll already be there eating a cheeseburger and fries. He'll come in and see you waiting for him alone at a table."

"No, I'll sit at the counter, too," she said.

"Okay. You sit at the counter, too."

"What time should I tell him?"

I looked at my Timex. It was six. I knew they lived on the West Side and that meant it would take him at least an hour by bus and a half-hour by car. He probably didn't have a car. I was hungry, though, and had already set my mind on eating a cheeseburger rather than macaroni-and-cheese out of the box.

"Tell him seven-thirty."

"Okay."

I went to my room. I didn't want to hear her talking to him in her soft whispering voice. I'd stopped listening some time before. I looked at the notes for homework and felt sick in the stomach at the thought of having to write that science paper.

A few minutes later my mother came in and said, "Okay. It's all set." She sat down on the side of my bed and folded her bony pale hands in her lap. "What should I wear?"

"Wear your green dress and the brown shoes."

"You like that dress, don't you?"

"I like that one and the black one with the yellow at the top. It's classical."

"You mean classy."

"Whatever I mean." I felt really grown that night.

"Here, Tommy, take this." She handed me five dollars, which she'd been hiding in the palm of her right hand. "Don't spend it all. Buy the burger out of it and the rest is just to have. If you spend it all in that hamburger place I'm going to deduct it from your allowance next week."

•

When I got there I changed my mind about the counter. I took a table by myself.

I was eating my cheeseburger and watching the revolving door. The cafe was noisy with shouts, cackling, giggles, and verbal warfare. The waitress, Miss Azibo, was in a bad mood. She'd set my hamburger plate down like it was burning her hand.

I kept my eye on the door. Every time somebody came in I looked up, every time somebody left I looked up. I finished my cheeseburger even before my mother got there, and, ignoring her warning, I ordered another and another Coca-Cola to go with it. I figured I could eat two or three burgers and still have most of the five left.

Then my mother came in like a bright light into a dingy room. I think she must have been the most beautiful woman who ever entered that place and it was her first time there. She had always been something of a snob and did not believe in places like this; I knew she'd agreed to meet Mister Kibbs here just because she believed in my right to the cheeseburger and this place had the best in the neighborhood.

I watched her walk ladylike to the counter and ease herself up on the stool and sit there with her back arched. People in that place didn't walk and sit like that. She was acting classy and everybody turned to look at her. I looked around at the faces, and a lot of the women had these real mean sneering looks, like somebody had broken wind.

She didn't know any of these people and they didn't know her. Some of them may have known her by sight, and me, too, but that was about all the contact we'd had with this part of the neighborhood. Besides, we hardly ever ate out. When we did we usually ate Chinese or at the rib place.

I sipped my Coke and watched Miss Azibo place a cup of coffee before my mother on the counter. She was a coffee freak. Always was. All day long. Long into the night. Cigarettes and coffee in a continuous cycle. I grew up with her that way. The harsh smells are still in my memory. When she picked up the cup with a dainty finger sticking out just so, I heard a big fat woman at a table in front of mine say to the big fat woman at the table with her that my mother was a snooty bitch. The other woman said, "Yeah. She must think she's white. What's she doing in here anyway?"

•

Mitch Kibbs came in about twenty minutes after my mother, and I watched him stop and stand just inside the revolving doors. He stood to the side. He looked a lot younger than in the picture. He was stooped a bit, though, and he wasn't dressed like a millionaire, which disappointed me. But he was clean. He was wearing a necktie and a clean white shirt and a suit that looked like it was about two hundred years old but no doubt made of the best wool. Although it was fall, he looked overdressed for the season. He looked like a man who hadn't been out in daylight in a long while. He was nervous, I could tell. Everybody was looking at him. Rarely did white people come in here.

Then he went to my mother like he knew she had to be the person he'd come in to see. He sat himself up on the stool beside her and leaned forward with his elbows on the counter and looked into her face.

She looked back in that timid way of hers. But she wasn't timid. It was an act and part of her ladylike posture. She used it when she needed it.

They talked and talked. I sat there eating cheeseburgers and protecting her till I spent the whole five dollars. Even as I ran out of money I knew she would forgive me. She had always forgiven me on special occasions. This was one for sure.

She never told me what they talked about in the cafe and I never asked, but everything that happened after that meeting went toward the finishing off of the affair my mother was having with Mitch Kibbs. He called her later that night. I was in my room reading when the phone rang and I could hear her speaking to him in that ladylike way—not the way she talked to me. I was different. She didn't need to impress me. I was her son. But I couldn't hear what she was saying and didn't want to.

Mister Kibbs called the next evening, too. But eventually the calls were fewer and fewer till he no longer called.

My mother and I went on living the way we always had, she working long hours at the factory and me going to school. She was not a happy woman, but I thought she was pretty brave. Every once in a while she got invited somewhere, to some wedding or out on a date with a man. She always tried on two or three different dresses, turning herself around and around before the mirror, asking me how she looked, making me select the dress she would wear. Most often, though, she went nowhere. After dinner we sat together at the kitchen table, she drinking coffee and smoking her eternal cigarettes. She gave me my first can of beer one night when she herself felt like having one. It tasted awful and I didn't touch the stuff for years after that.

•

About a day or two after the meeting in the hamburger cafe I remember coming to a conclusion about my mother. I learned for the first time that she did not always know what she was doing. It struck me that she was as helpless as I sometimes felt when confronted with a math or science problem or a problem about sex and girls and growing up and life in general. She didn't know everything. And that made me feel closer to her despite the fear it caused. She was there to protect me, I thought. But there she was, just finding her way, step by step, like me. It was something wonderful anyway.

# A Liar in Love

## Quinn Eli

When a black man sits down to write about black women and relationships, the reader is well advised to take cover. Because whenever a man writes about male-female relationships in the black community and, like some cross between Cupid and Rodney King, argues that we should "all just get along," chances are that writer has an agenda up his sleeve. And that agenda, concealed in some flowery language about "preserving our unity as a people," is almost always self-serving.

I should know. I'm a male writer who spent the last couple of years in a graduate creative writing program, spinning tales about blacks folks in love. Most of my stories had some pressing conflict at their center—certainly there are enough hateful forces in the world that conspire against black love—and so I would artfully depict the way my two protagonists, a black couple in Boston or Brooklyn or Philly, beat down the conflict that threatened to tear them apart, and, hand in hand, defeated the forces of racism, poverty, and joblessness that might otherwise have destroyed them and, by implication, the entire black community.

But as I look back now from my new position as a Ph.D. candidate, a four-eyed student of literature, I can't help but think that my earlier short stories were a little too self-righteous and too assured of their own political and artistic consequence. In other words, I'm starting to think that maybe my stories were full of shit. Young writers always think we have something terribly *deep* to say and that we're the first people who ever in the history of humanity to see the world so clearly, so keenly—and so I guess it would have been a miracle if I hadn't shoveled at least a little manure onto every page I ever printed out. But what's bothering me now is the thought that maybe the shit I was dishing out—and attempting to feed to a hungry, unsuspecting public—was manipulative and self-serving.

It's an awful thought to face. If it's true that I packed my stories with self-serving messages, my only comfort is knowing I wasn't alone. Whenever a black man writes about romantic relationships, it almost always seems he's trying to preach to black women about the way they should treat us black men: A little less attitude, goes the usual refrain, a little less giving your man lip, and black love will flourish and grow and eventually defeat the menace of racism.

Some nifty trick, wouldn't you say? Putting *all* the responsibility for black liberation from oppression and injustice onto the shoulders of black women? If y'all would simply get your act together, my own stories have suggested, and quit with the mood swings and humiliating back talk, maybe we could all finally come together as a people and overthrow the devil who keeps us in chains. In the short stories I wrote, all that stood between black folks and freedom was the black woman's refusal to emotionally support her man. And since life invariably mimics art, I believe I began to carry this point of view into my own romantic relationships. Before I'd even had time to consider the absurdity of my attitude, I found myself saying to the women I dated, This is why the white man is able to keep us down—'cause we ain't unified. Every time I say one thing, you gotta say another. But you and me oughta be on the same side, baby.

In these discussions, however, "the same side" I was referring to was actually my side. And so the gist of my message couldn't have been much different from anything my father had said to my mother, back in the fifties, when she thought she might like to go to college: "You figure if you get all that schoolin'," he reportedly told her, "you won't need me around?" Like him, I guess I was afraid that if the woman in my life developed ideas and opinions that differed from my own, she would eventually come to think of me as a fool and have no choice but to leave me. But because I was a man of my times, a member of the first post–civil rights era generation—well educated, politically astute, and passionate about social causes—I was able to disguise my fear with a language that would have dazzled my father. I would simply suggest to my partner that by clinging so tightly to her own point of view she was demonstrating a "slave mentality" and thus undermining our progress as a people.

And most of the time it worked like a charm. Not because the women in my life lacked the intelligence or common sense to see through my ruse—more often than not they were much more intelligent than me in every imaginable way—but because all it takes to push a lot of black folks' buttons is for one of our own to suggest that we ain't down wit' da cause, that we done lost what it means to be black. It wasn't their identities as *women* I was challenging—on that subject they were thoroughly confident and would've stood for no instruction from a man—but rather, their identities as *black folks*. I had come from a long line of black agitators (during the sixties my brother accumulated a record with the FBI as thick as a telephone book) and so I posed convincingly as someone who could speak on such matters and who had only the best interests of the black community in mind.

Could it be, though, that all I really had in mind was my own obsessive need to be always in control? I'm a diminutive man, bookish and jittery, and I could never have gotten away with the macho posturing that some of my larger male friends had adopted (I tried once, though, with a woman I met in the Bronx, who looked at me as if to say, Nigga, you *must* be crazy, and then sat laughing at me for something like an hour, so it's possible that maybe—just maybe—I used the power of words to transform my insecurity and crazy need to control into something that sounded politically urgent, as though our very survival as a people were at stake.

It's only fair to point out, however, that overly controlling behavior, whether it's a woman's or a man's, is something that is difficult to escape in the black community. And while the behavior should never be condoned or encouraged—God knows it can have unhealthy ramifications, draining a person both emotionally and mentally—it must at least be acknowledged and understood. Like a lot of folks, I grew up in a household where money was always tight and opportunities for a better life were scarce, and because of liquor, depression, and feelings of personal worthlessness brought on by social restraints, the relationship between my parents always seemed to me like a time bomb ticking loudly through our cramped apartment, likely to explode at any minute. It made for the kind of anxiety that is still with me from childhood, and which I detect in so many other black men and women. It is any wonder, then, that when we grew into adults we sought ways to keep that anxiety at bay, to maintain a tight grip over our lives so that nothing would suddenly fly apart or spiral out of control?

When my need to control met head-to-head with a partner's need to control, the struggle that would ensue was better than anything you'd ever see in World Federation wrestling. We'd fight like we were in the middle of Madison Square Garden, two dark adversaries circling the canvas of our apartment, both of us determined to pin back the other's shoulders, to drop the opponent to his or her knees. Most of all, we each wanted to leave the struggle without surrendering too much and with our sense of personal dignity still intact. And, as all black folks know, battles like these are loud, fierce, and never really end: some part of each one comes up again in the next battle between you, or leaves emotional scars that never quite disappear. In my struggles with women, it occurs to me now, I must have been a particularly cruel opponent—because whenever I thought I was in real danger and might not survive the fight, I trotted out that old broken-record business about black unity. It was, I guess, my secret weapon—the suggestion that the disarray in the black community was due to exactly the kind of shit she was pulling right now, refusing to see things my way. And more often than not it was this accusation that brought the fight between us to its sad, bitter conclusion.

Could it be that I came to this type of behavior all on my own? Certainly my friends had their own secret weapons, their own ways of lying in love. If I had wanted, I could have borrowed a line a friend of mine uses when the women in his life assume points of view different from his and in the process threaten his sense of control. "Fine, baby," he says. "Have things your way. But it seems to me you done worked too hard and too long pulling yourself outta the ghetto to go backslidin' now."

And, man, what a panicky response he gets from these women when he reminds them of their modest beginnings—the Section 8 housing and low-income projects that they fought tooth and nail to escape—and suggests that by refusing to follow his lead they could end up back at square one. "All I'm tellin' you," I've heard him say, "is that what goes around comes around." My friend understands that for many black folks, words like these can conjure up all our worst fears about our accomplishments— Maybe it's just an illusion, we think to ourselves, another hand-out intended to keep us from complaining or to pacify some white liberal's guilt. Our professional successes often seem founded on something as sturdy as, say, a butterfly's wing, and pointing out how easily any one of us could end up back in Bed Stuy or South Central doesn't necessarily make my friend a bad person, but pointing it out to keep a woman in line puts him in league with the master who warns his house slave that one false move will land him back in the fields. What I mean is, keeping somebody back in this particular way isn't something my friend invented; rather, it's a strategy as old as the hills, the one thing that oppressors have always done whenever they've feared the oppressed. And so it doesn't take a rocket scientist to figure out from whom my friend could have learned such behavior.

The only other "secret weapon" I've ever seen used was in fact used on me. A woman I knew had a way of convincing the men in her life that her unhappiness was somehow their fault—and that this inability to make her happy was related in some way to their masculinity. The suggestion was that a woman's spiritual fulfillment—like (I guess) her sexual fulfillment—was based on her man's performance, and so any man who couldn't get the first job done right sure as hell wasn't cutting the mustard in any other regard. So in my fights with her for dominance and control, she was almost always the victor, because as soon as she felt threatened enough she'd invariably call out, "You don't know shit about being a man." And, like a balloon stabbed abruptly with the tip of a pin, I would burst and then sputter to the ground.

Despite the grimness of my encounters with this woman, I get some comfort now when I think back on her behavior: it's nice to know I'm not the only black person who ever blamed somebody else for my own failings and insecurities, and for the hurt I've experienced at the hands of an intolerant society. And lately I've seen lots of other folks doing the very same thing. Here in my West Philly neighborhood, for instance, we've got brothers standing on street corners holding their dicks, each one still swearing to anybody who'll listen that it was Whitey that kept him from going to college and getting ahead in life. Or else it was some woman—usually his mother, but it may be the old lady he's sharing his crib with now—who (figuratively) emasculated him and made it impossible for him to function as a man. Or check out some of the magazine articles and current fiction aimed at (and written by) black women: You'd be having a happy life, a rich and fulfilling life, my sister, they all seem to suggest, if these brothers of ours would simply get their acts together.

It seems there's no shortage of places to assign blame for the emptiness and dissatisfaction so many of us experience in our lives. But more often than not we point our fingers in the wrong direction—we point them at one another. Because to look inside ourselves for ways to be happy in a racist society is, admittedly, a monumental task, and to take personal responsibility for our own individual failings is just too damn scary.

So we find somebody else to blame. Or, as in my case, we find some concept outside ourselves—for me it was black unity—and, pinning all our hopes for happiness on that concept, browbeat and bully those who appear to be rocking our boat. Confused by my own need to be in control and fearful of taking any scenic excursions into my own heart, I believed the thing that would bring me happiness at last was a unified black community. But the unity I was working toward had a tyrant at its helm—namely, me—and, like some Stalin of the ghetto, I thought I could determine happiness for *all* black folks according to my own terms. Which is why I would get so impatient with those women in my life who saw the world differently than I did and who had their own ideas about how to live a fulfilling life. Some of these women had ideas as suspect as my own (I once dated a woman, beautiful and dark-skinned, who thought she'd be happy at last if she could just get herself a chemical peel), but this doesn't mean they should have let me determine the course of their lives. Looking back, I'm ashamed at the number of times that I tried to convince them otherwise.

But back in those days there was so much at stake for me. If I were to give up the concept of black unity—a concept that is, by the way, as flawed as Afrocentrism or any other concept that discusses black folks as though we were some monolithic entity—I might have to look to myself for a way to be happy. And I damn sure wasn't going to do that. It was easier and much more convenient to assume that all that stood between me and my ideal were the women, the black women, who were undermining "the cause" by insisting on their own point of view. Like the street brothers who maintain that it's Whitey keeping them down, or like the sisters who swear black men are the ones making their lives so unhappy, I was content to point fingers and pass the buck about the pain I was in, without ever once stopping to wonder if I had brought any of it on myself.

I'd love to say that I suddenly had some dramatic experience that removed the blinders from my eyes, but that kind of stuff only happens in fiction—or at least it happens an awful lot in the fiction I write. In reality, the only thing that caused me to change my way of thinking and start taking responsibility for my own life was the everyday, ordinary business of living. But I guess there were two incidents that you could say put me on a better path.

A while back I was standing on a crowded street corner—my mind wandering as usual—and without stopping to look both ways, I stepped out into a rush of traffic; of all the people who were standing near me, only one reached out a hand to pull me back to the curb. That person was a woman, the only other black person in the crowd, and if I owe my life to anyone, then certainly I owe it to her.

More recently, I was feeling pretty bleak about my life, wondering what the hell to do when I was finished with grad school, and in the meantime drinking my evenings away. But one night in a bar, a brother asked me what was wrong and patiently listened to my entire sob story. Then he gave me the name of some people he knew who were hiring at a local school and, together with his wife, made it his personal business to cheer me out of my depression.

When I think back now to the kindness of this man—and then remember the woman from the street corner incident—it's clear to me that I spent too much time in the past believing it was necessary to mobilize entire armies against the devastating effects of racism, and not enough time considering how one person can help another person to heal from those effects. A chain, after all, is only as strong as its individual links, and it seems to me now that the way to help strengthen my community as a whole is to improve the quality of my relationships—romantic and otherwise—with the individual black folks I meet every day. To do this requires tearing down all the walls I've built around myself and taking a long, hard look inside; what I've already discovered, much to my surprise, is that the view isn't really all that bad.

So, recently I finished a new short story—another romantic saga about a young black couple in love. This time, though, neither of them is more responsible than the other for whether or not their love survives—or, by extension, whether or not the black community survives. They are, quite frankly, a lot more cynical than characters I've created in the past. They know the world is an awful place and not likely to ever get much better. But they also know they've got a pretty good thing going, what Alice Walker would call "a council between equals," so they spend each day showering each other with kindness and rescuing one another from the unfriendly climate of the world outside their door. And if there's a lesson to be gathered from these two characters of mine, I'm hoping I'll be the first one to learn it.

# The Sexual Diversion:
# The Black Man / Black Woman
# Debate in Context

## Derrick Bell

Rayford Logan, the great black historian, called the period at the turn of the last century the nadir for black people. Hundreds of blacks were lynched, thousands were victims of racist violence and intimidation, and literally millions were exploited on farms and at mostly menial labor where their pay failed to cover the food and other necessities they were often required to purchase from their employers.

For Dr. Logan, the nadir meant the bottom, a status that arguably was only a small step up from slavery itself. It is a measure of the fragility of our current condition that a great many thoughtful black people now worry that we are heading toward another nadir, this one marked by far more self-destruction than anyone living a century ago could easily imagine. The statistics supporting these concerns are all too familiar.[1] Maya Angelou transforms them into words that highlight the pain of our plight:

> In these bloody days and frightful nights when an urban warrior can find no face more despicable than his own, no ammunition more deadly than self-hate and no

target more deserving of his true aim than his brother, we must wonder how we came so late and lonely to this place.[2]

If African Americans are to survive the storms we are now experiencing—and those storms now brewing on the horizon—we must reconnect ourselves, eschewing in the process divisive behaviors that distract us from the dangers lurking outside our community, dangers we know all too well and prefer to deny.

It is sad but hardly remarkable that oppressed black people vent far more of their rage on other blacks than on their oppressors. The very power that defines the status of those on the top and those on the bottom serves to deflect frustrated rage from the perpetrators of oppression to fellow sufferers. Diversion is now, and likely has always been, an important tactic in preventing the oppressed from recognizing the true sources of their oppression. Those in power recognize the value of diversion to redirect victim rage away from themselves and seldom miss the chance to promote its paranoid permutations.

Once sown, the seeds of distrust and enmity seem to flourish on their own. Those in power need do no more than appear to favor one subordinate group over another to quell even a possibility that the feuding groups will either recognize the similar character of their lowly state or identify the source of their condition. The lowly ones engage in spirited expressions of hostility against each other, exhausting time, energy, and resources that might otherwise be employed against their oppressors. In the process, their squabbling provides their real enemies with a seemingly impenetrable insulation from intergroup strife among those who, while fearing their differences, are quite similar in their subordination. Subordination, by its very nature, generates beliefs and behaviors that lead to antagonism among subordinate groups. Victims often look for the less powerful and attempt to victimize them in turn. Those harmed seek to retaliate, and soon there is a vicious cycle of hostility that creates disorder and chaos among victims of the status quo while serving to ensure the position of those in power.

The stability and even the survival of the economic system in this country depends on maintaining divisions between people based on race, gender, and class. The success of this strategy can be measured in the fact that (for example) there is little outcry about the gap in income and wealth between the rich and the rest of us, even though this gap is larger than at any time in this century. The reason is not hard to find. Those at the short end of the income and wealth gap are easily convinced that they should vent their otherwise unfocused upset on those on welfare, newly arrived immigrants, those who commit street crimes, and the society's traditional scapegoat—black people. A great many whites across the socioeconomic spectrum are vocal in their opposition to affirmative action policies that they view as aiding less qualified members of minorities at their expense; there is no similar opposition to all manner of priorities and preferences aimed at privileging those who are already well-off.

It would be a most welcome but quite unlikely miracle if black people, we who from our earliest days in this country have occupied the very bottom of society's well, were able to avoid the victim's predisposition to battle others within our group rather than those responsible for our lowly status. Alas, it is likely that because of our long history of subordinate status in this country we are more rather than less prone to this affliction. Because sexism and patriarchy are deeply rooted in this society, all too many black men have fallen into patterns of physical and emotional abuse of women, behavior that black women understandably fear and resent.

For a generation now, a host of writers—many of them black women—have been telling the world about the inadequacies of black men. This often emotional testimony ranges from mournful frustration to flat-out rage. These revelations contain both deeply felt disappointment about what often is and a yearning hope about what might be. And while there are many, many black males who do not fit the woeful patterns, we know from statistics and personal experience that these criticisms are based in reality as well as myth. Rather than either condone or condemn, I want to examine this phenomenon in the context of a society where the deflection of oppression is the norm.

Who can deny it? Life for black men in racist America is devilishly difficult. Surely, a factor in our failings is the hostility we encounter at every level. While slavery is over, a racist society continues to exert dominion over black men and their maleness in ways more subtle but hardly less castrating than during slavery, when male-female relationships between black people generally were not formalized, and even when a marriage was recognized, the black man's sexual access to his wife was controlled by the master or his sons or his overseer.

Black women also suffered the pains of slavery. Black women were exploited, abused, and demeaned, and that harm was serious. Forced to submit to the sexual desires of their masters or to slaves selected by their masters, they then suffered the agony of watching helplessly as their children were sold off. Black men were also dealt a double blow. They were forced to stand by powerless and unable to protect black women from sexual access by white men, and they were denied access to white women as a further symbol of their subordinate status. The harm done black men by this dual assault has never been fully assessed. Moreover, the assault continues in less blatant but still potent forms.

James Baldwin asserts that "the action of the White Republic, in the lives of Black men, has been, and remains, emasculation. Hence, the Republic has absolutely no image, or standard, of masculinity to which any man, Black or White, can honorably aspire."[3] The vain effort to protect black males against this ever-present danger, Baldwin explains, results in what Andy Young calls "sorriness," a disease that attacks black males. Baldwin writes:

> It is transmitted by Mama, whose instinct—and it is not hard to see why—is to protect the Black male from the devastation that threatens him the moment he declares himself a man. All of our mothers, and all of our women, live with this small, doom-laden bell in the skull, silent, waiting, or resounding, every hour of every day. Mama lays this burden on Sister, from whom she expects (or indicates she expects) far more than she expects from Brother; but one of the results of this all too comprehensible dynamic is that Brother may never grow up—in which case, the community has become an accomplice to the Republic.[4]

Women may well respond that here is one more effort, albeit a well-written one, to blame male failure on female love. There is a chicken and egg aspect to this position. This society has not much loved either black men or black women, and debate as to whether society's hostility or parental efforts to shield males from this hostility is more damaging does not move us much closer toward the relief that both need. Even so, in Baldwin's view, "this dilemma has everything to do with the situation of the Black man in the American inferno."[5]

Black women do not accept racism as the reason for sorry behavior—they have experienced it firsthand, and for them it is an excuse, not a justification. Alice Walker's character Grange Copeland speaks her mind on this subject:

I'm bound to believe that that's the way white folks can corrupt you even when you done held up before. 'Cause when they got you thinking that they're to blame for everything they have you thinking they's some kind of gods! You can't do nothing wrong without them being behind it. You gits just as weak as water, no feeling of doing nothing yourself. Then you begins to think up evil and begins to destroy everybody around you, and you blames it on the crackers. Shit! Nobody's as powerful as we make them out to be. We got our own souls, don't we?[6]

In addition to rejecting the traditional, patriarchal notion that women must be protected by men, black women cannot see why black men must try to emulate the macho sexism of their white counterparts rather than work toward a more natural and healthy equality between the sexes. As a woman student wrote in an essay, quoting Fran Sanders's "Dear Black Man,"

Talk to me like the woman that I am and not to me as that woman who is the inanimate creation of someone's overactive imagination. Look at me with no preconceived notions of how I must act or feel and I will try to do the same with you. No presumption, no assumptions, no banal rhetoric substituted for real person-to-person giving and receiving. Look at my face when you speak to me; look into my eyes and see what they have to say. Think about the answers that you give to my questions. . . . I am a woman and you are a man and I have always known it. If you love me, tell me so. Don't approach me as you would an enemy. I am on your side and have always been. We have survived, and we may just be able to teach the world a lesson.[7]

That, of course, is a wonderful homily of how life should be for sexual partners, regardless of race. It is an ideal, and as is obvious from the charges and countercharges, a far from fulfilled ideal for many black men and women.[8] It can hardly be denied that black women bear much of the brunt of black male frustration and suppressed rage.

During my twenty-five years of law school teaching, I have listened to dozens of black women—and more than a few white ones—voice their disappointments with many black men. Much of the problem is due to the paucity of black men at the professional level rather than to their behavior. The statistics regarding the number of black men who fall by the wayside long before professional school are harsh. Most law school classes contain many more black women than men. This disparity heightens black women's sense of betrayal when potentially available black men choose white women. As one of my students put it, "We black women are always being reminded of how marginal and unworthy we are. We're never smart enough or beautiful enough or supportive, sexy, understanding, and resourceful enough to deserve a good black man."[9]

Another former student, Kirsten Levingston, makes clear that she would not encourage a black woman to stay with a black man if he made her unhappy, nor would she discourage a black man from marrying a white woman who makes him happy. Even so, she believes black Americans must do all they can to unite and develop. This unity begins at home with our children, and, she contends, "the key to producing strong and proud black children is to raise them in an environment with strong and proud black parents."[10] Ms. Levingston's call for unity may be unrealistic in a society where one-half of all marriages end in divorce, but hers is a view shared by many, perhaps most, black women.

Recently, while discussing this issue in a civil rights class, two black women prepared a fictional dialogue among friends regarding interracial relationships. As reported by the black woman commentator, the black and white law students discussed the tendency of handsome and promising black men to prefer or at least look with admiration on white women, while disliking ethnic hair styles and other Afrocentric "looks" on black women. They raised the often unspoken question regarding black women's suspicion that any expression of interest in them by white men is based on the stereotype of black women as super-sensual, and discussed the refusal of some black women to date white men for that reason. The narrator shares this concern, but feels trapped by it because the "bottom line is that there just aren't enough brothers to go around." She recognizes that many black men are not very sensitive to this dilemma, resent black women who date white men, and sometimes ask, "How come a garbage collector isn't good enough for you?" The fictional group discusses several variations on this theme and then the narrator closes with this observation:

As I took a sip from my wine glass, I realized that there were no definitive answers. I could say I am black, female, and bright in a white mediocre world, but that hardly explains why I sit on the beaches of St. Croix feeling so abandoned.

In the same class, a young Indian woman, after conceding the burdening nature of male hegemony in Indian culture, posed the question,

Why is it that struggle and racial adversity create strong black women and "weak and disempowered" black men? The African-American female has fewer job opportunities and just as many stereotypes heaped upon her as does the African-American male. Why does the most oppressed class, women of color, derive strength from oppression, whereas black men may scapegoat oppression to justify unjustifiable behavior (often against women of color).

Both my student's question and the issue deserve to be more firmly grounded in the societal environment out of which they come. I shared my student's observations with a black social worker friend, Gwen Jordan, who felt that the Indian woman posed an ultimate dilemma for all people of color. When we attempt to work through the difficulties in relationships that are fundamental to the preservation of our culture and well-being in public, within the view of others who do not share our cultural issues, we unconsciously place that struggle in the context of an alien culture whose values and mores do not support—and are often hostile to—the core of our definition and being. And then it is from this perspective that we evaluate and judge the quality of these relationships and the sincerity of our mates.

In Ms. Jordan's view, African-Americans in their relationships must struggle to achieve a level of unconditional love in a systemic context—racism—which places conditions upon our being. Within that context, we trivialize ourselves when we attempt to define African-American male/female relationships in terms of the prevailing culture: we attribute to black females mystical powers and strengths that become burdensome in their superficiality, and we attribute weakness and defeat to black males. These, according to Jordan, are really just more sophisticated versions of the stereotypes that we have carried since slavery. The result is that we disempower ourselves and imperil our capacity to love unconditionally and, through that love, to grow and create together.

The threat of disempowerment is certainly real, but the effort to define differences can be both revealing and strengthening in our understanding of how we function as male and female human beings. James Baldwin, for example, provides an enlightening statement about the psychological makeup of men and their weakness, too often masked by a show of muscle and—it must be said—all too often manifested in the physical abuse of those very women who would, if given a chance, love and care for them. Baldwin writes:

> One is confronted, first of all, with the universal mystery of men—as we are, of a man, as he is; with the legend and the reality of the masculine force and the masculine role—though these last two realities are not always the same. Men would seem to dream more than women do—always have, it would seem, and very probably, always will. They must, since they assume that their role is to alter and conquer reality. If women dream less than men—for men know very little about a woman's dreams—it is certainly because they are so swiftly confronted with the reality of men. They must accommodate this indispensable creature, who is, in so many ways, more fragile than a woman. Women know much more about men than men will ever know about women—which may, at bottom, be the only reason that the race has managed to survive so long.
>
> In any case, the male cannot bear very much humiliation; and he really cannot bear it, it obliterates him. All men know this about each other, which is one of the reasons that men can treat each other with such a vile, relentless, and endlessly inventive cruelty. Also, however, it must be added, with such depthless respect and love, conveyed mainly by grunts and blows. It has often seemed to me that men need each other in order to deal with women, and women, God knows, must need each other in order to deal with men.
>
> Women manage, quite brilliantly, on the whole, and to stunning and unforeseeable effect, to survive and

surmount being defined by others. They dismiss the definition, however dangerous or wounding it may be—or even, sometimes, find a way to utilize it—perhaps because they are not dreaming. But men are neither so supple nor so subtle. A man fights for his manhood: that's the bottom line. A man does not have, simply, the weapons of a woman. Mama must feed her children—that's another bottom line; and there is a level on which it can be said that she cannot afford to care how she does it.

But when a man cannot feed his women or his children, he finds it, literally, impossible to face them. The song says, Now, when a woman gets the blues, Lord / She hangs her head and cries / But when a man gets the blues, Lord / He grabs a train and rides.[11]

Even we black men fortunate enough to provide for our families must defend against the myriad forms of emasculation that the society has placed in our path. Success as the society measures it exacts a very real and often terrible price. None of us escapes, really, and those of us who feel we have established some limits to what we will put up with spend far more time than we should criticizing those who, by our measures, have been too willing to comfort whites in order to either get ahead or (usually) stay even.

Baldwin, I think, would urge more understanding—if not compassion—as he reminds us:

It is a very grave matter to be forced to imitate a people for whom you know—which is the price of your performance and survival—you do not exist. It is hard to imitate a people whose existence appears, mainly, to be made tolerable by their bottomless gratitude that they are not, thank heaven, you.[12]

Writer Jill Nelson speaks for many of us, men as well as women, when she describes how difficult it is to maintain one's ethical bearings in the job market. Following a series of interviews at a major, white newspaper that was considering her as a reporter, she wrote:

I've been doing the standard Negro balancing act when it comes to dealing with white folks, which involves sufficiently blurring the edges of my being so that white folks don't feel intimidated and simultaneously holding on to my integrity. There is a thin line between Uncle Tomming and Mau-Mauing. To step over that line can mean disaster. On one side lies employment and self-hatred, on the other, the equally dubious honor of unemployment with integrity. In the middle lies something like employment with honor, although I'm not sure exactly how that works.[13]

Jill Nelson got the job. Even so, it was a constant hassle, which she writes about with pain-filled humor. Increasingly, blacks—men and women—are not getting these jobs, or much of any work. The optimist might hope that frustrated employment hopes might bring humility and compassion to the Donnells of this world and their less talented brethren. Alas, for all the reasons Baldwin asserts, it usually does not. And it is unlikely that the relations between some black men and black women will improve until societal conditions improve. Even so, we must not ignore the fact that despite all the barriers, a great many—dare we say most?—black men marry and stay with their wives and families through thick and thin. Here, again, Baldwin says it well:

A stranger to this planet might find the fact that there are any Black people at all still alive in America something to write home about. I myself find it remarkable not that so many Black men were forced (and in so many ways!) to leave their families, but that so many remained and aided their issue to grow and flourish.[14]

This positive observation provides an important foundation on which to plan the coming struggle for our survival in a society in transition, one that appears more than ready to sacrifice our interests, our well-being, even our lives, in a desperate effort to avoid the dangers inherent in change. The black man/black woman debate should continue, but participants must be aware of the ever-present temptation of diversion and its potential to twist that debate in a way that comforts our enemies and betrays ourselves.

# Notes

1. Typical are the figures issued by the U.S. Justice Department, reporting that young black men were almost 14 times more likely to be murdered during 1992 than the nation's general population. In that year, black males ages twelve to twenty-four were victims of homicide at a rate of 114.9 per 100,000, compared with 8.5 murder victims per 100,000 of the general population. They constituted 17.7 percent of all homicide victims, even though they were only 1.3 percent of the U.S. population. Black males age sixteen to twenty-four, were 1.5 times more likely to be victims of all types of violent crime (source: "Around the Nation," *Washington Post*, 9 December 1994, A = 10).

2. Maya Angelou, "I Dare to Hope," *New York Times*, 25 August 1991, 15.

3. James Baldwin, *The Evidence of Things Not Seen* (1985), 21.

4. Ibid., 19.

5. Ibid., 20.

6. Alice Walker, *The Third Life of Grange Copeland* (1970), 207.

7. F. Sanders, "Dear Black Man," in *The Black Woman: An Anthology*, ed. T. Cade (1970), 73, 78–79.

8. Compare Wallace, "A Black Feminist's Search for Sisterhood," in *All the Blacks Are Men, All the Women Are White, but Some of Us Are Brave*, ed. G. T. Hull et al. (1982), 5–8 ("Whenever I raised the question of a Black woman's humanity in conversation with a Black man, I got a similar reaction. Black men, at least the ones I knew, seemed totally confounded when it came to treating Black women like people"), with Staples, "The Myth of Black Macho: A Response to Angry Black Feminists," *Black Scholar*, March / April 1979, 24–32 (While black males are not free of sexism, most black men lack the institutionalized power to oppress black men, and it is their lowly societal position that most disturbs black males).

9. I used this quote in the story "The Last Black Hero," in Derrick Bell, *Faces at the Bottom of the Well: The Permanence of Racism* (1992), 75.

10. See "Racial Reflections: Dialogues in the Direction of Liberation," ed. Derrick Bell, Tracy Higgins, Sung-Hee Suh, *UCLA Law Review* 37 (1990): 1037, 1083.

11. Baldwin, *Evidence of Things Not Seen*, 20–21.

12. Ibid., 44.

13. Jill Nelson, *Volunteer Slavery* (1993), 10.

14. Baldwin, *Evidence of Things Not Seen*, 21.

# Music, Darkrooms, and Cuba

## Richard Perry

When the waiter had taken their or-
ders, Adrian glanced at his companion's throat, dazed by his behavior and
the realization of how long it had been since the translator had entered his
dreaming. Even more time had passed since he'd seen her in the flesh,
thirty-something years; she'd be well past fifty now, age he couldn't imagine her wearing.

·

The translator had come into his life
in 1960, during a summer of ill-tempered heat. Residents of midtown
speak fondly of that time, for on those occasions when they left air-
conditioned spaces they could walk without jostling neighbors or having
to confront the not yet documented homeless. Still, despite these lifestyle
improvements for the well-to-do, the truth was that the summer of 1960
was insufferably hot, which is why folks in the inner city remember it as
one that drained lovers of appetite for touching and drove old women to
sprawl naked in the dark. What relief there was came from window fans,
refrigerated drinking water, sponge baths, and dreams of ice.
All during that summer, Adrian found himself across aisles from

women who fell asleep on subways, lips parted, thighs gaped beneath the pleats of pastel dresses. He'd never guessed that the world was so densely populated by women with compelling thighs, and though he thought of that summer as the year of the translator, he also remembered it as a time when thighs didn't touch, the year when he took two chances.

The first was on the "A" train, when he stared into the smoked eyes of a girl who had caught him exploring the dark cave between her knees. The second was that evening. Fired by a stranger's cunning smile and a hard rain's hammer at his window, he'd asked his wife to turn over so he could mount her from behind.

Two weeks later Adrian was part of a crowd in front of the Hotel Theresa, standing in a street whose light had been stolen from cathedrals. The day was stifling. Dense with rain's undelivered promise, a pewter sky slid down to gaunt trees lit by birds who would neither sing nor fly until dawn, then fell onto the shoulders of black boys slumped by lost desire for basketball. Adrian glanced at the man on his right. The man had an undeveloped beard. He wore a pink shirt and sucked a grapefruit wedge, a union that would have brought Adrian's camera to his eye had not the Cuban visitors chosen that moment to spill from the hotel door. The press, baffled that a head of state had deigned to stay in Harlem, surged forward, obscuring the photographer's view. Efficiently, he elbowed an improvement in his position and plunged forward into a moment defined by light shining in his eyes without the blinding. Music surged—flute, bassoon, a saxophone; he felt pain in his mouth, and his feet twitched with wanting to dance.

There at the side of Fidel Castro was a creature so arresting that Adrian had suppressed an outcry only by biting his lip. Trembling, he shot a roll in black-and-white, advancing the film so fast that his thumb would be sore in an hour. She was, simply, the loveliest woman he'd ever seen. Her nose was African, skin a deep shading of loam, hair a black sweep at her shoulders. She had full lips and hands that searched for harp strings. Only once did she frown at the stupidly shouted questions. Twice she waved away smoke from Castro's foul cigar.

When the press conference ended, the translator, on her way to the limousine, looked directly into Adrian's face and winked. Her eyes were green, and when she smiled he saw that her teeth were bad. Before he could regret this, she threw her head back, exposing a throat he'd forever insist was inviting him to weep. He didn't weep, because to do so would call attention to himself, and because in his haste to witness history he'd left home without a handkerchief. Instead, he drew deep breaths that tasted of cigar smoke and promised to protect the translator from all harm forever.

Of course he knew it was strange to be drawn to protection rather than desire, and had not the occasion been so moving, he'd have stopped to think it through. But he was pleased with the depth of his feeling, and so he only acknowledged it in the way the well-adjusted accept compliments from strangers. Then he went home beneath a clearing sky that tried to distract from its unkept promise with fabric borrowed from an old man's willing heart. On his way to the subway he walked a street where men sat listlessly on stoops. All the buildings had green plants growing stubbornly at windows, and doorways wild with shadows and a trumpet's thin spun gold. Adrian saluted the plants' persistence, forgave the men their indolence, knowing that by evening they'd look up at the translucent sky. Hard on the heels of that certainty came the bliss, so unaccustomed a feeling that it took a while to name it. He thanked God for beauty in the world, and while he did, the trumpet healed his lip and lifted his feet in dance.

Inside his Bronx darkroom, heart racing like a first-time lover, he bent to process the film. In a little while he moaned, cupped a hand to his mouth, staggered to the bathroom where he sat on the toilet and sucked his throbbing thumb. Then he lay his face against the warm, smooth sink, feeling stupid and unworthy.

None of the photographs had developed. At first he thought he'd left the lens cap on, but when he checked, the cap was in his pocket. So the film was defective. He stared at the celluloid, understanding that nothing in his life would ever match this day for disappointment. He knew this with a certainty so quiet his heart had to lean forward to hear it. He was about to say it out loud when his wife sailed into the apartment, carrying two novels and whistling a tune by Ellington.

•

Here in the restaurant, Adrian's companion was waiting with the patience of a woman who knew not to interrupt a man reliving failure in the darkroom. Twenty minutes ago, she'd stepped from shadow on the corner of 26th Street and Third Avenue, materializing like an image from solution. Shadows loomed behind her; street light nested in her hair. Her coat was blues-song red, her shoes, brown tasteful oxfords, sensible, like her hands. It wasn't until she asked if Adrian knew a decent place to eat that her head moved to reveal her throat, not until then that music flowered—an oboe, a trumpet that sang of potted plants. This time the song didn't say to dance. This time the song said that if this woman's teeth were bad, what was left of his life would change.

The street was deserted—small shops, apartment buildings—it was evening, just past seven; March was in decline. The day had been rich with a spring's soft promise, but the night bloomed raw, sliced by a wind that should have been arrested as an enemy of the people. Adrian looked again at the woman's throat and felt the impulse to protect. It wasn't that he mistook her for the translator (he was shaken by the similar appearance, but he knew she wasn't); he was overwhelmed that the ability to feel was still in him. So he chose not to think, in the way that one paralyzed by heights goes to meet his love across a bridge without looking at the water. In this way he was able to accomplish something he'd not done since the evening more than thirty years ago when he'd asked his wife to turn over. He took a risk. He invited the woman to dine with him, around the corner in a small Italian restaurant.

•

Now he listened to her voice, flat, clipped, rising at the ends of sentences. Her name was Norma Fillis, and this was her first time in New York. She'd worked for sixteen years as a practical nurse. Most of her clients were elderly, although once there'd been a young woman in a wheelchair who kept a greenhouse in which she obsessed over grapefruit that grew no larger than her fist. Norma was from Marietta, Ohio, a small city known for its prison, a maximum security facility from which, apparently, no one had ever escaped, and it was also known for its widows who tilled gardens so luxurious that in spring the entire metropolis grew sick of the smell of roses.

The words struck Adrian's forehead like frozen rain. By now, braced by a glass of chenin blanc and the smell of tomato sauce, he'd begun to recover from his folly, which was, simply, that he'd disregarded what he knew. And what he knew was this: he was old; life was armed and extremely dangerous; the only way to survive the world was to hide within it, be film that refused to develop. He'd mastered the tones of anonymity, or so he'd thought, and now he was trying to adjust to color in his life (a coat the red of blues songs), and to having invited a stranger to dinner because he was moved by her throat. He shivered at what might have happened—an accomplice hidden in a doorway, a knife, a pistol's circle frozen at his neck.

Norma paused in mid-sentence. In the interval her words collected—*Ohio, Marietta, nurse*—and Adrian swallowed and forced himself to talk. He'd been born in Paterson, New Jersey, had lived his adult life in the Bronx. He'd worked, before retiring, as a photographer.

"A photographer," Norma said, as if the profession were exotic. She leaned toward him, movement that fired the scent of avocado. "What kind of pictures did you take?"

"I worked in the garment center."

"The what?"

"It's here in New York. An industry that makes and sells clothing."

Norma lifted her wine, a red bordeaux even though she'd ordered fish. "You photographed fashions?"

"No. I photographed women modeling lingerie. For mail-order catalogues. It was all I could get then," he said, and looked past her at a silver tray that seemed glued to a waiter's fingers. He'd had some talent—a good eye, a deftness in the darkroom; he'd wanted to be another Van der Zee or Parks, but he'd had no chance to share his gift. People who bought photographs didn't see the world as he did—shades of black and white, complex and frightening. And one had to eat. Even when the white models had complained about his presence and he'd been forced to take his pictures from behind a screen, even then he'd done what he must.

When it became difficult to work without grinding his teeth, he imagined he endured this humiliation for his wife, who taught school with a devotion that inspired in her students a love for reading that caused them to turn from television and ride past subway stops. The truth was that his wife's life was nicely filled with work and books, and affection for other people's children, and when Adrian realized there was no one for whom he could do, he would think of the translator, imagine she needed money to escape from Cuba, or to fix her teeth, or was heartsick for someone to love her.

Dinner came, for him, veal in a wine sauce, for his companion, broiled flounder, linguini on the side. Norma dug in, eating with the enthusiasm of a man, then, a fork of pasta like a bee's nest at her mouth, she paused.

"How could you take pictures like that?"

"There are ways to hold the camera. I had an assistant, white, who spoke directly to the models, arranged the poses. I'd tell him what I wanted. He'd tell them."

"What did you feel?"

"It was a job."

"The women, what were *they* like?"

He shrugged. "Ordinary."

"It would have made me crazy," Norma said. She devoured the nest of pasta. "I'd have hated them. Are you married?"

"She passed away. Ten years ago."

"What was *she* like?"

"A good woman. Self-sufficient."

"Children?"

He shook his head. "Are you married?"

"Never." There was a note in her voice, strident, as if the idea had plucked a vocal chord.

"Why?"

"*Adrian.* What a question to ask a lady. I declare," and she smiled, revealing perfect teeth. Then she cocked her head to one side so that her throat was lit at an angle only just invented, and bent to attack her food. He couldn't remember the last time he'd talked to someone about his life, and though self-revelation was unsettling, it also made him feel worthwhile, concrete. Now he considered telling Norma about the translator, how once he'd have promised anything to see her, how at times the thought of her existence was all the motivation he could find for getting out of bed. But Norma might be confused, in the way the translator must be at how life had changed in Cuba. The beaches were still white, but the country was gripped by bad fortune. He'd read in the *Times* that there were shortages of food and medicine. The young people wanted to go to America; they piled into unsafe boats and drifted toward Miami, where in full view of flamingo-colored buildings they were turned away by soldiers barely old enough to vote.

Outside, a siren keened, faint, then came closer, swelled and burst in the street. Norma touched a napkin to her mouth. "Ambulance?"

"Or police."

"I've heard," she said gravely, "about your police."

"Oh?"

"That they can be brutal. That they have no respect for anyone who has no money, who isn't white."

Adrian frowned. "We have black police, you know."

"I heard that few of them are different."

"You can't," he said gently, "always believe what you hear. I'd guess they're like policemen everywhere . . . but imagine what life would be *without* them." He paused, fixed by the vengeance with which a man at a nearby table thrust his spoon into a grapefruit.

". . . Coming here, I took the train. There was a woman wearing purple sneakers, maybe fifty, a scar on her left cheek, skin the color of mahogany. When she got off she left behind a *Daily News*. I picked it up. On the fourth page, in the lower left-hand corner, was a woman's photograph. She'd been found in a vacant lot in the Bronx, in the shadow of the elevated train, her neck broken. Strangled by someone of strength. No purse. Estimated motive, robbery. It happened two blocks from my house."

"That was an old paper," Norma said.

"Old?"

"I read about it. I'd been here two days. The dead woman was a nurse. Someone saw the photograph and identified her."

"I don't usually read the *Daily News*," he said.

His companion leaned back in her chair, her eyes on the remains of her flounder. "Why would a woman carry an old newspaper? She works hard and gets behind? She found the paper, like you, and read old news to pass the time? Or was she just out of touch?

"You know, I haven't been here but what my boss-lady calls 'a New York minute,' but it's long enough to see the madness in this city. Yesterday I'm pushing the baby along the avenue, and coming toward me is this white woman, dressed to kill. She stops to put a coin down near the knee of a homeless man who's sleeping in a vestibule, on a poster for Aruba, then she walks on. Her head's dancing to some no-beat private song. She had a white glove on one hand and she was holding the other one, and with her bare hand she's running her finger along the side of a building and licking it. We were on Madison near 82nd. No one else noticed. When she passed, I heard the sound her mouth made. Like kissing."

"I've seen people like that," Adrian said. "I always imagine they're disappointed."

"At what?"

He shrugged. "Life?"

"I think they're weak. You have to be strong to live in this world."

When Adrian didn't respond, she said, "Are *you?*"

He blinked. "Strong?"

"You have a strong face."

He touched his face.

"You touch your face like a stranger."

"It's not a good face."

"I declare. What a thing to say about your own face. What's wrong with it?"

"The eyes are too close together. The chin too narrow. The mouth belongs on a taller man."

She laughed. He'd have thought her laugh would be controlled and sensible, like her shoes, but this spilled from her lips in a cackle that turned heads in the room and rekindled his discomfort.

"Well, I like your face."

"Thank you," Adrian whispered. He'd not meant to whisper.

Norma lit a cigarette. "Which way is Harlem?"

He pointed. The waiter mistook the gesture; Adrian ordered coffee.

"Why do you eat here?"

"I eat all over."

"Do you eat in Harlem?"

"Not any more. When I was young, it was the place to be. Alive. Safe. Once Fidel Castro came to visit. Did you know that?"

"Why's that so special?"

"Because now he wouldn't."

"Why?"

"It's . . . different."

When she asked how it was different, he explained that it was mostly the young, the disrespect they had for elders, boys with their hats on backwards, girls lean and hard, immodest, the booming music, sound meant to intimidate, to make it impossible to ignore them. Instead of baseballs, they carried guns, invented opportunities to use them, and their faces, nearly always furious, were those one would never photograph in color. Even their laughter disturbed him, a pitched substitute for rage.

What Adrian didn't say was how hard it was for him not to despise these children, less for their music or their hats than because they didn't understand the darkness toward which he headed. It was as if they had no old folks in their lives, as if they were strangers to death and disillusionment except as seen on screens in front of which they hunched in speechless worship. Worst of all, they killed one another with the same impunity with which they'd fire on passers-by. He was convinced that despite the slaughter, despite the blood left pooled on the pavement, which screamed their suspicion that life wasn't worth it, they didn't believe that death was real, or forever.

"Well, it isn't so," Adrian would mutter when he passed them, "death *is* forever." His voice, then, was taut with loathing, with love and the desire to be loved, with fear for the moment of their discovery and a greater fear that they'd never understand at all.

But the children didn't hear him. The truth was that they seldom saw him. It didn't matter that he was sixty-seven, and kind, or that his bitterness at having to die was all mixed up with his longing for connection. They wouldn't have cared that once he'd fallen in love with a translator from whose absence of image in his darkroom he'd not recovered.

"Well," Norma said. "They're not *all* our kids. Some of our kids are coming up right, we just don't hear about them. Lots go to college and make something of themselves. And some of what you talk about is nothing more than style. When I was coming up we had the Afro, remember? And my mama and daddy talked about my hair like I'd sold my soul to the devil. It's what the young *do*: they set their parents' teeth on edge. Then they become parents, and the same thing happens all over again. Think about it. What was the rage when you were a kid? Zoot suits? Conked hair?"

"I never," Adrian said stiffly, "straightened my hair."

"But you had a zoot suit?"

He nodded, full of shame.

"And what did your daddy say?"

"That I looked like a gigolo."

"See?"

He wanted to say, But we weren't *killing* one another.

"Anyway," Norma said. "I want to see Harlem. I'd have gone already if I had someone to go with. The woman I work for said not to go by myself. She said the Village was okay, but not Harlem. Will you take me sometime? And I want to see where you live."

"Excuse me?"

"I'm off until tomorrow. And to tell the truth, Adrian, I'd rather not spend it alone. I'm tired of alone."

He didn't understand. Then his heart stepped off a shelf, took its sweet time looking for a bottom. "I'm not prepared," he said.

"Prepared? For what?"

"For . . . guests."

"You don't have a couch?"

He nodded, and his face made her laugh again. "Adrian. Are you afraid of me?"

He shook his head. "Should I be afraid of you?"

She reached for her purse; he gathered himself. "Of course not."

"Well, then." She held an almost empty pack of cigarettes, lit one, blew smoke into his eyes. "Listen, Adrian, do you believe in things happening for a reason? Like they're fated? I think we're meant to be friends. I think something or someone brought us together. And don't worry. I'm not crazy, or *weird*, or anything like that. I'm just lonely."

He was struck by how easily she said this. He wanted to say, I am, too, and while he considered making that confession, Norma said it again, as if its persistence in her life confused her.

•

                   The night had sharpened. The wind came from the north, driving debris with the rhythms of an untuned engine. Norma smoked another cigarette. Her arm in his was heavy, unfamiliar—*he* was unfamiliar. The familiar was what he counted on to fill the empty in the life, to stave off danger and aloneness: patterns, schedules, the *Times* reassuringly on his doorstep in the morning. He had no thirst for change, and now his throat was dry and his heart looked for a bottom.

They moved in silence toward the corner, past a black man huddled in a doorway, who, in summer-ripe falsetto, sang a haunting lullaby. The song filled the doorway and made Adrian think of warmth and safety. At Third Avenue he looked into rushing lights and waved his arm, bracing for the inevitability of cabdrivers who would ignore him. But it was different tonight, as if the red length of Norma's coat demanded service.

As was his habit, Adrian glanced at the driver's license, committing the number to memory before he gave his destination. The driver was Palestinian. What an unfortunate country that is, Adrian thought, and told the driver to take the highway. When they reached 116th Street he said, "That's Harlem, on your left."

She twisted, sent the faint smell of avocado up his nose, said it seemed peaceful.

•

                   Inside the apartment, Norma stood a moment before the photograph of Adrian's dead wife's face, then moved to a living room window, looked three stories down into the street. A rumbling rolled past the building.

"What's that?"

"The elevated train."

"You live with that racket?"

He said he'd grown used to it. He took her coat. "Would you like a drink?"

"No, thank you."

She sat on the couch, slipped off her shoes. "It's very comfortable. Two bedrooms?"

"One's a darkroom."

"May I see?"

The light was harsh. Equipment lined one wall; the others were covered with black-and-white photographs of faces. Most looked away from the camera, so that in the moment Adrian's eyes adjusted to the light he had the feeling of being ignored. A thin layer of dust covered everything. He was tired, his behavior pulled at him like a sodden winter coat. A woman was in his house, in stockinged feet. She stood in the darkroom's center, watching averted faces, then with a wan smile turned, walked back into the hall. Adrian left the light on, shut the door.

"That's your bedroom?"

Reluctantly he nodded. She went into the parlor, returned with her purse, and marched into the room he slept in. The room seemed different, as if the furniture had darkened since the morning. Behind the window, a gate cut off the fire escape.

"How long has it been since you've had a woman?"

Adrian couldn't remember her name. "Eight years," he blurted. In a clear moment the odor of that woman came to him, her flesh sheened with sweat, a musk perfume that made him think of Muslims. Norma was stepping out of her dress. She had a dancer's body, one of strength. Her hands were on his shoulders, driving him to the bed.

"Please. I'm an old man."

"Adrian." She pointed to his head. "Old is here."

"It's not safe."

She was fumbling for her purse. "Oh, but it is."

He shut his eyes, allowed her to undress him. As she sheathed his member in latex, her fist like a vise at his groin, he shivered but didn't watch. Confused, but hard inside her, he let himself be taken, flat on his back, open hands above him, thinking that if there were music in the room he'd find distraction. But there was no music, only her breathing, a bed spring's rhythmic protest, the tropical smell of silence in the dark behind his eyes. In that silence men on stoops sat beneath green plants while Adrian marvelled at the wonder in his feet. It was all as he recalled from more than thirty years ago—the fragile sky, the heat—except for the smell and that there was no music.

·

In the morning her touch against his cheek awakened him. She'd pinned up her hair and wore his old brown bathrobe. "Breakfast?"

He smelled coffee, nodded.

"I'll put the eggs on now."

When she left, Adrian swung from bed, took his blue robe from behind the door. In the bathroom he washed and looked at his face and didn't think. Norma called to him; he went obediently into the kitchen. The train groaned by. He was hungry, ate without speaking. She talked of jobs she'd held: a house by the sea in Oregon, a ranch in Colorado. Adrian suffered her speech as a man endures his captor's conversation. When she excused herself and went into the living room, he began to plot his escape.

"I'm out of cigarettes. Do you have any?"

He told her where. Coming back, she moved as if she lived there. She lit the cigarette from the stove.

"My God," she coughed. "How old are these?"

"Old?"

"They're stale. Something awful." She held the cigarette beneath the open faucet. Adrian cringed when she dropped it in the sink. "I'll have to go get some."

"I'll go."

"No, finish your coffee. Where's the store?"

He told her. She hummed her way to the bedroom, came back dressed. "I just ring the buzzer to get in?"

"Yes."

"You need anything?"

For an alarming moment he considered being rude, but he only shook his head.

"Back in a minute."

And she left, taking with her all that energy, leaving a space into whose silence Adrian allowed himself to fall. Shoulders hunched, he recreated the night leading to this morning, saw her step from shadow, the light alive in her hair. She could have been a thief who smirked while the old man made a mess of emptying his pockets. He'd been lucky, and his relief ballooned so heavy that his head dropped.

Yolk from the fried eggs dried on his plate, a sickly yellow that clashed with the red in the flatware's oval center. He pushed away from the table, went to the sink and retrieved the soggy cigarette, tossed it into the trash, wiped his fingers on a towel. There was an ache in his groin and things were moving several ways inside him, a fugue of feeling more intricate than Bach—one of those complex tunes by Ellington, one that his wife used to hum, the stereo a sound-lamp on a sunlit Saturday morning. What was the name of that tune, and why had his wife died and left him? How long had it been since he'd asked *that* question? And why was he so tired and lonely and yet desperate for alone?

"Translator," he said. "Please comfort me."

In the living room, open on the low table, sat Norma's purse. When she returned, he'd ask her to leave. It was his house, his unyielding pattern; she'd disturbed it. He sat on the couch, head against the cushion, eyes closed. Her body formed behind his eyelids, strong, brown, and very hot, and his face was wet and now her thighs were tight around him, her head thrown back, laughing that strange, ungodly, high-pitched laugh, the glow of her cigarette just before he slept, too tired to say, Be careful, please, don't smoke in bed. . . .

•

He awoke into a sense of danger. Disturbed, he trudged into the kitchen, checked the clock. One-thirty. They'd eaten breakfast at eleven. He drifted back to the living room windows, opened one. The sun threw shadows across the midday roofs of cars; the air felt like October. Adrian closed the window, fumbled questions. Where was she? What had happened?

The bathroom was empty. The opening door moved dust through gloom that huddled in the darkroom's corners. He switched off the light, forced himself into the bedroom. The bed lay stained and crumpled, the way it looked after they'd come for his wife, after her gasping, her face fixed in the agony his fingers couldn't change.

He fled that room. Norma's coat still hung in the hallway closet. In the light of day it was closer to orange than red. He'd slept through the buzzer and she'd given up and gone home. There could be no other explanation. He closed his eyes and witnessed a scene that drained strength from his knees: a body in a vacant lot, skirt raised, spread-eagled thighs; birds flew from a bloodied, teeth-ruined mouth, a sky the color of water.

"No," Adrian whispered. He grabbed the purse, rummaged through it. A handkerchief, not used, a mirror with a smudge of fingerprints, a wallet. Fifty-seven dollars. Her name was Norma Fillis. A small bottle of white pills. Two condoms. A scrap of paper, a telephone number in a barely legible scrawl.

He sat waiting for the phone to ring, the hole widening in his belly. Norma knew his name. And where he lived. It was beyond his control; there was nothing he could do. For the first time that day he experienced a feeling that was tolerable. There was nothing he could do.

•

When he went again to the window the shadows were longer, the street deserted except for a woman in a yellow scarf who pawed in garbage cans. He went through Norma's purse again, read the number on the paper, took it to the phone and dialed. After three rings a voice answered.

"Hello?" It was an old man's voice.

"May I speak to Norma Fillis, please?"

"Who?"

"Norma Fillis."

"Ain't no Norma Fillis here."

Adrian explained the number in her purse. "Sorry," the voice wheezed, "ain't no Norma Fillis here."

"Excuse me," Adrian mumbled, and hung up. The buzzer growled. He answered it, moved to the front door, waited. When the steps halted at his apartment, when the bell rang, he called, "Who?"

"Me. Norma."

He opened the door. It was unlocked; he could have been set upon by thieves, by murderers. She swept past, had let her hair down. "It was nice out before," she said, "but now it's chilly."

"You were out all day?" His voice was querulous, old; it spoke of patterns interfered with.

"Well, hardly all day. A couple hours. When I came back the first time you were sleeping. Someone was coming out of the building and let me in. I'd left the apartment door unlocked. You were sleeping so good I decided to take a walk. I went past the lot where they found the woman. Is it time for lunch yet? Are you hungry?"

"No."

"Let's go to Harlem tonight. Something inexpensive. I'll treat. But for now," she said, and winked, "let's go back to bed."

He wouldn't look at her.

"Are you all right?"

He nodded.

"No, you're not. What's wrong?"

"Nothing."

"Nothing? Look at you." Her voice was patient; she touched his shoulder. "I enjoyed last night. Did you?"

"No."

She took her hand away.

"Who are you?" he rasped.

"Why, Adrian, I declare. Who *am* I?"

He could hardly speak for shaking. "That number in your purse. A man answered. An old man . . ."

"Number? What number?"

He showed her.

"Oh, Adrian, that's my sister's number. In *Ohio*. She moved and called me . . . see? That's what you get for going through a lady's purse." And she laughed that awful laugh. "Adrian, what's wrong? What are you afraid of?"

"Nothing . . . not afraid." It was difficult to breathe.

"Look at you."

"I'm not afraid."

She tried to catch his eyes with her own, but he wouldn't let her.

She said, "You wear fear."

"What do you know? I'm an old man. Leave me alone."

"Old?" her mouth tightened. "What's old?"

The room gathered shadows. Her face seemed luminous, thrust shining out of darkness. "I took care of a man once, in good health, all of him dead except the fear, and that lived like small animals in a cage inside him. Don't be like that. We all have to die. But we don't have to do it in installments."

"Leave me," Adrian barked. "I don't need your pity."

"Pity?"

"Go."

"Adrian."

"Leave me alone."

She moved to her toes, her mouth set. He feared she'd leap and hit him; he remembered her strength. But once she reached the height her toes would take her she sighed and shook her head, and the light released her face.

"If you insist."

Her voice, her feet, were flat and practical again. She collected her purse, her coat from the closet. Places she touched shook in Adrian's vision, left pools of darkness in her wake. When she went past him, he caught, for the last time, the smell of avocado.

The door clicked behind her. Adrian sat on the couch. The slip of paper still lay on the table, and he picked it up, but the room was too dim to read it. There was a lamp at his shoulder, but he wouldn't turn it on. He needed to move, to drive away his heart's strange, sudden pleading. So he began to walk, not outside where there was space and cool; he walked his empty, stale-aired rooms. Bathroom to bedroom to kitchen to hallway, back again, cramped steps, but he was moving, driven by the pleading of his heart, by desire so long thwarted it was screaming, and outside the train went by.

"Translator. Oh, translator," he said, and walked, carrying his heart like dead fish wrapped in newsprint, like an infant whose fever wouldn't break. He slumped to the couch, leaped up as if he'd sat in fire, raced toward the darkroom, banged against the doorway as he entered. There he retrieved from a strong box the film he'd shot on the day the translator had come into his life. He lay the waxed envelope on the counter, fixed the reeking chemicals, slid the strips of negatives from their sleeves, blew dust away, lowered the film into the pan and waited.

While he waited evening fell. When it had come to rest against the city he went downstairs to get the *Times* that had been on his doorstep since morning.

# ( ( part four ) )

OUR LIVES TOGETHER

(from *Out of the Madness*)
# Cool Brother


## Jerrold Ladd


By the summer of 1978, I had al-
ready begun to develop strong self-reliance traits. I was coming to grips
with my reality. We were children in abject poverty, separated from real
America. We had parents who were trying every morning to deal with
the man or woman in the mirror. The first law of nature, self-
preservation, prevailed for them. They became wrapped up in big balls
of grief and left us to fend for ourselves. But my mother, even in her zom-
bielike condition, was there when I needed her the most.

She would come out of her dope trance, utter her powerful wisdom,
then disappear without a trace: "Don't hang around the wrong crowd.
Don't stay out too late." Times like that made me wonder how my mother
would have been if she had not been put through so much, if her mother
had let her go to school, if the father of her children had not abandoned
her.

When she confronted me about stealing food from the shopping center
(mother's intuition), she explained in two quick sentences, nothing more,
nothing less, how it could devastate my life: "Jerrold, whatever I do, I'm
not gonna raise you to be no thief. When people find out you're a thief,
they'll never trust you again."

But I was driven by hunger and had no concern for what others thought. I had experienced enough hunger headaches to know that you can't do anything when you're cramping and swelling and every cell in your body is screaming for a bread crumb or something. It almost paralyzes you.

•

The boy who introduced me to stealing, Bad Baby, was sixteen, short, and lean. He was aggressive and would act quickly on his beliefs, which were good ones. The young girls loved his long Afro and the sharp clothes his mother, who had a speech defect, piled up for him. Of course they were a minimum-wage family, and they lived next door. Their apartment had nice cheap furniture, pictures, pots, plants, and wall-to-wall carpeting on the floor. The apartment also stayed cool and pleasant from the air conditioner in the window.

"Jerrold, are you coming over for dinner?" Bad Baby often asked.

"Naw, man, I'm not hungry," my shame would say.

"Come on over and eat, Jerrold. There's no reason to be ashamed, little brother. Ain't nothing wrong with eating at a friend's house."

Bad Baby had this kind of sympathy for my brother and me because even the poorest kids now talked about how dirty and ragged we were. They had given us nicknames. They called me Dirt Dobbler, and Junior, Dirt Mieser. But Bad Baby wasn't like them. Instead, he did nice things and never talked bad about me.

Bad Baby was also good at building bicycles from used parts. He also stole them. At times, when his mother let him, he would ride his bike out of the neighborhood. I didn't have a bike of my own, like kids from the minimum-wage group, so he would carry me along on the back of his bike. We went to visit his aunt across Hampton. We ran errands to the store. But on one trip Bad Baby took me across the Hampton bridge. It was the first time.

With Prescott, Bad Baby's older brother, we rode alongside the traffic on busy Hampton Road until we came upon a residential area. As we turned down several different streets, Bad Baby and Prescott checking in all directions, I noticed small bikes, toys, and chairs unattended on front lawns. They stopped at one corner, where Bad Baby ushered me off and pointed to a bike lying in someone's front yard.

He said, "Jerrold, this is the only way you'll ever have a bike. Go get it, man."

"I don't want to," I told him.

He and Prescott stepped away for a second, talked, and returned.

"Jerrold, you'll never have a bike unless you do it this way," he lectured.

"Bad Baby, take me home."

"If you don't get the bike, we're gonna leave you here."

Seeing that I wasn't budging, they sped off. I ran after them but they were too fast. Scared, I turned back around, hopped on the bike, and pedaled in the direction they had ridden. They stood around the corner, waiting for me. We hurried back past the traffic and back across the bridge. Along the way, Baby Baby told me that the people had plenty of money and would never miss the bike. To keep me from being whopped, he told my mom he'd built it for me. And I kept it.

.

Bad Baby had always observed what went on at our house and had always been concerned. So it was no surprise when he found out my mother was on drugs. After he gradually became closer to my brother and me, he convinced us to run away and sneak into his house late one night, even though it was only next door. He thought things would be better if my mom was reported.

Since our mother had traded the upstairs room with Junior and me, Bad Baby had to creep onto the ledge under our window and above the back door. After he was inside, he tucked clothes under our blankets to look like sleeping people, and helped us out the window. The next day, authorities from Human Resources came. This funny-looking white man, dressed in a suit, took us to our apartment. He identified himself to our mother and told her he alone would question my brother and me. She gave him a nervous "okay" and looked at us sadly, as if she knew her wrongdoing had finally caught up with her. Before the white man started, I whispered to my brother to tell the man we were okay. My brother looked disappointed.

As for me, I had gone along reluctantly with Bad Baby's plan, but this was too much. From snatches of conversations at the corners with the dope dealers, I had heard about these strange white people from the state who destroy black families. I had been warned to avoid them at all costs. But more than any verbal admonishment, my instincts compelled me not to trust them. She was my mother. This was our home.

In our room, with the door shut, the man began talking with that soft, soothing voice, the kind psychiatrists use to relax people. "Now, I don't want you to be afraid of what will happen to you boys, because no one's gonna hurt you. I just want you to tell me the truth, and I'll see if I can make things better for you, okay?"

"Okay," my brother said, already falling under the spell. But I was not to be taken. The white man began his questions.

"Now, does your mother feed you?"

"Yes, sir," I said quickly. "We eat very well."

"How often do you attend school?"

"Ooh, we rarely miss days. I love school, my momma always helps me."

"Does she take care of your sister?"

"Yes, sir."

"Does she do drugs?"

"Ooh, no, sir," I told him.

The white man started looking confused, as if he couldn't understand why neighbors would report something wrong with such happy kids and such a good mother. Before leaving, he apologized to my mother. And we never heard from the state people again.

Thereafter I was forbidden form talking with Bad Baby. Before the summer ended, he and his family moved across Hampton to the shack houses. I later learned that Prescott, Bad Baby's brother, was murdered there. His throat was cut.

•

My quiet brother, who also was experimenting with self-reliance, had learned to steal during his own adventures in the camp he'd gone to. And together, on days when our hunger would not let us rest, we stole food from the shopping center. We stole things that were easy to conceal, like cans of sardines and small packages of rice. A bowl of rice and a tall glass of water was enough for our indiscriminate stomachs.

Another hustle we used to get food was going into the shopping center late at night to steal TV guides. The newspaper companies dumped hundreds of papers on the sidewalk. So Mark, another kid named Big Mark, my brother, and I would get there about one in the morning. We would quickly sift through the piles and pick out all the TV guides. Then, when we had gathered all we could carry, we would scurry back to the lake to take the hidden trail. Back in the projects, we would go from door to door, selling our magazines for a quarter apiece.

We weren't thieves, just hungry children. Work, when we could find it, took the place of stealing. Each morning Junior and I would rise early and go looking for jobs, walking up Industrial, up Singleton, up Hampton Road. Consumed with our attempts to find work, we would stay gone all day without eating. Most places would not hire us because we were too young, just eight- and ten-year-olds. Occasionally we did stumble upon a place that needed temporary help. And my brother once landed a job for a service station that paid him about thirty dollars for a full week of work.

We worked at the shopping center, too. All day my brother and I would be at the Tom Thumb with Syrup Head and Three Finger Willie, roaming around. We would ask customers if we could carry their groceries but would not ask for a fee; instead we would just stand there, looking dirty and hungry. When we were done, some would tip us, others wouldn't. We could make a good seven bucks after a long, ten-hour day. We gave our mother sometimes all, sometimes half the money; the rest we spent on food or candy. We also dug through the trash cans behind the DAV store in the shopping center, looking for clothes, toys, change, and good pairs of shoes.

I still played Deadman, but not as often, because a body had been found in the Deadman vacant units. Between the stealing and scavenging, though, I was managing to stay away from the house, where things weren't getting any better. A bootleg family had moved in next door to us. They bought cases of beer from South Dallas, a wet part of the city, and stored it in their house. From their back door they sold each can for a dollar. Nighttime traffic was steady in and out of their house. On the corners, the heroin dealers were in full force.

•

I was on my Huffy bike all the time now. I often rode it down Fishtrap and Shaw streets, near the two candy trucks, and on Apple Grove and Morris, up and down the sidewalks and trails on the block, not stopping for the common fistfights that crowds gathered to watch or the young boys burning mattress cotton at nightfall to keep the mosquitoes away.

I would even ride my bike where rapists had once attacked me. Each time I did, a black man sitting on a porch watched me curiously. Sometimes a woman was with him. I made a mental note to keep an eye on him. If he were another rapist, I would not be his next victim.

Riding my bike on the other end of the block, I grew closer to Eric, a boy I played Deadman with. He and I were the same age and both had heroin mothers, so we had a lot in common. Eric was afraid to live in his house, a problem he discussed with me. He knew something bad was going to happen there. He told me he kept his bedroom window open, in case he needed to make the two-story jump to safety. He dreamed, he often said, of the day when his parents would stop selling dope and they all could leave the projects forever. To pass the time, we would sit out at night on the swings the authorities had built. We would swing our souls away late into the dark, starry nights. Both our young mothers had stopped coming home.

Eric also knew of the muscular, dark man who had been watching me. I pointed him out one day while he sat on Eric's porch. Eric was surprised. He said that the man had been with some of the prettiest women in the projects. He was no rapist. He was one of those settled, cool brothers, the smooth ones who know a lot about women.

One evening, instead of going up Morris, I rode past the man's house, where he was sitting on the porch with his girlfriend. He stopped me and asked what my name was, said he knew about my mother and my home situation. He said he used to be just like me when he was a boy. Looking into my eyes with his own black rubies, he told me I was good-looking.

"Women will take care of you when you're older, if you know how to move a woman's heart," he said. His girlfriend just sat there and smiled. The man wasn't threatening, and he aroused my curiosity too much for me not to go back. So I did go, all summer long.

I don't think he had children, because I never saw any. I know he didn't work. The apartment, which belonged to his woman, was sparsely furnished and had only two dining-room chairs and a couch. It was still a project unit, so it had the small rooms, which stayed hot. Everything was kept tidy and clean, even the tile floors, which required a lot of mopping. His backyard had the same wire clotheslines and red ants.

He kept food, a lot of vegetables, greens, and fish, but none of the disgusting pig feet, pig ears, and things my mother cooked from time to time. He never fried his food and said he didn't eat pork because it was worse than putting heroin in your blood. He, not his girlfriend, cooked their meals; I found that odd. Until he moved away, he gave me food, which I ate like a starved animal.

But what I recall most is his bedroom. The windows were covered by heavy blankets, forever blackening out the sun. It stayed totally dark in there. A dull, red light, like one blinking on a dark stormy night atop a tall tower, revealed the shadow of a small table next to his bed. That light and the reefer smoke made the room an enchanted setting.

While the deep rhythms of the band Parliament and Bootsy's Rubber Band softly played out of four speakers in each corner of the room, I would sit, light-headed from his reefer smoke, absorbing the almost spiritual music, and listen to this black man, who wore a net cap over his small Afro. I clearly remember two of his imperatives: "Always love your woman's mind" and "You have to take care of her, so she'll hold you up when the white man wants to crush you." Not until years later would I come to understand his advice or the rare kind of black man he was. Over time I grew to respect him because, unlike many of us, he seemed content and at peace, seemed to know some secrets about the projects, perhaps their purpose, perhaps why we were in them, that made him seem not subdued, at least in many ways.

After the sweet brother piqued my interest in women, it wasn't long before I met my first female friend, Gloria, on the day she and her family moved to West Dallas, near my unit, on the row behind Biggun's. My friendship with Eric had been dwindling away naturally, like friendships between little kids do, so Gloria came along on time.

From the first day I saw her at the candy truck on Fishtrap, Gloria was beautiful to me. Too beautiful. She was thin, her skin gleamed with natural health, and her eyes were pearls shaded by shoulder-length hair. Not even her old clothes and weathered shoes could overshadow her beauty. After I gathered enough courage I introduced myself.

"My name is Jerrold, you must don't live around here."

"How'd you know?" she asked.

"Because you're shopping at the high candy truck. If you want to, I'll show you where the cheap one is."

"That'll be nice," she said, looking as if she knew she had met her first friend. And from that day forward, that's the way Gloria and I would get along, simply, openly, and cheerfully.

I walked her back home from the candy truck and offered to help her and her family move in.

•

With the work of moving, Gloria was helping as much as her girlish strength would allow, carrying bags of clothes and boxes of pots over the barren ground, between much-needed rest periods. Her sisters, on the other hand, were bulky, strong women who could help the men carry the heavy pieces. They all worked under the admiration of the older boys, who stood around watching. Enough of them had already volunteered. And her mom, who was thin like Gloria, helped also.

Over time I learned that Gloria's two sisters had babies and her mother was on heroin. I didn't know much about her father—who mostly stayed to himself—except that he had a job somewhere and was the only support the family had. Gloria's mother shouted at him all the time. He seemed to be on heroin, too.

I admired the young girls as much as I could at that age, but Gloria was beyond them all because she was kind, gentle, and sweet, all at the same time. I can't recall ever hearing one bitter word come from her mouth or one angry expression on her face. The older boys longed for her ripeness with lusty stares. But of all of us, she liked scrawny me.

She was my first intimate contact with a woman. To share feelings and play games became the order of the day. And though we would not see each other for weeks or months, we would still say that we were going together. We would sit around together and talk on her back porch, after I climbed the tall tree back there, which was equally as important. Sometimes we held hands, being sure to stay away from the minimum-wage group, who would have teased us. We occasionally sat alone under the dark nights. We kissed only once, and I thought I experienced a little bit of that healing my cool friend had talked about, for even at that age blacks were real mature about relationships between men and women.

Sometimes Gloria would express her disappointment at her mother, who she thought could do a lot better. I would overhear Gloria questioning her mother about women things. But her mother, who didn't want to be bothered, always responded unkindly, angrily, sometimes frantically. Something else I picked up on was Gloria's serious weakness. She lacked self-reliance, something all kids had learned was vitally necessary. I hoped Gloria would also gain the skill, in time.

But for now she looked to her mother for guidance, to shape her into the fine woman she was destined to be. Gloria was enduring the projects the way my brother had when he first arrived: remaining quiet, sweet, and sensitive, even to her mother. No need to worry about Gloria, her loveliness would see her through.

Toward the end of the year 1978, however, I let a boy and his sister peer-pressure me into picking a fight with Gloria. I wanted to be accepted by the bullies, even at the cost of my love. I figured this was the better long-term investment, an example of those self-reliance skills. After they dared me, I walked up to Gloria, her knowing all along what was going on, and blackened her eye.

The two who'd put me up to it "oohed" and "aawed" and giggled. But Gloria, devastated, was crying softly. When she walked away from me that day, I saw the pain and hurt in her eyes. She wouldn't speak to me for weeks, and the bullies still chased me home. I felt terrible for months afterward. But Gloria eventually forgave me. She stopped me one day as I walked in front of her house and told me I was wrong for doing that. But when I apologized, she smiled. Regardless, we would never become close friends again. Gloria and her family would soon leave the projects. Her mother was about to have a nervous breakdown.

After apologizing to Gloria that day, I went home and found a small crowd gathered across from my window. They were watching as a black man was being wheeled from the Deadman units by paramedics. A sheet hid his face. He was Gloria's father.

# Palm Wine

## Reginald McKnight

This was fourteen years ago, but it still bothers me as though it happened day before yesterday. I've never talked about this with anyone, and I'm not talking about it now because I expect it to relieve me of painful memory but because, as they say in Madagascar, the bad is told that the good may appear. So. I was in Senegal on a graduate fellowship. I was there to collect and compile West African proverbs. This was to complete my Ph.D. in anthropology, which, I'm afraid, I failed to do. The things I'm going to talk about now had as much to do with that failure as did my laziness, my emotional narrowness, and my intellectual mediocrity. I was a good deal younger then, too, but that's no excuse. Not really.

Anyway, one afternoon, instead of collecting proverbs in Yoff village, which I should have done, I went to Dakar with Omar the tailor—a friend of a friend—to buy palm wine. I'd craved palm wine ever since I'd read Amos Tutuola's novel *The Palm-Wine Drunkard* in college. Tutuola never attempts to describe the taste, color, or smell of palm wine, but because the Drinkard (whose real name is Father of the Gods Who Could Do Anything in This World) can put away two hundred and twenty-five kegs of it per day, and because he sojourns through many cruel and horrifying worlds in order to try to retrieve his recently killed palm wine tapster from Deadstown, I figured palm wine had to be pretty good.

As Omar and I boarded the bus, I dreamed palm wine dreams. It must be pale green, I thought, coming from a tree and all. Or milky-blue, like coconut water. I had it in mind that it must hit the tongue like a dart, and that it must make one see the same visions Tutuola himself witnessed. A creature big as a bipedal elephant, sporting two-foot fangs thick as cow's horns; a creature with a million eyes and hundreds of breasts that continuously suckle her young, who swarm her body like maggots; a town where everything and everyone is red as plum flesh; a town where they all walk backwards; a town full of ghosts.

I really had no business going that day. I was at least a month behind in my research because of a lengthy bout with malaria. But I excused myself from work by telling myself that I had no Wolof proverbs on the subject of drinking and I'd likely encounter a couple that day. I took my pad, pencils, and tape recorder along, knowing I wasn't going to use them.

On the ride to town, I could scarcely pay mind to matters that usually fascinate me. For instance, I would often carefully observe the beggars who boarded the buses to cry for alms, their Afro-Arab plaints weaving through a bus like serpents, slipping between exquisitely coiffed women and dignified, angular men, wives of the wealthy, daughters of the poor, beardless hustlers, bundled babies, tourists, pickpockets, gendarmes, students. A beautiful plaint could draw coins like salt draws moisture.

Some beggars not only sang for indulgences but also sang their thanks. "*Jerrejeff*, my sister, paradise lies under the feet of mothers. A heart that burns for Allah gives more light than ten thousand suns." Some of them sang proverbs from the Koran. "Be constant in prayer and give alms." "Allah pity him who must beg of a beggar." Some of them merely cried something very much like "Alms! Alms!" And some of them rasped like reptiles and said little more than "I got only one arm! Gimme money!" and the proverbs they used were usually stale. They were annoying, but even so I often gave them alms, and I recorded them. I guess it was because I liked being in a culture that had a good deal more respect for the poor than my own. And I guess I tried hard to appreciate art forms that were different from the ones I readily understood.

But, honestly, as I say, that day I could think of little more than palm wine. It would be cold as winter rain. It would be sweet like berries, and I would drink till my mind went swimming in deep waters.

We alighted from the bus in the arrondissement of Fosse, the place

Omar insisted was the only place to find the wine. Preoccupied as I was with my palm wine dreams, they weren't enough to keep me from attending to Fosse. It's an urban village, a squatter's camp, a smoke-filled bowl of shanties built of rusty corrugated metal, gray splintery planks, cinderblock, cement. It smelled of everything: goatskins, pot, green tobacco, fish, overripe fruit, piss, cheap perfume, Gazelle beer, warm couscous, scorched rice, the sour sharpness of cooking coals. People talked, laughed, sang, cried, argued—the sounds so plangent I felt them in my teeth, my chest, my knees. A woman dressed in blue flowers scolded her teenage son, and the sound lay tart on my tongue. Two boys drummed the bottoms of plastic buckets while a third played a pop bottle with a stick, and I smelled *churai* incense. Two little girls danced to the boys' rhythms, their feet invisible with dust, and I felt them on my back.

A beautiful young woman in a paisley wraparound pagne smiled at us, and I rubbed Omar's incipient dreadlocks, his wig of thumbs, as I called them, and said, "Hey, man, there's a wife for you." Omar grinned at me; his amber eyes were crescents, his teeth big as dominoes. "She too old for me, mahn," he said.

"Oh, please, brother, she couldn't be older than eighteen."

"Young is better."

"Whatever. Letch."

I didn't really like Omar. He insisted on speaking English with me even though his English was relatively poor. Even when I spoke to him in French or my shaky Wolof he invariably answered me in English. This happened all the time in Senegal and the other francophone countries I traveled. People all around the globe want to speak English, and my personal proverb was, Every English speaking traveler will be a teacher as much as he'll be a student. I suppose if his English had been better I wouldn't have minded, but there were times it lead to trouble—like that day—and times when the only thing that really bothered me about it was that it was Omar speaking it.

Omar the tailor man, always stoned, always grinning, his red and amber crescents, his domino teeth, his big olive-shaped head, his wolfish face, his hiccupping laugh jangling every last nerve in my skull. He perpetually thrust his long hands at me for cigarettes, money, favors. "Hey, I and I, you letting me borrow you tapedeck?" "Hey, I and I, *jokma bene* cigarette." He was a self-styled Rastafarian, and he had the notion that since the U.S. and Jamaica are geographically close, Jamaicans and black Americans were interchangeable. I was pretty certain I was of more value to him as a faux-Jamaican than as a genuine American.

He was constantly in my face with this "I and I, mahn" stuff, always quoting Peter Tosh couplets, insisting I put them in my book (I could never get him to understand the nature of my work). Moreover, it took him six months to sew one lousy pair of pants and one lousy shirt for me, items I was dumb enough to pay for in advance. Between the day he measured me and the day I actually donned the clothes I'd lost twenty-six pounds (constant diarrhea and a fish-and-rice diet will do that to you), but I wasn't about to ask him to take them in—I only had a year's worth of fellowship money, after all.

Omar always spoke of his great volume of work, his busyness, the tremendous pressure he was under, but each and every time I made it to his shop hoping to pick up my outfit, I'd find him sitting with four or five friends, twisting his locks, putting the buzz on, yacking it up. "Hey, I and I, come in! I don't see you a long time."

In northern African they say, Bear him unlucky, don't bear him lazy. But I bore Omar anyway because he was a friend of my good friend and assistant, Idrissa, who at the time was visiting his girlfriend in Paris. I went with Omar to get the palm wine because Omar, who knew Fosse a great deal better than Idrissa did, insisted that that day was the only time in palm wine season he would be able to make the trip. He told me that Idrissa wouldn't be back till the season was well over. Originally, the three of us were to have made the trip, but Idrissa's girlfriend had sent him an erotic letter and a ticket to Paris. And money. We blinked; Idrissa was gone. And since Omar was so "pressed for time," we wasted none of it getting to the city. As I walked the ghetto with Omar I reflected on how Idrissa would often fill things in for me with his extemporaneous discussions of the history, economics, and myths of wherever in Senegal we happened to be. Idrissa was self-educated and garrulous. My kind of person. He was also very proud of his Senegalese heritage. He seemed to know everything about the country. As Omar and I walked, I told myself that if Idrissa had been there I would have been learning things. (What did I know?)

On our walk, Omar seldom spoke. He seemed unable to answer any of my questions about the place, so after about ten minutes I stopped asking. We walked what seemed to me to be the entire ghetto, and must have inquired at about eight or nine places without seeing a drop of palm wine. Each inquiry involved the usual African procedure—shake hands all around, ask about each other's friends, families, health, work; ask for the wine, learn they have none; ask them who might, shake hands, leave. It was getting close to dusk now, and our long shadows undulated before us over the tight-packed soil. I was getting a little hungry, and I kept eyeing the street vendors who braised brochettes of mutton along the curbs of the main street. The white smoke rose up and plumed into the streets, raining barbecue smells everywhere. I said, "Looks like we're not getting the wine today. Tell you what, why don't we—"

"Is not the season, *quoi*," Omar said as we rambled into a small, secluded yard. It was surrounded by several cement-and-tin houses, some with blanket doors, insides lighted mostly by kerosene or candles. Here and there, though, I could see that some places had electricity. Omar crossed his arms as we drew to a stop. "We stay this place and two more," he said, "then I and I go."

"Aye-aye," I said.

Four young men sat on a dusty porch, passing a cigarette between them. Several toddlers, each runny-nosed and ashy-kneed, frenetically crisscrossed in front of the men, pretending to grab for the cigarette. Until they saw me. Then they stopped and one of the older ones approached us, reached out a hand, and said, "*Toubobie*, mawney." Omar said, in Wolof, "This man isn't a *toubob*. This is a black man. An American brother." I answered in Wolof, too. "Give me a proverb and I'll give you money." The boy ran away grinning, and the men laughed. I drew my cigarettes from my shirt pocket, tapped out eight, and gave two to each man.

"Where's Doudou?" Omar asked the men.

They told him Doudou, whoever he was, had left a half-hour before, but was expected back very soon. One of the men, a short, muscular man in a T-shirt and a pair of those voluminous trousers called chayas, detached himself from his friends and walked into one of the houses. He returned carrying a small green liquor bottle. I felt my eyebrows arch. The stuff itself, I was thinking. I imagined myself getting pied with these boys, so drunk I'm hugging them, telling them I love them and, Goddammit, where's old Doudou? I miss that bastid. The man in the chayas unscrewed the lid with sacramental delicacy, drank and passed the bottle on. I watched the men's faces go soft when each passed the bottle on to his brother. I took the bottle rather more aggressively than was polite, and I apologized to the man who'd handed it to me. Omar winked at me. "You don't know what bottle is, *quoi*?" Omar had the irritating habit of using the tag *quoi* after most of his sentences. He did it in English, French, Wolof, and his own language, Bambara. It wasn't an uncommon habit in French West Africa, but Omar wore it down to a nub.

"Paaalm wiiine," I said in a low, throaty voice, the way you'd say an old love's name. My God, what was wrong with me? I was behaving as though, like the Drinkard himself, I had fought the beast with the lethal gaze and shovel-sized scales, or had spent the night in the bagful of creatures with ice cold, sandpapery hair, like I'd done some heroic thing and the stuff in the green bottle was my reward. As I brought the bottle to my lips, Omar said, "It's no palm wine, I and I." I drank before Omar's words even registered, and the liquid burned to my navel. It was very much like a strong tequila. No, that's an understatement. If this drink and tequila went to prison, this drink would make tequila its girlfriend. "Is much stronger than palm wine," said Omar.

My throat had closed up and it took me a few seconds before I could speak. All I could manage was to hiss, "Jeezuz!" And abruptly one of the young men, a Franco-Senegalese with golden hair and green eyes said, "Jeezuz," but then he continued in rapid Wolof and I lost him. Soon all five of them were laughing, saying, "Jeezuz, Jeeezuz," working the joke, extending it, jerking it around like taffy. My blood rose to my skin, and every muscle in my back knotted. I squinted at Omar, who looked back at me with eyes both reassuring and provocative, and he said, "He saying he like *Americain noire* talk. You know, you say—*quoi*—'Jeezuz,' and 'sheeee,' and 'mahn,' *quoi*. We like the *Americain noire* talk." His mouth hovered this close to a smirk.

I was furious, but I had no choice but to grin and play along. I lit a smoke and said, "Jeezuz," and, "Jeezuz Christ," and "Jeezuz H. Christ," cuttin' the monkey, as my dad would put it. My stomach felt like it was full of mosquitoes. My hands trembled. I wanted to kick Omar's face in. His hiccupping giggles rose above the sound of everyone else's laughter, and his body jerked about convulsively. Yeah, choke on it, I thought. But I didn't have to endure the humiliation long, for soon an extremely tall, very black, very big-boned man joined us, and Omar said, "Doudou!" and fiercely shook hands with the giant. Doudou nodded my way and said in Wolof, "What's this thing?" and I froze with astonishment. Thing? I tried to interpret Omar's lengthy explanation, but his back was to me and he was speaking very rapidly. As I say, my Wolof was never very good. Doudou placed his hands on his hips and squinted at the ground as though he'd lost something very small. The big man nodded now and then. Then he looked at me and said in French, "It's late in the season, but I know where there's lots of palm wine." He immediately wheeled about and began striding away. Omar followed, then I.

The walk was longer than I'd expected, and by the time we got to the place, the deep blue twilight had completely absorbed our shadows. After seven or eight months of living in Senegal, I had become used to following strangers into unfamiliar places in the night. But even so I felt uneasy. I watched the night as a sentry would, trying to note every movement and sound. There was nothing extraordinary about the things I saw on the way, but even today they remain as vivid as if I'd seen them the day before yesterday—a three-year-old girl in a faded pink dress, sitting on a porch; a cat-sized rat sitting atop an overflowing garbage crate; a man in a yellow shirt and blue tie talking to a bald man wearing a maroon khaftan; a half-moon made half again by a knot of scaly clouds; Omar's wig of thumbs; Doudou's broad back. I wasn't thinking much about palm wine.

It was an inconspicuous place, built from the same stuff in the same way that practically every other place in Fosse was. Perhaps half a dozen candles lit the room, but rather than clarify, they muddied the darkness. I couldn't tell whether there were six other men in the place or twelve. I couldn't make out the proprietress's face, or anything else about her, for that matter. The only unchanging features were her eyes, an unnatural olive-black and egg-white, large, perpetually doleful. But was her expression stern or soft?

As the candlelight shifted, heaved, bent, so did her shape and demeanor. At times she seemed as big as Doudou, and at other times she seemed only five-foot-two or so. One moment she looked fifty, a second later twenty-three. Her dress was sometimes blue, sometimes mauve. I couldn't stop staring at her, and I couldn't stop imagining that the light in the room was incrementally being siphoned away, and that my skull was being squeezed as if in the crook of a great headlocking arm, and that the woman swelled to two, three, four times her size, and split her dress like ripe fruit skin, and glowed naked, eggplant-black like a burnished goddess, and that she stared at me with those unchanging olive-and-egg eyes.

It's that stuff I drank, I kept saying to myself. It's that stuff they gave me. Then, with increasing clarity I heard a hiss as though air were rushing from my very own ears, and the sound grew louder, so loud the air itself seemed to be torn in half like a long curtain, until it abruptly stopped with the sound of a cork being popped from a bottle; then everything was normal again, and I looked around the room half embarrassed, as if the ridiculous things in my head had been projected onto the wall before me for all to see, and I saw that Doudou was staring at me with a look of bemused deprecation. I felt myself blush. I smiled rather stupidly at the giant, and he cocked his head just a touch to the left but made no change in his facial expression. I quickly looked back at the woman.

( ( speak my name ) )

She told my associates that the wine was still quite fresh, and she swung her arm with a graceful backhand motion before ten plastic gallon jugs apparently full to the neck with the wine. It was very cheap, she said. Then she dipped her hands into a large plastic pan of water on the table that stood between herself and us. She did it the way a surgeon might wash her hands, scooping the water, letting it run to the elbows. In the same water she washed two bottles and laid them aside. Next, she poured a little palm wine into a tumbler, walked to the door, then poured the contents on the ground outside. I could feel excitement sparking up again in my stomach. "Is ritual," said Omar, but when I asked him what it meant he ignored me.

The woman returned to the jug, filled the bottom half-inch of her tumbler with wine, and took two perfunctory sips. After that she slipped a screened funnel into the first bottle's neck, filled the bottle, then filled the second bottle in the same way. Omar lifted one of the bottles, took a whiff, then a sip. I closely watched his face, but his expression told me little. He arched both eyebrows and nodded a bit. The woman handed the second bottle to Doudou, and he did pretty much what Omar had. I don't recall noting his expression. Then Omar handed me his bottle.

It was awful. It was *awful*. It was awful. Though Idrissa had warned me about the taste, I had had the impression that he was trying to prepare me for the fact that it doesn't taste like conventional wines. I was prepared for many things—a musky flavor, a fruity flavor, dryness, tartness, even blandness. But for me, the only really pleasant aspect of this liquid was its color, cloudy white, like a liquid pine cleaner mixed with water. It had a slightly alcoholic tang and smelled sulphuric. It had a distinctly sour bouquet that reminded me of something I very much hated as a kid. If you could make wine from egg salad and vinegar, palm wine is pretty much what you'd get.

Really, the stuff was impossible to drink, but I did my best. The ordeal might have gone more easily had Omar not been Omar—singing reggae music off key, slapping my back, philosophizing in a language he didn't understand, toasting a unified Africa, then toasting the mighty Rastafari, toasting me, then Doudou. But the thing that made the ordeal in the bar most unpleasant was that Doudou glared at me for what felt like ten unbroken minutes. He stared at my profile as though my face were his property. I couldn't bring myself to confront him. He was just so fucking huge. He was not merely tall—perhaps six-foot-eight or so—but his bones were pillars, his face a broad iron shield. He gave off heat, he bowed the very atmosphere of the room. Wasn't it enough I had to drink that swill? Did I need the additional burden of drinking from under the millstone of this man's glare? Just as I was about to slam my bottle to the table and stalk out, Doudou said in French, "An American."

"Americano," I said.

"Amerikanski," he said.

"That's right. We've got that pretty much nailed down."

"Hey," Omar said, "you like the palm wine?"

Before I could answer, Doudou said, "He doesn't like the wine, Omar."

"Who says I don't?"

Doudou cocked an eyebrow and looked at the low-burning candle on our table. He rolled the bottle between his fingers as if it were pencil-thin. "I tell you he doesn't like it, Omar." Then he looked at me and said, "*I* say you don't." I felt cold everywhere. A small painful knot hardened between my shoulder blades, as so often happens when I'm angry.

"You know," I said, stretching my back, rolling my shoulders, "I'm not going to argue about something so trivial." Then I turned to Omar and said in English, "Omar, the wine is very good. Excellent."

Omar shrugged, and said, "Is okay, I think. Little old."

We were silent after that, and Doudou stopped staring, but it got no more comfortable. Two men started to argue politics, something about the increasing prices of rice and millet, something about Islamic law, and when it got to the table-banging stage, Omar suggested we leave. I had suffered through two glasses of this liquid acquired taste, and Omar, much to my regret, bought me two liters of the wine to take home. I did want to go home, and said so, but Doudou said, "You must stay for tea." Omar said yes before I could say no, and I knew it would be impolite to leave without Omar. We walked back to Doudou's place and I saw that the young men were still quietly, getting happy on the Senegalese tequila. Doudou sat in a chair on the porch and sent the young man in chayas into the house; he returned with a boom box and a handful of tapes. He threw in a Crusaders tape, and immediately two of the men began to complain. They wanted Senegalese music, but Doudou calmly raised his hand and pointed to me. The men fell silent, and I said, "I don't have to have American music."

"Sure you do," said the big man. He leaned so far back in his chair that its front legs were ten inches off the porch and the back of the chair rested against the windowsill. His feet stayed flat on the ground.

"Your French is good," I said.

"Better than yours," he said. He was smiling, and I couldn't see a shred of contempt in his expression, but that remark burned up the last of my calm. It was full dark, but I could see his broad, smooth face clearly, for the house's light illuminated it. It hung before the window like a paper lantern, like a planet. Looking back on it, I can see that I must have offended him. He must have thought I was evincing surprise that, he, a denizen of Fosse, could speak as well as he did. Actually, I was just trying to make conversation. When the bottle came my way I tipped it and drank a full inch. "Thanks for the hospitality," I said. Doudou folded his arms and tipped his head forward, removing it from the light. "Amerikanski," he said. One of the men chuckled.

Omar sat "Indian-style" a foot to my right. He rolled a very large spliff from about a half-ounce of pot and an eight-by-ten-inch square of newspaper. He handed it to the man sitting across from him, the Franco-Senegalese with the golden hair. The comedian. "Where's the tea?" the man asked in Wolof. "Eh?" said Doudou, and then he pointed to the boom box. The man in the chayas turned it down. The golden-haired man repeated his question. Doudou's only reply was, "Ismaila, get the tea," and the young man in the chayas rose once again and came back quickly with the primus stove, the glasses, the sugar, and the tea.

"Omar tells me that you're an anthropologist," said Doudou.

"That's right," I said.

"The study of primitive cultures." Doudou said this as though he'd read the words off the back of a bottle. A dangerous sort of neutrality, as I saw it. It grew so still for a moment there that I jumped when Ismaila lit the stove; the gas had burst into blue flame with a sudden *woof* and I found myself glaring at Ismaila as though he'd betrayed me.

I cleared my throat and said, "That's only one aspect of anthropology . . ." I struggled for words. When I'm nervous I can barely speak my own language, let alone another's, but I managed to say, "But I study the living cultures." There, I thought, that was nice. I went on to explain that the discipline of anthropology was changing all the time, that it had less to do with so-called primitive cultures and more to do with the study of the phenomenon of culture and the many ways it can be expressed.

The light from the stove's flame cast ghostlight over the four of us who sat around it. A short man with batlike ears sat behind me and Omar. He was in silhouette, as was Doudou, up there on the porch. The man with the strange ears tapped my shoulder and handed me the spliff. I took a perfunctory hit, and handed it to Omar. "Ganjaaaa," said Omar.

"I knew an anthropologist once," said Doudou, "who told me I should be proud to be part of such a noble, ancient, and primitive people." He paused long enough for me to hear the water begin to boil. Then he said, "What aspect of anthropology do you think he studied?"

"Couldn't tell you," I said.

"Too bad."

"Maybe," I said, "he was trying to tell you that primitive . . . I mean, that in this case 'primitive' means the same thing as 'pure.'"

"Really. 'In this case,' you say."

"I can only—"

"Was I supposed to have been offended by his language? Are you saying we Africans should be offended by words like 'primitive'?" He placed his great hands on his knees, sat up straight. It occurred to me that he was trying to look regal. It worked. I could feel myself tremulously unscrewing the top of one of my palm wine bottles, and I took a nip from it. My sinuses filled with its sour bouquet. "Well . . . you sounded offended," I said.

"Who studies *your* people?"

"What?"

"Do you have anthropologists milling about your neighborhood? Do they write down everything you say?"

"Look, I know how you must—"

Doudou turned away from me. "Ismaila, how's the tea coming?" he said.

"No problems," said Ismaila.

"Look here," I said, but before I could continue the man with the pointed ears said, "I get offended. I get very offended. You write us down. You don't respect us. You come here and steal from us. It's a very bad thing, and you, you should know better."

"What, because I'm black?"

"Black," said Doudou.

"Is fine, I and I. Is very nice."

"What the fuck's that supposed to mean, Omar?" I said. "Look, I'm trying to help all black people by recovering our forgot things."

"Your 'lost' things," Ismaila said quietly as he dumped two or three handfuls of tea into the boiling water.

"'Lost' things," I said. "My French is pretty evil."

"Your French is poor."

He removed the pot from the flame and let it steep for a few minutes. One of the men, a bald, chubby man with a single thick eyebrow, rose from the ground and began fiddling with the boom box. He put in a tape by some Senegalese group and turned it up a bit. The guitar sounded like crystal bells, the bass like a springy heartbeat; the singer's nasal voice wound like a tendril around the rhythm. As Ismaila sang with the tape, he split the contents of the pot between two large glasses, filling each about halfway, and dumped three heaps of sugar into each glass.

While he worked, I kept nipping at the palm wine like a man who can't stop nipping at the pinky nail of his right hand even though he's down to the bloody quick. The more I drank, the odder its flavors seemed to me. It was liquid egg, ammonia, spoiled fish, wet leather, piss. The taste wouldn't hold still, and soon enough it wholly faded. The roof of my mouth, my sinuses, my temples began to throb with a mild achiness, and if I'd had food in my belly that evening I might have chucked it up. Ismaila began tossing the contents of the glasses from one glass to the other. I could see that Omar was following his movements with great intent.

"What's all this about, Omar?" I said in English. "Why are these guys fucking with me?" I hoped he'd understood me, and I hoped that no one among his friends would suddenly reveal himself as a fluent speaker of English. I also ended up wishing Idrissa was there when Omar said, "No worry, I and I, the tea is good."

"Things lost?" said Doudou. "That must mean you're not pure, *quoi*. That you think you can come here and bathe in our primitive dye."

Omar and I exchanged looks, our heads turning simultaneously. I was encouraged by that speck of consanguinity. It emboldened me. "Want some palm wine?" I said to Doudou. "It really tastes like crap."

The giant shifted slightly in his chair. He said nothing for maybe fifteen seconds. "How does it feel," he said, "to be a black *toubob*?" I felt my face suddenly grow hot. My guts felt as if they were in a slow meltdown. I took a large draft of the wine and disgust made me wince. "By *toubob*," I asked, "do you mean 'stranger' or 'white'? I understand it can be used both ways."

Doudou leaned forward in the chair and it snapped and popped as if it were on fire. It appeared for a moment that he was going to rise from his chair, and everything in me tightened, screwed down, clamped, but he merely leaned and said, "In Wolof, 'toubob' is 'toubob' is 'toubob.'"

The blood beat so hard beneath my skin I couldn't hear the music for a few seconds. I tried to breathe deeply, but I couldn't. All I could do was drink that foul wine and quiver with anger. I stared for a long time at some pinprick point in the air between me and Doudou. It was as though the world or I had collapsed into that tiny point of blackness, which, after

I don't know how long, opened like a sleepy eye, and I realized that I'd been watching Ismaila hand around small glasses of tea. First to Omar, then to Doudou, then to the golden-haired man, then to the man with the bat ears, then to the chubby bald man with the uni-brow. Ismaila didn't even look my way. I sat there with blood beating my temples. Their tea-sipping sounded like sheets tearing.

Then Ismaila brewed a second round of tea, but I received no tea in that round, either. When everyone finished Ismaila simply turned off the stove and began gathering the cups and things. It was the most extraordinary breach of Senegalese etiquette I'd seen in the year I lived there. No one, not even Omar, said a word. Omar, for his part, looked altogether grim. He leaned toward me and whispered, "You got no tea, huh?" I could hear the nervous tremor in his voice.

"It's no big deal, Omar."

"I and I, you tell him for give you the tea, *quoi*."

"Skip it."

"*Quoi?*"

"Forget about the tea. I got this." I raised the bottle and finished it.

"He *must* give you the tea."

"Omar, that big motherfucker don't have to 'must' shit."

Omar relit the spliff and said, "Is bad, mahn, is very bad." He offered me the spliff, but I waved it off and opened up my second bottle. Omar often displayed what one could call displacement behavior when he didn't understand me. He'd swiftly change the subject or say something non-committal. You might think that this was one more thing that bothered me about him, but actually I found it rather endearing, for some reason. "Is bad, I and I. He do bad."

"Fuck it."

The other men had moved closer to the big man. Two sat on the ground, two squatted on the porch. They spoke quietly, but every so often they burst forth with laughter. I drank and stared at the bottle. "Listen in you ears, I and I," said Omar. "You must strong Doudou. You must put him and strong him."

"Speak French, Omar."

"No, no. You must. He do this now and every day—*quoi*—every day. Only if you strong him he can't do it."

I took this to mean that unless I "stronged" Doudou he would treat me badly every time he saw me, but I wasn't figuring on seeing him again and I whispered as much to Omar—in French, so there'd be no mistake.

"And besides," I said, "as your countrymen say, The man who wants to blow out his own brains need not fear their being blown out by others." I raised the bottle but couldn't bring myself to drink from it this once.

"No, mahn, strong him. He do this and then 'nother man, then 'nother, then 'nother man. All the time. All day."

"Sheeit, how on earth could—"

"Believe in me, I and I—"

"—anything to do with how other people treat me, man. Let's get out of here. I can't just—"

Omar clutched my knee so firmly I understood—or thought I did—the depth of his conviction. "You make strong on him now, and it will be fine for you." Then he removed his hand from my knee and touched it to his chest and said, "For me, too."

It was then that I realized that the incident with the tea was meant for Omar as much as for me. Omar had brought me as an honored guest, or as a conversation piece, or as his chance to show his friends just how good his English was. But why was it up to me, either as symbol or as a genuine friend, to recover his luster? I was the guest—right? I told myself to just sit there and drink, then leave. But suddenly the men around Doudou burst into laughter again, and I distinctly heard the golden-haired comedian say, "Jeeezuuuz!" and I felt my body rising stiff from the ground in jerky motions. I walked straight up to Doudou, dropped my half-empty bottle at his feet and slugged him so hard I'm sure I broke his nose. I know for certain I broke my finger.

Doudou went tumbling from his chair and landed face down on the porch. He struggled to get up, but fell forward, his head rolling side to side. His blood looked like black coins there on the porch. All the men rushed up to him, except the chubby man, who shoved me off the porch. I went down on my ass, but sprang up almost immediately. I was still pugnacious, but in a very small, very stupid way. Omar removed his shirt and pressed it to Doudou's nose.

I said, "Is he okay?"

No one replied.

I said, "We can get him a cab, get him to a doctor. I'll pay for the cab. I'll pay the doctor." And someone told me in Wolof that I could go out and fuck a relative. I stepped closer to the lot of them, out of shame and concern rather than anger, but Omar handed his shirt to Ismaila, stepped toward me with his palm leveled at my chest. "You go now," he said.

"But I thought you said—"

Our Lives Together

195

"You are not a good man." He turned back toward Doudou, whom they'd moved to the chair. The man with the strange ears left with a plastic bucket to retrieve fresh water. They all had their backs to me. I stood there a good long while, sick to my stomach from palm wine or shame, or both. After some minutes, Omar turned toward me for the briefest moment and said, "Don't come again, Bertrand." He said this in French.

I left the little courtyard and immediately lost my way. I wandered Fosse for what must have been ten years. On my way, I encountered an army of headless men who chased me with machetes. Blood gushed from their necks like geysers. Later I was eaten and regurgitated by a creature with three thousand sharp fangs in its big red mouth; it had the head of a lion, and its long snaky body bristled with forty-four powerful baboon arms. Months later in this strange new world, I discovered a town where everyone ate glass, rocks, wood, dirt, bugs, etc., but grew sick at the sight and smell of vegetables, rice, couscous, fish. They captured me and tried to make me eat sand, but I brandished a yam I'd had in my pocket, and when they all fell ill at the sight of it I ran away. In another town I met a man who was handsome and elegant in every way, and I followed him to his home simply to jealously gaze at him. But while on the way to his own home, I saw him stop at other people's homes, and at every place he stopped he'd remove a part of his body and return it to the person from whom he'd borrowed it. At each place he'd leave a leg, or an arm, or a hand, and so forth, so by the time he got home I discovered he was but a skull, who rolled across the ground like a common stone. It made me sad to see his beauty vanish so, and I walked all the way back to my home in Denver with my shoulders rounded and my head bent low. And when my people asked me what I found on my long, long journey, I told them, "Palm wine. But it wasn't in season, so I have nothing to give you."

# The Black Family

## Amiri Baraka

Take this as a note from a black man
reflecting on the fundamental social unit in which most of us (bm) exist. Therefore
this is meant as a clarifying basis for any serious discussion of "the black man,"
impossible without identifying the socioeconomic and cultural matrix, the basic
human context, in which he exists, and drawing from that the politics which defines
that context.

The black family, in its nuclear or
extended form, is the most ancient family unit in the world. And as such
it has reflected the entire history of human social change on earth!

The most ancient family structure was the communal family, the
*horde*, in which all males and females could mate. The children, obviously, were part of the collective, but could trace their parentage only
to the mother.

Ancient communalism, so-called primitive communism, was the earliest form of social organization. And women held a predominant and naturally powerful status in that kind of society and in that kind of family.
They were the only known parents, and lineage naturally flowed through
them.

As social relationships changed, based on economic and political changes in society, the structure of the family reflected these and changed as well. Many other variations precede the nuclear monogamous family.

The pairing family, the Punuluan family, were changing models, as the single hordes got larger and larger, eventually dividing, excluding the parents from collective sex, then, later, brothers and sisters.

Women in all these early family units were powerful, as groups of women controlled the home and the newly developed sciences of agriculture and the domestication of animals (developed by women). When the societies developed *surpluses* and these surpluses (larger herds of cattle and the bounty of the new, metal-tipped spears) and wealth became privately held, usually by men, this was the beginning of the end of the matrilineal development of society. It was also the beginning of classes in society.

It is the private ownership of wealth (by men, in the main) that is the catalyst for the social revolution that ends communalism and brings in the mode of production called *slavery*.

With slavery (ancient slavery, worldwide), the family structure undergoes a radical change, reflecting the radical change of society itself! The overthrow of communal society brought an overthrow of *motherright*. The matrilineal structure of the mainstream of human development was overthrown, and women were, literally, enslaved. They still are.

The overthrow of women and motherright, and the emergence of slavery as the dominant mode of production also accompanied the overthrow of Africa and the "southern cradle" (i.e., the origin of humanity and human civilization), and the rise and ultimate world rule of peoples from north of the Mediterranean.

With each change of the mode of production (how society produces food, clothing, and shelter), the structure of the family changes as well.

Monogamy, as Engels said in *The Origin of the Family*, *Private Property*, *and the State*, has existed only for women; prostitution rises with monogamy. The purpose of monogamy is to fix the line of inheritance, of wealth and power, through the male. (The Greek word for "housewife" is neuter, it has no sex. Homosexuality becomes an observable social feature of ancient slave-holding, post-matrilineal societies.)

As world society has gone through its development past slavery to feudalism and past feudalism to capitalism, the family has changed as well. By the end of feudalist society, Africa was the source of a new world-enslaved population. The rise of capitalism corresponds to the decline and enslavement of the African peoples in Africa and worldwide.

The enslaving of Africans and the colonization of Africa (and indeed of the whole Third World) has made historic, profound, and tragic changes in the black family. The slave trade has existed since the fifteenth century; the triangular trade (Africa–New World–England) was the basis for world trade, the Industrial Revolution, and the primitive accumulation of wealth responsible for U.S. and European world domination!

As modern slaves, black people were *chattel* slaves, owned as *property* by their masters. The estimated number of Africans who died in the Middle Passage and slavery is 50,000,000 (Du Bois), 300,000 (Toure).

The African family, even in its feudal state of development and its placement of women as less powerful and subservient to men, still maintained many essentials of its matrilineal character. And the black queens—the Shebas, Nzingas, Aminas, Cleopatras—attest to the prominent place of African women throughout history.

Under Western slavery, the black family was *legally* destroyed. Marriage between slaves was illegal (and, to the slavemasters, even the occasion for slapstick "coon" comedy).

As property, black people had no humanity, they were part of the means of production—tools, machines. The U.S. Constitution ruled us three-fifths of a human being. The Dred Scott decision (1859) said we had no rights the United States had to recognize!

Children produced by slaves were the property of the slavemasters, to be dealt with by them as they desired. Families were routinely separated, parents sold in one direction, children in the other. Genocide and social degradation always accompany slavery. Self-consciousness is dangerous and history the dim analogy of religious parables. Education for blacks is outlawed, along with the *drum* (witness the inherent politics of our art!). Marriage itself becomes a subversive activity, only practiced "underground," like the railroad that led to freedom. "Jumping the broom," we called it. A ceremony held in the forests surrounding the plantation, through which, even as slaves, black people defied slave society by declaring the continuing sanctity and sacredness and will to self-determination of the black family.

Chattel slavery and the slave trade are together the single most destructive assault on the black family in the history of the world! Any working-class family is weakened and dispersed by the negative pressures of capitalism. Even in the nineteenth century, Marx and Engels showed how child labor and long work hours for parents away from the children contributed to the weakness of English working-class families. Consider that for black people this class assault was added to by slavery and the national oppression that followed it and still continues to this day. (In the

United States we have been slaves for 244 years and "free" for only 127 years!)

It was the struggles of the African American slaves and the antislavery movement that ended slavery, and this should have marked a great positive step for the black family toward stability and self-determination. But Reconstruction was always partial and insincerely attempted. (There are "loopholes" and still unpracticed aspects of the Thirteenth, Fourteenth, and Fifteenth Amendments—and Ralston-Purina and *them* got our forty acres and a mule!)

By 1876, Reconstruction had been destroyed (by the Hayes-Tilden compromise, the repeal of civil rights bills, the installation of the racial-fascist "Black Codes," the withdrawal of the Union armies, and the rise of the KKK).

By the end of the century, segregation—U.S. apartheid—was the law of the land (1896, *Plessy v. Ferguson*), ratified by Booker T.

Throughout our history in the United States, the Afro-American people have struggled for freedom, equality, self-determination, democracy! As a result of our struggle, there are three distinct eras of Afro-American history. Periods in which our continuous struggle reached high peaks: the nineteenth-century antislavery movement, the early twentieth-century Harlem Renaissance, and the Civil Rights and Black Liberation movements of the 1950s and 1960s. American apartheid did not legally end until 1954 (*Brown v. Bd. of Ed.*), and you know the reality of that!

The rising and falling motion of black struggle I characterize as the *Sisyphus syndrome*, after the Greek myth of the man punished by the gods by having to continuously throughout history roll a huge boulder up a mountain, only to have it rolled back down on him at the end. As soon as we have managed to mobilize a sharp, revolutionary upsurge in our struggle, as in the three periods mentioned, the forces of reaction and white supremacy forcibly roll the rock back down on us, though hopefully not as far down as before. Langston Hughes called this phenomenon "white backlash."

The nature or status of the black family reflects almost directly the rise and fall of our national "fortunes" here in the United States. When the Afro-American people are in periods of vigorous and progressive advance, through the focused intensification of our struggle, our lives are improved, even amidst the shouts and chants, marches and gunshots, and the confrontations of the period. (For instance, the 1960s black income was higher than it has been since—jobs, housing, education, etc. See *The*

*Social and Economic Status of the Black Population, 1790–1978*, U.S. Department of Commerce.) Political confrontation forces concessions. No struggle, no progress, to paraphrase Fred.

When the upsurge comes to an end and the negative aspect of the Sisyphus syndrome dominates, then the fortunes—the structure, the political and economic conditions, the social stability—of the black family are also under assault and clearly weakened!

Compare the black family, in its most recent period of self-consciousness, unity, and political focus (the 1960s) with the condition of the black family today. The condition of the black family today is directly attributable to the same state assault, corporate cooptation, and class betrayal that sent the Black Liberation Movement into decline.

No one should have to be told that, of the black family, black youth are most directly under attack—pushed out of schools, unemployed, stereotyped as public enemies and with blacks in general as a criminal class, often locked up, assaulted even by each other and by the police, and even killed (by police and racist civilians alike)!

The black woman is *triply oppressed*, by race, class, and gender—the slave of a slave.

The weakness of the black family is a direct reflection of economic exploitation and the national racial and social repression of the Afro-American people.

To strengthen and stabilize the black family it is necessary to strengthen and stabilize the whole of the black nation!

The first focus must be political! The gaining, maintaining, and use of power. Political organization is key. The term Black Power was put forward in the 1960s, but it came to be coopted by black petty bourgeois politicians, including the Black Congressional Caucus, to mean electoral politics under the wing of the Dems or the Reps, two wings of the same vampire.

The larger black family of the Afro-American people must be brought together, including all of the various class and ideological forces in the black nation. This united front, joining together all segments and sectors of the people in collective struggle around concrete issues—in this case, our own self-determination—is the strong political "kinship" necessary to reunite and strengthen our big national family, to strengthen and create a developmental paradigm for our smaller families and a powerful instrument of change.

We know also that the even larger black family of the Pan-African peoples must be brought together in the same manner, to create both an OAU and an OAAU that see one African American nation as well as one Africa and one Pan-African family.

The largest family of all includes the peoples of the whole world. And all but those uninformed by history should know that (as quiet as it's kept) this too is a *black* family—every human being on the planet is of African descent!—even though quite a few of the chi'ren backward and some even dangerous. Eventually, this is the largest challenge of family reorganization and reunification there is!

# Fade to Black: Once Upon a Time in Multiracial America

## Joe Wood

*New Orleans.* It was late and the show was finished. We were hungry and drunk. Adolph said Mulé's was probably closed by now but he knew a place to eat on the other side of town. "Maybe you'll see some of *them* over there, too," he said. Adolph is a scholar of African-American history and politics, and he was raised in New Orleans and knew how *they* looked and where *they* ate. They liked Mulé's, a seventh-ward diner that serves the best oyster rolls in the city. The other place, Adolph said, was also good for observations, but far below seventh-ward culinary standards. It turned out to be an all-night fast-food joint, lighted too brightly, with a listless crowd of party people waiting in broken lines for some uninspired fried fare.

For a moment I forgot entirely about *them* and *they*. I wanted to try an oyster roll but there were none left, so I ordered a chicken sandwich "dressed" with lettuce and tomato and mayonnaise. The woman at the cash register seemed bored by my enthusiasm, and sighed, and in response I noted her skin color. She was dark. I turned my head and checked out two sleepy-eyed girls in the next line. They looked tired in their frilly prom dresses; their skin was waxen, the sad pale finish of moonlight. I knew—oh, I hesitated a moment, because I could see how a hasty eye might have thought them white, but *I* knew. Turning to

Adolph I whispered "creole" and made a giant drunken nod in their direction. Adolph looked and confirmed it: they were, in fact, *them*.

And they were us, black like us. I bet that virtually no one in the crowd had any trouble spotting the girls' African blood, and not only because we happened to be standing in an establishment that catered to black people, and not only because the girls did not look scared or determined not to look scared, as white girls in such situations usually want to. We all knew because we all were in some elusive sense family, and family can—or imagines it can—recognize itself, detect itself, see its own self no matter the guise.

So there stood the girls, their tired moonish looks telling us everything. Now I really eyed them and discerned the secret layer of brown just underneath the surface of their faces and arms. With practiced accuracy my eyes took in the other hints: a certain weightiness of hair, a broadness of lip, a fullness of hip and nose. (When I was a child it was something of a sport to fish for evidence of our presence, to seek ourselves in the faces of "whites" such as Alexander Hamilton or Babe Ruth.) Each detail made plain the girls' "blackness" as surely as a look in the mirror, and gave me the old sense of triumph, until a moment passed and I remembered why we could never really be the same: we were in New Orleans and these girls were creole and I am not.

•

Adolph, you hold the key to this story. The reason—you and I are family, but you are on the other side of the creole difference, a strange distinction made of nothing but stories and lies, lies and stories, the forces that conjure family. While you and I would both like to think of the creole tale as one more plotline in the black story, because that's all it is, really, we both know that true believers say creole is a separate thing altogether; you and I know how they say, Look at us. How they say, Watch us go. How they enjoy being them, and not us.

Them and us. How strange. I realize now that we have never talked about the differences in our looks, your light and my dark. Neither of us, I suspect, has consciously *avoided* this discussion. It simply hasn't been an issue: there are so many things to talk about—why waste time on such foolishness? But there it was, during the trip down home to New Orleans, there was the difference stuck in our faces. It broke our silence, compels me to speak on the absurd—let me first describe our looks with as cold an eye as I would any character.

I have chocolate-brown skin, generous lips, the kind of ordinary kinky hair many black women still get mad at. I wear a goatee and sometimes glasses. I am thirty years old and I'm not in great shape because I don't like working out. You've got a couple of decades on me but you're probably in better condition. I don't recall seeing too many gray hairs on your head last time I saw you, though your hairline is ebbing. Your hair is straight and heavy like a South Asian's; your skin is amber brown, your features are round but strong: You've even been mistaken for a countryman by several natives of India. But you are black, definitely, and creole.

We've been friends for several years now, and though there is no explaining friendship, there are a few reasons I want you to know I see. We both love to watch people do their hustles. We laugh at the same absurdities, and mostly get hurt by the same absurdities. We have similar politics, and we aren't sellouts. (Which is not normal, which is why the sellouts call us cynics.) There is a lot more, of course. The stories of people's affections are oceanic in number and complexity. In this way we are very ordinary.

But the subject at hand is the black and the brown. Surely this is one of the stories that makes us up, as it makes up every other African American, and with any examination, every white or Asian or Latino or anybody else on these shores. Though we haven't talked about our own colors, you and I have talked about how much social meaning is attached to shade difference, even today. You've lived it and tried to forget it because the debate is absurd. I don't like tracking that stuff inside, either. I've cracked jokes about those confessional pieces describing the pain of being dark, or the pain of being light, or the pain of being mixed and in-between—seldom is anything real said. We've laughed about how white people eat up that stuff, but for the moment I will stop laughing because I've decided to put in mind that conflict.

·

My sister is light with broad features. Adolph, you and she have met, but you don't know how much she favors my mother. They are both light—my mother says her father had a lot of Native American in him. In the photograph she keeps in the basement he looks creole. Mom told me that several of his brothers and sisters were so light they lost the mossy accent and turned Jewish or Italian or WASP, and vanished into the white world. Mom's mom was as dark as navy blue, and she couldn't hide her slave history. We don't name the rest of the races that made her, but you can bet she had some other tribes inside.

Remember that Tito Puente concert that night in the municipal ballroom by the waterfront? Remember checking out all those Latinos, those creoles, those light-skinned black people? Remember the way I eyed Jeannine, her light color? I remember thinking of a brotha I know whose skin is very dark, and then I could *see* him at the table. I could hear him, too, accusing me—I felt for a second like a Negro banker hunting for a suitable wife.

Of course this was an easy comparison. Everyone knows that the powerboys who choose "suitable wives" are sick about this sort of thing, and everyone knows that the young Negroes in the theater on 125th Street who laughed when Alva Rogers was on the screen in Spike Lee's *School Daze* are sick, too. You and I know that the equation between femininity and light skin is ubiquitous in the culture, as is the equation between light skin and intelligence, and light skin and beauty. Negroland's self-described iconoclasts, especially the boys, are no less sick this way. You've seen brotha writer and brotha artist and brotha filmmaker walk more proudly holding the hand of the Mulatto Ideal. And why not? In the movies or on television brotha man's semen always produces a mulatto child, no matter the skin color of the mother. At bottom, light skin and white features and *multiracial* make males in Hollywood happy, and most employers in America happy, and many social planners and other futurists, too; I had to wonder whether the same story fashioned my desire.

I took refuge in the way the story failed to determine my sense of my own body. Each day this "I" of mine faces the mirror; I blindly see *me*, and fail to wonder enough what the brownness means to others. Usually I even forget that old refrain "the darker the berry the sweeter the juice," its equation between dark skin and blackness, the way it insists that one's fidelity to the race rises directly with an increase of melanin. I suppose my being dark makes it relatively easy to see through that old affirmation; I know it is not as easy for lighter sisters and brothers, who are often made to feel as if they should pay us in blood for their skins. But I think a more fundamental reason is that I, like most everyone else, don't really like to live racially. No one I know takes much pleasure in trying to measure how racism shapes his or her life; no matter how much folks celebrate or hate being black, they ordinarily forget about it. Who has the time when thanking God that the newborn is not deaf, when worrying about why the tax man is phoning you at work, when marveling at the way the sun lights up the metal on the scaly top of the Chrysler Building? Of course, there *are* those moments when you and I are forced to shoo away un-imaginative opinions about who we are: the veteran cop, the prospective landlord, the Afrocentric professor often make judgments that follow tired and expected patterns. But most of the time I, like you, dispose of such takes the moment they enter the skull, because I live here.

There is, of course, much more and much less to say about all this. Here is another story about Adolph and me. A beginning and an end and another beginning.

•

One of the last nights I was in New Orleans, Adolph took a bunch of friends to a bar in the seventh called Pampy's. It was the kind of speakeasy you find in black neighborhoods all over the country. There was a jukebox against the wall playing old r & b songs; the walls were seasoned with posters for local concerts and handwritten signs about "house rules"; the drinks were poor. A gang of dressed-up people in their forties sat on stools at the bar, hungry, bathed in an encouraging red light. Even so, I could guess everyone's complexion, including the guy sitting at the other end of our table.

Gary was just a little bit darker than the light-skinned girls at the beginning of my journey, and I was already pretty certain he would call himself creole—no, by now I *knew* he'd say he was. Still, I asked. Gary and the woman sitting next to him both said yes. It turned out that they were lovers. She was darker than he, the syrupy brown of coffee with extra sugar mixed in, brown like me, so her claim surprised me a little. But I didn't say anything out loud. Maybe, I reasoned, she's a genetic specter; even the best cultivation fails sometimes.

I could tell that Gary was a nice guy, though his looks made it hard to take him seriously. His face was almost perfectly flat; its most active feature was his mouth, a messy thing. He wore his dental bridge a little too high on the upper gum, which would have been all right if his incisors didn't hang down the way they did. Each time he opened his trap he looked like a clownish Dracula, and even though he spoke with considerable honesty and earnestness, it was hard not to laugh.

Gary had grown up nearby, in a project where poor creoles lived along with noncreoles. That equation of higher class and lighter skin—not necessarily. Class status didn't, however, seem to cause Gary much anxiety. Now in his late twenties, he was a waiter at a downtown hotel, and, from the looks of it, doing fine. His girlfriend didn't really talk much, except to say again that she was creole. I asked one more time about the differences between creoles and other blacks. "Sometimes they like to blame us for looking good. We look good," he said, in a sincere drawl. I noticed that Gary's eyes were a little too high on his face and his hair was a little too low; I considered how the difference between looking inbred and not is a question of millimeters.

"Like my hair. I got good hair," he continued, smiling in the generous red light. He pulled a comb smoothly across his scalp. "Not like yours." I recalled something Adolph once told me about *them*: the first questions people ask when a baby is born is what kind of hair, then what color is it, then does it have two heads or whatever. Gary was a nice guy, and he didn't especially mean anything by "good hair" or "like yours," he was just repeating the things he'd heard; he was saying, Look at me—can't you see?

I could only laugh. A few minutes later Gary and his girlfriend left. I recounted the scene to Adolph, and he just doubled over laughing about how the nigga was so low-class he didn't even know enough not to say that absurd shit. So that's why you're laughing? I thought as I laughed, too—it was very, very funny. I stopped when I remembered that Gary had been very kind to utter his family's open secret, its story of itself, and I realized the smugness of my own laughter. Then I sensed with horror the oldest future, its familiar story: *Our family is better than yours.*

# Where We Live: A Conversation with Essex Hemphill and Isaac Julien

## Don Belton

At the twentieth century's close, independent filmmakers Marlon Riggs, Isaac Julien, and poet Essex Hemphill are likely the artists/activists whose work most richly articulates and extends the represented range of black gay men's identity. Their daring interventions advance the project of healing the whole of black masculinity by celebrating acts of dialogue, compassion, and love between black men across the spectrum of sexual orientation, as well as between black men and black women.

Riggs's landmark documentary *Tongues Untied*, along with Julien's *Looking for Langston*, a cinematic meditation on the life and legacy of the closeted Harlem Renaissance writer Langston Hughes, served stunning notice that black gay male silence and invisibility had ended. For two decades, Hemphill has crafted elegant poems that illuminate the life-giving geography of black men's love and grief.

Riggs died on April 5, 1994, of complications due to AIDS. In December of 1994, I brought Julien and Hemphill together for a conversation around the completion of Riggs's film *Black Is . . . Black Ain't*, which explores the nexus of black identity and masculinity. Hemphill appears in the film, along with cultural activists bell hooks, Michelle Wallace, Cornel West, and Angela Davis. I met with Julien and Hemphill at

Hemphill's apartment in West Philadelphia. Hemphill showed an advance cassette copy of the film. The following is excerpted from conversation between Julien and Hemphill that afternoon.

HEMPHILL: I find myself resisting popular notions of black masculinity while at the same time being attracted to them. Early on, I learned ways to protect my masculinity or, I guess I should say, my homo-masculinity. I wasn't inclined to be athletic. In the black neighborhood I came from, there was an emphasis on being able to play basketball or football. I, instead, was attracted to gymnastics because of the way the body looked. But I knew instinctively that if I had said, "I want to be a gymnast," among the fellas I ran with I would have been labeled a sissy. As an adult, I've had to resist the idea that I'm not a man because I don't have children or a woman.

JULIEN: I think this is a good place to start. Initially, masculinity was about living up to the fiction of normative hetereosexual masculinity. Growing up, I remember men in the community who were a part of my parents' circle commenting in Creole about how I was such a *petit macqot*, which is a small boy, *un petit garçon*. It was also a way of calling a young boy a sissy. A means of saying he's already displaying feminine traits. Maybe I wasn't interested in trying to conceal that part of my identity. So, in a way, it began a war early in my life, but not a bloody war. It was a war of positions in the sense I did not want to totally participate in being a straight black male in the conventional framework. My feelings for boys my age happened very early on—I must have been eight years old. In the playground, I saw the shorts fall off the goalkeeper's waist during a sports match. I remember feeling very erotically charged by the image. There was already in circulation the idea of black men having this hypermasculinity that was tough and resilient. It was tough growing up in London in the 1970s. You had to be tough to physically contest the everyday racist treatment by the police, by various authority figures and institutions. Therefore, you understood that this toughness was a mask and a defense. Questions around being black and male came to the forefront for me when I began to pursue my education and most of the other young men around me were being arrested.

HEMPHILL: We're faced with redefining what masculinity is. We're faced with constructing a masculinity for all of us, one that will be useful as opposed to disempowering. I think that, given issues like economic oppression, we feel safe holding onto the model constructed out of athletics, around street toughness and other conventional models of masculinity. You know, "My gun's bigger . . ." The gun is supposed to be an extension of you or your anger, and it's the bullet that strikes, not the fist. I can't think when I last saw two black men physically fighting. And not that I'm endorsing fighting, but I think the gun has become an apt metaphor for our isolation from our own rage and frustration. Our increasing isolation from one another's humanity. Then there's the masculinity that we're getting via television, film, and magazines. We need a masculinity that brings us more into contact with one another. A masculinity that is intimate and humane. A masculinity that allows if I feel like being soft my softness won't mean I'm a sissy or a punk.

JULIEN: In *Black Is . . . Black Ain't*, bell hooks and Michelle Wallace talk about the language of sexism and the presumptions around gender. That's really where everything begins to shut down. We both grew up experiencing scenes in which black men could not cry or express fear. Growing up, I very much identified with trying not to reproduce the dominant ideas of being a man. There's an overvaluation of strict gender codes in the black community. "Only sissies cry." When that was told to me, I said, "Fuck this. I'm not going to live like this." Those stories or fictions of "real" masculinity are learned early in life and then become ways of toughening young boys. That sort of information isn't useful to our community. I think there should be more of an investment in unlearning those codes, because they end breeding a certain inhumanity. Our redemption as a people is *not* a "dick thing," as bell hooks points out in the film.

HEMPHILL: I believe that many of the destructive lessons taught in our childhood homes is the result of the desperation of our parents. They were children at one point and were made to learn those same lessons. I don't know how we begin to unlearn that behavior.

JULIEN: Well, it's true that the codes we're meant to adhere to—masculine and feminine—are prescribed in childhood. As black boys and girls growing up in families attacked by racism from the outside, we are made to feel a kind of double restriction on the expression of ourselves in any way that might go against the grain of dominant ideas. We, as black men especially, are supposed to instill and police these codes within ourselves. But where are these codes coming from? I think that in America, but not only in America, there is this obsessive concentration on the family—the notion that everything can be resolved within the family. But this middle-class notion of "family" seems to me the space where we first learned how to fear one another and to fear the free expression of ourselves. As a result, the debate around black masculinity in the U.S. has become so topical with films like *Jungle Fever* and *Boyz in the Hood*. One of the problems with the *New York Times* article / symposium on black men [*Who Will Help the Black Man? New York Times*, 4 December 1994, v. 1, 74:1] is that it is exclusively a discussion by and about black middle-class, presumably heterosexual men. The question at the center of that discussion is really, How can we get black people, black men in particular, to get over in the American Dream? It should be obvious by now that's just a poor question. I also think the street tough machismo identity is bankrupt. It's just producing a competitive, nihilistic environment for black men to destroy themselves and each other. It's difficult to have a position on this without talking about the disappearance of real economic opportunity for the black working poor and the infiltration of drugs in our communities in both the U.S. and London. Marlon's film carries an important critique of black manhood along these lines.

HEMPHILL: Yes, and the critique bell hooks provides [in the film] of the black macho pose of the 60s and 70s is so powerful because if the sum of black political struggle is about empowering the black phallus at the expense of all other cultural issues, we cannot succeed. Or else that success will have no meaning. Our masculinity must encompass diversity and nuance. There should never be a question about whether Sally can drive a rig or whether Tommy can raise the children. There are also important class issues. The *Times* piece represented the black male middle class. I'd like to see that [discussion] take place with representatives from a broader range of possible black male identity. I'd have loved to have heard someone who flips hamburgers for minimum wage talk about how he views himself as a man. A construction worker. An emergency room doctor. I had problems with one of the participants in that article referring to working-class blacks as "black trash." Its a simple-minded analogy he was trying to draw—that you have white trash and you have black trash. Well, come on, baby [laughs], . . . who says any group of society is to be regarded as trash? So for me the *Times* piece was not a broad enough conversation. It was a safe conversation for the *New York Times*. Safe for the particular men who were included. And self-serving.

JULIEN: It became a spectacle, a symbolic discussion of black masculinity in a white newspaper, a discussion where very little was actually said. The patronizing and vindictive tone toward black working-class people, even by the one speaker who actually does work with young black men from impoverished backgrounds. . . .

HEMPHILL: The absence of debate on gender issues. . . . The absence of any gay voice. . . .

JULIEN: It's a question of power. Black men have been rendered powerless by the dominant society, and it's that drive to have power at any cost, no matter what is silenced or dismissed. It isn't very different from ways in which blacks are excluded from the representation of "true" American masculinity.

HEMPHILL: Yes. It's important to realize it isn't black women who are gunning down one another. Black women are not gunning *us* down and beating us to death. *We* are doing this.

JULIEN: We won't be able to abate this hatred and annihilation of self by flattening out and silencing differences within our community. These differences are vital to our mutual survival.

HEMPHILL: In a recent issue of the Nation of Islam's newspaper, *The Final Call*, Louis Farrakhan called for a "million-man march" on Washington, D.C. A march of one million black men on the nation's capital. The call itself is historic, though I've heard nothing about it in the mainstream press. But who's going to be on the stage when those one million black men assemble in Washington? You? Me? Would Marlon have been invited to speak? Hardly. It will be men who are considered safe. Safe for me equals ineffective—men who will not take risks in their intellect and who will not take risks in their compassion. I think of the ending of *Black Is . . . Black Ain't*, where bell hooks speaks about replacing the notion of black unity with the notion of communion. The root meaning of communion suggests that our union is based on a willingness to communicate with one another. It's a beautiful idea to pursue. [In the film] Michelle Wallace says, "I always get the feeling that when black people talk about unity and community that it's a turf war thing, you know—we're gonna get together and this is gonna be our block, and if you come on our block, you know, we're gonna kick your ass." Michelle says, "I always think I'm gonna be the one whose ass is gonna get kicked." I've always felt like that as well. I'm as black as anyone, but not by the criteria the nationalists construct.

JULIEN: It's about wanting attention and power in the system. Farrakhan demands this march on Washington. It's about another spectacle of middle-class black straight men claiming ownership of blackness. It's just another bankrupt political discourse.

HEMPHILL: But if this march happens, it will have historic ramifications. A new kind of power will be unleashed—a power that shows us the possibility of unity among black men. I think black gay men need to at least bring the issue of our participation to the table. We should press to have gay voices at the podium.

JULIEN: I think that within a Farrakhan march of black men on Washington, anyone attempting to read its meaning in any way that could be considered homoerotic would be dealt with. I don't see where the intervention can be made there.

HEMPHILL: Given some of the dangerous places gay men are often willing to go in the name of love or desire, why would intervening at the Farrakhan march be any less dangerous?

JULIEN: I say just the opposite. I would say we should be going back to the communities we are a part of and working on a grassroots level to get the black community to challenge hetero-normative assumptions. I think that would be the way from a grassroots level to change destructive assumptions about blackness, gender, and sexual identity. Otherwise, we just become a part of Farrakhan's spectacle.

HEMPHILL: I still think we need to bear witness in the representation of black male identity. Those black men who will march will largely be lower- and working-class men—your grassroots level. The march may not be framed around their identities, but they have always been the essential part of the Nation of Islam's political base. Of any black political base. For that reason, I believe we ought to try to participate. So at least, for the record, there is the fact that we were there to claim our membership in our communities.

JULIEN: Why should we try to claim membership in black masculinity through the Nation of Islam?

HEMPHILL: Big spectacle-oriented groups like the Nation of Islam are winning minds and support among everyday black people. Either we are a part of black communities or we aren't. Our presence has always been crucial to our communities, yet within those communities and the larger society we're still rendered as nonexistent. We're still considered to be not interested in something like this. There is a danger in that. As black gay men we need a politic that touches the vast majority of our brothers where they're at. Otherwise as gay men we only represent a breakdown. . . .

JULIEN: I think failure is something that should be celebrated. I don't want to be in a formation of black male identity where one has to hold oneself in a rigid way—as in a march—even against how we might feel about ourselves in terms of our pain, our skepticism, lack and self-doubt. All these things are as much a part of black male identity as the things we might want to parade, like toughness and unity. We have to be willing to engage in a process of thinking through our failure as black men in this society. Black masculinity has always been a "failed masculinity" in relationship to white male colonialism. Black macho discourses of empowerment will never truly reach us where we live. There is something interesting we can learn from our so-called failure, because our failure also contains our resistance. Failure to live "up" to oppressive masculinity is a part of what it means to be queer. That's what my work has been about. What your work is about. Being black itself is seen as a failure in the white world. We want to remember that, and there is a way we can use that failure to critique white supremacy. If you want to be a black version of white supremacy, of course you end up with a Farrakhan.

HEMPHILL: So where do we intervene?

JULIEN: Use the media. If you're going to make the intervention it would be, "This is a problem, and you know . . ." If, when they march, you have an interview on CNN, and CNN runs it only five times that day, then you'd have a larger audience than their march on Washington.

HEMPHILL: Definitely, yes. But I still come back to the power of the possibility of black men coming together. I'm not being romantic here. When Marlon was working on *Black Is . . . Black Ain't*, I went with him to a theater in South Central Los Angeles to film a meeting between the Bloods and the Crips gang members. It was historic. Some of that is in the film. I will never forget stepping out of the van when we arrived at the theater and looking up, and along the rooftops of the theater and the houses on the block were these SWAT teams of uniformed policemen holding guns. There were at least one hundred men, most of them white, which underscores this nation's real terror of black men cutting back on the violence against one another and creating a space to come together.

JULIEN: But what are these black men coming together to do?

HEMPHILL: Don't quash it yet, Isaac, [Isaac laughs] without taking into account that an agenda would have to be defined. Maybe it's desperation that draws me to the march despite my aversion to Farrakhan. We can't just attack his ideology. What good is that? I can't look at television without seeing negative representations of a black male. He's either in handcuffs or he's been shot by one of his brothers over whatever foolishness is out there.

JULIEN: I don't think it's a matter of desperation. The desperation is that people are looking for black straight men to provide political leadership against white patriarchy. The problem is with these very selective representations. We're dealing here with white society's own anxiety and fear about black men and about the black underclass, the working-class populace.

HEMPHILL: How can we control it?

JULIEN: That question is part and parcel of the postslavery experience. I don't know how one negotiates oneself out of it.

HEMPHILL: I don't think you addressed my concern [about] whether or not there's a necessity for black men to assemble anywhere in this country.

JULIEN: I just question the whole premise. I can see a homoeroticism in it, perhaps, but I have to see it for what it is—a fantasy.

HEMPHILL: You're not in any way interested in a million black men assembling?

JULIEN: No.

HEMPHILL: Okay. I guess that's our first point of contention. [Both laugh.] So what is the perfect site for our resistance?

JULIEN: An intervention like *Black Is . . . Black Ain't.*

HEMPHILL: What about the troublesome issues of Marlon's dying of AIDS and his sexuality? There are public television stations and schools that won't run it because of Marlon's candor.

JULIEN: You have this distribution out of, say, Sony Classics. That film can be seen in twenty cinemas in New York alone. That sort of intervention would be profound, and it could be marketed toward black people.

HEMPHILL: This isn't about art cinema. I'm talking about addressing raw black life.

JULIEN: Yes, and that's what I'm addressing as well. I'm talking about the apparatus of mass culture. Which is Sony. Miramax. We don't own the means of production. Even certain aspects of our blackness are being experienced through what comes through the marketplace.

HEMPHILL: I see your point, and I respect that. But, I guess, with your hypothetical way for intervening . . . what comes to mind is that I come to the table with an idea and you come with an idea, but now we have to take our ideas to something that doesn't come from us, the media, corporate distribution. . . . For me, the way I live, my blackness is the priority. Period. Be it my identity as a gay person or as a person with AIDS or my identity as a writer . . . I'm still dealt with as black, first and foremost.

JULIEN: I think it's a product of segregationist thinking about sexuality and gender that we have to prioritize our identities.

HEMPHILL: I don't want you to misunderstand me. In 1991 or '92, when I was on tour in England, I had trouble with customs, and the trouble I had had everything to do with me being a black man in bomber jacket, in jeans and construction boots. All these other people are flowing by me in customs with no problem, but they stopped me every time, because I fit a certain profile. That's why my blackness has to be there first for me. It's a battle around that place where I am desperate and wanting to see some of the dying stop.

JULIEN: But a march won't stop that. Anyway, I think the image of one million black men marching on Washington is phallocentric and misogynist. I don't know. Maybe I'm just cynical.

HEMPHILL: I don't think it's cynicism. We share a similar concern and pessimism. I think we articulate it differently. I agree with you about the phallocentrism and misogyny. . . . I stopped three or four young brothers on my street last spring, and they were bigger than me. It was after school, after business hours. These young fellas had taken magic markers and written all over the storefront windows. And something in me just snapped. I'm sick of there being no intervention. I told them, "Don't do that. That's a black business. You're destroying property." I was scared to death, but I wasn't going to my apartment and locking my door. The truth is I might not be sitting here now because of that act. Even a simple intervention could cost our lives.

JULIEN: Generally, there's a breakdown of the civil society in America.

HEMPHILL: Various horrifying themes occur in all our communities. Why is there such tremendous disrespect among black men towards women, regardless of our sexual orientation? Even a statement like, "Miss Thing is gonna take me to a new level of sensuality." I was wondering why it's never "*Mr*. Thing." Why is it "*Thing*"?

JULIEN: I thought "Miss Thing" was about a parody of a sexist comment.

HEMPHILL: Think about the things you've heard among gay brothers about women. How much different are some of those statements from the ones by some heterosexual brothers? There hasn't been much discourse among black gay men about that. But I know sisters are anxious for that. Not just conversation, but deliberate work. I don't think current notions of masculinity work for any male. I don't think they work for anyone.

JULIEN: I think the social complexities around contemporary male identity are just deepened by issues of blackness and gayness.

HEMPHILL: This is why, for various reasons, including expediency, I've elected not to take a white lover when that option has been there. I feel like this is the worst country to try to love outside the race. I can't imagine what you deal with in your relationship [Mark Nash, Julien's life-partner of seven years, is white].

JULIEN: My experience being in America with Mark has not been one where I've been rejected. If blacks or whites want to reject me, they're not my friends and I don't feel I've lost anything.

HEMPHILL: It seems so incredibly important, the way that Marlon's use of the slogan "Black men loving black men is *the* revolutionary act" in *Tongues Untied* has been so fucked by so many people [because Marlon's partner, Jack Vincent, is white].

JULIEN: I just don't agree with a slogan like that. Who's to say what *the* revolutionary act is, anyway? Who can prescribe that? If I'd grown up in America, I don't know what I would be like. The positioning of a slogan like that—the way it is positioned in the film—is fine, I suppose, but when it's used as some kind of moral code to police interracial desire, then I think it's really about our shame about the range of our own desires.

HEMPHILL: The act of black men loving black men isn't only about our sexual expression. It means everything, including intervening downstairs when those young black men were defacing their neighborhood. That was about my love for them. If I didn't love us, I wouldn't care. You know—"Just go ahead. Get your magic markers and do the block. Do the block!"

JULIEN: I think it's very complicated, the discourse of love in relationship to yourself. Unlearning self-hatred and fear is hard work. I've had to be in America to really begin to understand that, being so marginalized here.

HEMPHILL: In some ways, I think we *have* failed.

JULIEN: We have to be willing not to reject that failure out of hand. That's essential to experiencing humanity.

( ( part five ) )

HEROES

# Voodoo for Charles

## Don Belton

On Christmas morning in 1991 I telephoned my nephew. I have two nephews: Charles, who had only just turned nineteen the week before, and Wayne, Jr., who is somewhere in his middle twenties by now. These are the children of my brother's first marriage. My nephews grew up in Newark, New Jersey, where much of my early childhood was spent, but that was before the conflagration of the 1967 riot and the razing of what remained of the city by the local, state, and federal governments in the name of an urban renewal which is yet to come. While Newark was not an easy city to live in, it was still, in any case, from the late 50s to the mid-60s (when I lived there with my great-grandmother in the black district called the Hill) a city. Today Newark is the ghost of a city. Its statistics for AIDS, black-on-black crime, infant mortality, and unemployment bear witness to dissolution.

Charles was living in Newark in 1991. I had not spoken to him in over four years. I hadn't seen him in a longer time. The last time we'd spoken was by telephone. (For several years now, I seem to talk to the members of my family only on the phone.) By 1991 I still felt unresolved about our last conversation. I had been visiting my parents' house in Philadelphia, while they were away on a trip. "Uncle Don," Charles had said to me on the phone back then, "Where's Grandad and Gramma? I want to tell them I got shot."

His father had divorced his mother when Charles was six. My brother had married again after renouncing the street life he'd embraced almost his entire youth. His second marriage was to a middle-class black woman nine years younger than he (and one year younger than I). She was a preacher's daughter. My brother soon became an evangelical preacher himself. Since my brother has renounced what he often calls, from the pulpit, the sin and shame of his former life, he has also, tragically, renounced his sons. He is uncomfortable with them. It is as if they are his doubles. They *are* him, but with a frightening difference. They are projections of all the parts of himself that he has disowned in order to achieve his new life. They still know little more than the brutal reality of the streets he fled. They also remember him as the junkie who beat their mother, and they still bear the mental and spiritual wounds of that. He does not talk to them, any more than our father spoke to him, because to talk to them might mean confronting the past from which he is always running; allowing that past into his present. Instead, he quotes the self-hating apostle Paul when I criticize his abandonment of his sons, proclaiming himself a new creature in Christ. "All old things," he assures me, parroting Saint Paul, "are passed away." My brother now has three young daughters with his new wife. When his new wife was pregnant with the last girl, she called me on the phone and said, "Your brother wants a boy, but I pray it's another girl. It's easier for black girls than it is for black boys."

In the four years since I'd spoken to Charles, his mother had been murdered in the housing project where both she and her children were raised. Had it been easier for her? After having been shot (almost fatally, for refusing to run drugs for a neighborhood syndicate), Charles recovered and began his career as a drug lord in Newark. Recently he had been sentenced to three to seven years in prison for attempted murder, a sentence from which he was on the lam on Christmas, 1991. He was *nineteen*.

The phone rang several times before there was an answer at the number that another relative had provided. The voice that answered was a man's, husky, low. I wondered if this was the new voice, the man's voice, for the mercurial black baby boy whom I'd helped to raise. I asked if Charles was there.

"Who is this?" the voice asked, gruff.

"I'm sorry," I said. I'd been told he was in hiding. "This is his uncle, Don."

"Uncle Don?" I listened to the voice come alive, filling with pleasure, softening, turning into a boy's. "Uncle Don?"

Suddenly I was afraid, awed by the power of the telephone to create the illusion that pushing a sequence of buttons was all that was required for me to reach Charles. He was, after all, now speaking into my ear—this was his voice, we had each other on the line. I also felt regret that it had taken me so long to complete such a simple action.

He wanted to know where I was calling from. He said he'd heard I lived in Maine. I told him I live in Saint Paul, Minnesota.

"Minneapolis?" he asked. "Where Prince lives?"

"Yes."

He told me he'd seen the book I'd written, at his great-aunt's house in Newark. He said he wanted to read it. I promised to send him a copy. I told him I was writing another, a section of which I had dedicated to the memory of his mother when it was published in a literary journal. I don't really know much that is certain about his mother, though I knew her, except that she was mellow-voiced and pretty when she was young. Her skin was the color of yellowed ivory, she had freckles, and her name was the same as my own mother's.

"You're a teacher, aren't you? At a college?"

"Yes," I said. "I teach literature."

I wonder what Charles thinks of my life. I know he's been told I am a success, though I doubt he understands why. I doubt he knows mine is a success I sometimes can barely feel, though I live in a multicultural (predominately white, middle-class) neighborhood, where my white heterosexual neighbors tolerate my homosexuality, my blackness, my intellectual bent. A number of the neighbors have adopted children of color from the American South, Peru, Korea. Others are busy making babies. The parents accept me ostensibly, but they make certain I never babysit. I wanted to tell Charles I'm gay. I came out to most of the adults in my family years ago. I wanted him to learn from me that his uncle loves men.

I also wanted to tell him what it has been like for me teaching at a college whose faculty I joined in 1990, a college that has failed to tenure a single black professor in twenty years, about the stress of sometimes confronting a racism so covert and insidious our ancestors could not have imagined it. I wanted to tell him that although I was preparing a lecture I would give in a few weeks in Paris at the Sorbonne, my life felt permeated by a soul-sick sadness I inherited from my father and my father's father (both of whom were named Charles) and share with my nephew's father. Obviously Charles is a part of this, and I believed that if I could discuss this sadness with Charles (surely he was now old enough for this conversation), could share my names for it with him and hear the names he gave to it, then we might touch that hurt together and help each other heal. But something prevented me. I wasn't afraid that he would cease to look up to me if he knew my life isn't the magazine of success our relatives want to pretend it is; I was afraid of the incoherence that stretched out before me when I thought of naming the pain we were both a part of. Any words I might speak would have to be words used in faith, since I did not know their exact power to hurt or heal. To speak them I would have to trust myself and trust Charles, trust love. And I was unable to speak those words of faith that morning.

I did the best I could. I opened the door as wide as I could to my nephew, hoping he might, because of his youth or recklessness, push it further. "So how are things with you?" I asked him. "I haven't seen you in so long. Talk to me."

I listened as my nephew brought me up to date on his life with the same adolescent mixture of nonchalance, anxiety, and wonder with which I had once reported to my parents about a backpack trip to Quebec City in 1975, life in my college dorm, or meeting James Baldwin at his brother David's apartment on Manhattan's West Side when I was a sophomore.

Trying to listen beneath my nephew's words for his feelings—for his life and my own—my mind wandered over all I already knew of Charles's life. He had been out of my life for so long, and more importantly, since he had once been in part my responsibility, I had been out of his. I wondered would I even recognize my nephew were I to pass him by chance on the street in my city, or see his face in a video clip accompanying the all-too-familiar TV news narration about another anonymous (even when named) young black male criminal murdered, imprisoned, standing trial, beaten.

I thought about the times when my nephews were little. Even though I was only thirteen when Wayne, Jr., was born and sixteen when Charles was born, I took my role as their uncle quite seriously. My brother had become a junkie shortly after Wayne, Jr., was born, and though my brother was clean when Charles was conceived, he'd begun using again before Charles was delivered. Between the births of my nephews, my star had begun to ascend. I received an academic scholarship to an exclusive Quaker boys' school in Philadelphia. Education, it seemed, was the sword I could use to vanquish racism. If I hewed the assimilationist line, studied and got good grades, dressed and spoke properly, went to church, I would become something better than a criminal or a corpse. I soon tried to pass these values on to my nephews—even though I had begun to feel a certain amount of ambivalence, distance, and irony in relation to these values even then. I knew instinctively from the moment I first saw my nephews that they were born into a world full of trouble.

I used to take them everywhere with me whenever I could be with them. I dragged them to the library, bookstores, plays. I remember, later, the train trips down from my exclusive New England college, arriving at Newark station—a monstrosity always under construction and restoration, a sad remnant of the populuxe shrine to mobility I'd traveled through when I was a child, the times I shuttled back and forth between Philadelphia and Newark, between belligerently bourgeois parents and my Southern immigrant great-grandmother, a hickory-skinned crone with long, puff-of-smoke hair.

When I took the train down for my nephews, it was invariably a trial to find a cabdriver—black or white—willing to transport me to the notorious housing project where my nephews lived. I remember walking up stinking stairways and through dark hallways to find their apartment, sometimes finding their mother high on drugs with her boyfriend and her sister, or finding no one at home at all.

"Oh, Uncle Don," Charles was saying on Christmas morning in 1991, "did I tell you Aunt Geraldine died of AIDS?"

I remember searching the grounds of the project when no one was home, and finding Wayne and Charles in some glass-strewn play yard amid the wild bedlam of unsupervised children—unsupervised except for the foxlike vigil of men and women whose preying on children takes various forms, all deadly. I would take my nephews to a friend's place in the country or to the city, to a planetarium, a museum, a movie, a historical site, *any*place that said to them there is someplace—some *way*—other than this.

By the time I moved from college to graduate school, I was spending more time with Charles because he was still young enough to be at home, while Wayne, Jr., grew harder to locate during my visits. Wayne, Jr., was running with a bad crowd, picking up the legacy his father had escaped and left for him in Newark's streets. When I did see my oldest nephew, I realized that in my absence he was rapidly becoming a man I didn't understand. (This was before the violent, misanthropic music he now favored and the disaffected style of dress he'd adopted was appropriated and commodified by the white media.)

I was worried about Wayne, Jr., increasingly unsure with him now that he was becoming a man. I went back and forth, reaching out to him and hoping he would reach out to me. I worried that it might not be good for him to spend too much time with me anymore, that I knew too little about that street world in which he was striving. I knew that though I'd come from Newark, the destruction waiting in its streets had not remained the same. It had metastasized. In that world he would have been my mentor. I might encourage his tenderness, and that might be his undoing in that world. I couldn't give him what he needed to survive there. He knew that. I hoped to share with him some of what he might need to get out. If he wanted it. And I'd hoped to give him that from the first time I carried him across a room.

But Charles was still a child. He clearly needed me. I struggled to give him everything I'd given his brother too late, the experience of being prized. It had been an experience I'd somehow created or been given, perhaps by my great-grandmother, in my own early childhood. My storytelling, "part-Indian" great-grandmother with the smokecloud hair was off-and-on my primary care-giver from my birth until I was nine years old. She chose me, chose me to invest with her stories and accumulated legacy, which is to say she loved me. With Charles I was in a hurry, because I knew that the world I left him in every time I returned him to his mother's apartment was a world in which children became old abruptly, without warning.

I told him the same stories I'd taught his brother. I told him about his great-great-grandfather on my mother's side, who moved his wife and children all over South Carolina before he came to Philadelphia around the turn of the century, always a step ahead of the Klan, because he refused to accept the large and small indignities white men meted out to colored men. In Saluta, South Carolina, he'd been the first black man to attend the auction of cotton he raised on his homestead, not because he was granted a special permission but because he demanded a basic right. In Philadelphia he had a "contract" with movie princess Grace Kelly's father, John B. Kelly, the brick magnate, to supply the work crews for building operations, though I cannot imagine what a contract between a black man and an Irishman looked like in the early nineteen teens. He moved his family into a big house in the once-progressive neighborhood near Girard College in North Philadelphia.

I once took Charles to the ruin of this house, near Girard Avenue. We stood at the entrance and called our ancestor's name. We could see from the entrance to the backyard. A tree was growing through the kitchen into the second floor. For a time Great-Grandfather had rented the house next door to help an ongoing chain of relatives from the South relocate and find work. He lost his mind after the unionization of his trade empowered newly arrived white ethnics and ousted black men from the professions of carpentry and masonry. My mother grew up with him living on the third floor of her family home, a withdrawn, bitter, old man who occasionally came to life when he took his fiddle down from the mantle and ordered his grandchildren to dance until they went crying to their mother, "Please, make Grand Pop behave!"

Charles learned old songs from my collection of reissued recordings by Louis Armstrong, Bessie Smith, Cab Calloway, Ethel Waters. There was one Waters song that always broke him up; it had the spoken line *Take it easy, greasy, . . . you got a long way to slide*. Charles loved singing and language. He was a miraculous dark bird when he was little, always echoing and articulating. Before he turned two he had a good command of adjectives and adverbs. He was always narrating his experience. I am told small children usually exhibit exceptional verbal skills or advanced physical skills early. Charles exhibited both. He loved to run and climb and dance. He was fondest of his push toys. When he was four or five, I bought him toy boxing gloves and we practiced his jabs and footwork. I'd make the sound of the opening bell and he would start bobbing, weaving, and hooking. He had the classic combination down pat: the left jab followed by the right cross. I called him Kid Chocolate, after the legendary 1920s black boxer. I used to tell him his boxing technique was pure voodoo.

Charles was my heart. I was his uncle, almost his father, even if only for the day, the weekend, the week or summer we were together.

Once Charles fell riding his tricycle and split his tongue. I rushed him to the hospital emergency room and had to curse out the receptionist before he was admitted. "We can't admit him without the consent of his parent—that means a mother or father," the receptionist had told me from a barred cage. I was standing there with Charles's blood drenching my polo shirt. "*I'm* his goddamned parent!" I railed. "What's it to you? What kind of shit is this?"

I believe I am being objective when I say Charles was the most beautiful baby I have ever seen, more beautiful than his brother, who was perfect, and, if pictures are any indication, more beautiful than his father or I had been. His skin was darker than ours at the same time it was more brilliant. He shone. His was a preternatural blackness dedicated to the light. His round face was like a thundercloud with the lightning of his eyes and teeth flashing constantly inside it. Charles was the resurrected promise of all our childhoods going back generations for our manhood. I loved that boy better than my life. He was my life. Only better. Even before he was born, I was always talking to him, reading to him. When his mother was pregnant with Charles, I used to sit by her and touch her stomach and read to him inside her womb. I read him James Baldwin's letter to his nephew from *The Fire Next Time:* "*You can only be destroyed by believing that you really are what the white world calls a* nigger. *I tell you this because I love you, and please don't you ever forget it.*"

But as I've said, by the time Charles was born, his father was back on heroin. My brother tried many times to save himself, to heal, to redeem himself, and no one knows better than I do that he was born into a world of trouble. And maybe the reason I loved his sons so much was because I loved my brother and I hoped I could redeem him if I could help redeem them.

•

The following is one of my earliest memories. It emanates from both my memory and my imagination. It is literally true, however, in terms of the organic infrastructure informing my life, it has the quality of supertruth. Once, when I was four and staying in Philadelphia for the summer, my brother and I were walking home from Sunday school. The afternoon was sultry-hot. We were in no hurry to get home. I held his hand, as I always did when we walked down the street together, and he swung our arms in a jovial way. Soon we heard thunder and saw the zig-zag lightning. The swinging of my arm slowed. As we walked, we were caught in the downpour.

The rain pounded so hard it hurt my small body. I had never been outside in weather like that, away from home, in the street, without my mother or my father. All I had was my brother to protect me. He was lanky, athletic, almost as tall as my father. We began to run. The rain poured like a mirror of heaven. My brother held my hand tight. Lightning flashed, thunder rumbled, and I began to scream and cry.

I stopped running, and my brother stopped. I couldn't move. I was too terrified. I believed I would die. God was angry. He was tearing up the world and washing it away. I fully realize now what I only realized then in part, that my brave fourteen-year-old brother was terrified too. But he said, "It's all right. I'm with you. I'll get you home." This vow was punctuated by a burst of thunder so loud it threatened to crack open the street before us. My brother took me and ran first in one direction and then another. We rushed along the flowing curb. Then we were standing near a tree. We had reached the elementary school building two blocks from our house.

"We're almost there," my brother shouted over the ringing wind. "Do you want me to carry you?"

"No," I said, "I'm scared."

"All right," he told me. "We'll rest for a little while."

We ran from the tree to the awning leading into the school building. As soon as we came up against the closed glass entrance, there was a big burst of lightning. For an instant the world went white. The skin of my neck and arms tingled. We held each other. I felt his heart leaping just above my head, but he held me, and I didn't cry. We stood there holding each other until the rain slowed. Then we walked home in silence.

My father was sitting in the living room, reading the newspaper. My mother came out from the kitchen. I was excited. I wanted to tell them how my brother had saved me from the storm and brought me home safe like he promised. "You better take off those wet things," my mother said immediately. "Go on upstairs." As we turned on the stairs, my father said my brother should leave his clothes off when he removed the wet things and remain upstairs in the bathroom. He said that he'd received a call from church, that Wayne had stolen money from the Sunday school collection. My father had also found money missing from the coin collection he kept hidden in our basement. He was going to whip my brother.

The terror I'd felt in the storm returned. My father was a strong but soft-spoken man. I waited in the bathroom with my brother until our father came in with the piece of ironing cord. Wayne and I had been sitting on the rim of the bathtub. He was naked except for his blue jockey shorts. I had dressed myself in my Daniel Boone outfit. I held my brother's hands, telling him not to worry. His saffron body was still marked from the last beating he'd received from our father that summer.

Our father put me out, but I turned and stood at the door. I could see him through the slightly opened door, lashing my brother's legs and back with the cord. At first Wayne fought back and my father lost his balance for a moment near the sink. He righted himself and bore down on my brother, muttering and striking him, lashing him into the floor with the ironing cord. I ran downstairs to my mother in the kitchen. I told her to call the police. I said Daddy was killing Wayne. She did not move. Had she ceased to be our mother? It was a long time that we stood in the kitchen, listening to the lashing and crying upstairs before she said flatly, "He's got to learn. Your father is beating him because he loves him. He's beating him so the police won't have to."

The last time I saw my nephew Charles he was fourteen or fifteen years old. I had taken him to lunch at a restaurant inside the John Wanamaker department store, an historic, illustrated text of upward mobility in downtown Philadelphia. I had been told by his mother that he was having trouble in school. This was nothing new. From the time Charles began school, though he entered able to read, write, count, multiply, and divide, he was labeled a problem child by teachers who were either unwilling or unable to address the accelerated needs of a child like Charles in an overcrowded Newark classroom.

At Wanamaker's, I talked to him about school, which he thoroughly hated by then, and about his young life, which he was coming to hate as well. As I listened to him I could hear that he had already arrived at his youth's end. His voice grumbled with loss.

"Listen here, Kid Chocolate," I said, about to launch into my value-of-education talk.

"Don't call me that," he pleaded. "I hate my color. I hate it. I wish I was light-skinned like you, Uncle Don."

"Baby. Man," I said, "first of all, your uncle is *not* light-skinned," and I laughed (*how could I?*), "and even if I were, you're beautiful, man. You've always been beautiful."

But he wouldn't laugh. Not even for me. I think he even hated me a little that afternoon for trying to turn the light on his dark brilliance, since to be conspicuous by one's brilliance in the world to which he was always returned was only, to him, another liability.

I should have shaken him right in that restaurant in the bright, white department store. I should have shaken him. Held him. Rocked him. I should have told him what my great-grandmother told me in one way or another every day we were together, "*You're* the one the ancestors prayed for. *You're* all our hope." I should have told Charles, "You're the one. It belongs to you. You can't give up. You better win. Remember the Kid. Kid Chocolate. Knock that mean shit out. Where's your footwork, baby? Weave. Let me see your combination. Where's that spooky jab-hook-jab? Where's your voodoo?"

But I could see the enemies of my nephews and me knew how to manufacture the antidote to our voodoo and were now able to kill a black manchild's spirit early—and the work had already been accomplished in Charles. It was harder and harder for a black boy in Newark to slip through the system as I had done—which is not at all to suggest that my passage had been an easy one or that this nation sets no other snares for young black men besides ghettos.

Four years later, on Christmas morning in 1991, Charles was living with a thirty-year-old woman, waiting for his first child to be born. "As soon as the baby is born," he was telling me, "I'm going to turn myself in. I can do three years stiff. I'm not saying it's going to be all that easy, Uncle Don, but I can do it. Most of my friends from around the way are already in prison anyway."

"Guess what," he said, after I told him I loved him, that I believed he could still turn his life around, though I had no idea what I was talking about. I think I was in a mildly shocked state. I'd been hearing my own voice speaking to Charles as if from a distance.

"Guess what," Charles said again with a cheerfulness that finally undid me. "Now in Newark they even have surveillance cameras in the street lights."

We both realized it at the same moment: He was already in prison. He's been in prison most of his life. And because he, my heart, is in prison, so am I.

When I hung up I turned off the telephone. I sat at the house until it was dark, listening to records. Jelly Roll Morton. Marvin Gaye. Wayne Shorter. Sam Cooke. The Soul Stirrers. Albert Ayler. Jackie Wilson. Dexter Gordon. It was as though, through the voices of these black male artists I was calling a phalanx of ancestors to rise and protect my nephew. In the evening I made a light meal. I had planned to attend a dinner party. I plugged in the telephone long enough to excuse myself. "I'm fine," I assured my hosts. I said "Merry Christmas" and my hosts and I made plans to get together "soon."

Next, I cleaned my house. I swept dust from corners. I moved furniture, sweeping. I got on my knees and scrubbed the floors in the kitchen and the bathroom. I put clothes I no longer wore away in boxes, ready for the next week's trash collection. I did the wash and changed my bed. When I was done I felt better. I got into bed and fell into a hard sleep.

I awoke when it was still dark, the sheet and blanket twisted around my torso. In my sleep I had been dreaming and conjuring. I had awakened myself shouting, *"I'll get you home."*

# The Black Man: Hero

## Walter Mosley

1.

I recently watched a TV nature show in which a very small mouse was confronted by a large snake in the dead end of her own hole. The mouse, instead of giving in to fear, leapt on the snake's head, confusing him momentarily, and then ran up the length of his body to escape.

This tiny mammal proved herself as a hero. That is, she faced up to and survived against an overwhelming foe. It was real heroism: life under threat of death as it occurs every day for every species—including our own.

The mouse not only overcame the snake but she soon returned to her nest. You see, that was the only home she had and she was pregnant. That death trap was also a home for her future babies.

Later on I saw the same mouse (or one that looked a lot like her) kill another mouse and eat his brain in order to enrich her milk with the high nutritional content of that organ. That was a bloody scene, and it did not make me like her more, but neither did it alter her as a hero in my mind. Survival is a dirty business and heroes are not saints.

The end of the show was this dainty mother teaching her young to defeat and devour tarantulas, darkling beetles, and scorpions. Not all of the babies would survive this schooling.

It's a tough life.

•

It seems appropriate to begin an essay on black male heroism with a female example. Appropriate because heroes come in all forms and all of those forms are related.

The truth is that heroism isn't defined by male or female, good or bad, black or white. Heroism isn't even limited to humanity. Heroism, to my understanding, is simply survival. And, to make my very human definition even more so, it is really only the attempt to survive.

Heroism is in our blood, life itself—at least in part.

It is not my purpose here to say that black men are more heroic than others. It's not my goal to make saints out of men who are anything but saints. Neither do I want to exclude our mothers or even our enemies from this discussion.

I hope that this gesture of inclusion might invite others to open their minds to include some of the great tragic heroes of American history— African-American men.

2.

Heroism, as a rule, is not a studied thing—one does not risk his own life if he has other options. It's when we are cornered, like that mouse, that we stand up and try to do the impossible. And survival is the most impossible thing because death is waiting for all of us—evilly, without sense, without memory, without even a name.

Without a name.

Black American men and women were robbed of their true identities centuries ago, so long that one might wonder why we haven't gotten over it yet. One might wonder, that is, if they didn't know history, if they hadn't followed the history of the slavery, violence, and humiliation that have been visited upon black bodies and black minds from the seventeenth century up to, and past, Rodney King.

We lost—and have been systematically kept from—our names and our cultural memories for generations. All we have left, then, are our sensations. The senses have been our strongest link to life.

But even in this realm, our experience has often been nearly unbearable. Lives filled with pain, poverty, hunger, extreme violence, and love so harsh that it might just as well have been hatred.

Sometimes the pain would subside—temporarily: *a kind* master inherited the plantation; a moment of elation after the false emancipation.

In those moments we created the blues, we built the South, we wrought prayers that became a foundation for faith. And when we finished, the pain returned and what we had made was taken from us.

Robbed and then robbed again; the scene was set for heroes to emerge. But you must remember—one man's hero is another man's villain. When that mouse murdered another rodent for his brain she didn't do it to be remembered fondly by his clan.

3.

Black women and men have been driven down different paths to heroism toward a shared survival.

Women have been the nucleus, the producers of children and the beasts of burden. Raped and reviled, they became the roots of what culture we could approximate. They held the home and church together and made politics work. They stood strong because there was no place to run with children to be raised. They surpassed themselves with intellect, emotional strength, and, when necessary, with physical strength too.

Men were shorn early from their mothers. We became solitary laborers, silent martyrs of pain. Black men became the economic and cultural warriors of the new world. Juke-joint poets, cowboys, sharecropping fools. Black men danced to the sounds of grunts and wails—all the while whispering our tales on street corners, in elaborate codes that became the secret rhythms of the whole world.

Together black men and women not only survived, we also made names for ourselves. We did the impossible and we wept with joy and pain.

•

These acts of heroism are not chronicled properly in the literature of America. They aren't because we weren't supposed to do all that we've done. Our women were supposed to be the nursemaids of their rapists (an interesting irony), while the men were destined for loose-lipped whining and shuffling, afflicted with large genitals and no intelligence to speak of.

For generations these stereotypes were forced on us. We were humiliated and oppressed. Only in our secret hours and our secret hearts could we make our names. And even in those moments we chafed against each other and fought.

We had great cultural heroes such as Marcus Garvey and Langston Hughes. We had great sports heroes like Jack Johnson and Joe Louis. George Washington Carver rejuvenated the whole South, black and white, with his chemistry.

(There were women, too. There are always black women. Sojourner Truth, Mary McLeod Bethune, Zora Neale Hurston. But I'm talking about men right now.)

These men were all heroes, great not only in their actions but also in their ability to succeed against hatred and the threats of American white racism.

These were great men whose battles to maintain their names are heroic epics worthy of Homer.

These heroes were denied access to the mainstream of culture. Their words went out of print almost as soon as they were published, their deeds were never recorded in "serious" works of history. They were called primitive because they did not have the benefits of Western progress. And so these heroes moved forward like ancient men carrying fire in the night and burning their bodies to protect their burden from the rain. So many stories and dreams were extinguished. But still we survived. We passed on our stories wrapped in the hatred for our oppression.

Hatred because they tried to kill our dreams. Dreaming itself became a threat to life. Dreaming could bring death; success became synonymous with demise.

Hank Aaron received death threats for approaching Babe Ruth's record. Fats Waller and Bessie Smith died because no white doctor would admit them to the hospital.

You wake up one morning and find a snake the size of a fire truck in your home. What do you do?

4.

*His name was Raymond but we called him Mouse because he was small and had sharp features. We could have called*

*him Rat because Ray really wasn't very nice, but we liked him and so the name*
*Mouse stuck on him. . . .*

These lines were the first words in a series of stories that I've been writing about a fictional L.A. hero named Ezekiel "Easy" Rawlins. Easy is a friendly, introspective kind of guy who believes that he has a right to make it in this country in spite of his color (which is black). He is courageous, articulate, and, most of all, empathetic. He understands pain and wants to make a better world.

When Easy says that Raymond wasn't very nice, he means that Mouse is a remorseless killer who could gut a man and then sit down to a plate of spaghetti. Raymond is a thief, a great lover, fast with a smile and a story. Raymond is cold inside and unable to care about the pain of others.

Mouse and Easy are friends because the world Easy inhabits is hard and unfair. In the Deep South and deep in the ghetto black men often find that they need someone to cover their backs, and Raymond is better coverage than any insurance policy you could buy from the Rock.

I've written quite a bit about Easy and his world. Often Mouse enters into the tale. And when Mouse comes around everyone knows that there's bound to be blood—innocent blood, ignorant blood, usually the blood of black men born from black mothers.

•

When I talk to my readers they often ask me, Why does Easy maintain a relationship with Mouse? My pat answer is that Easy needs Mouse because when somebody's out after him, 911 just won't work. That answer is true enough, but there's another answer that has come to me over the years—Easy chronicles the world of black America in the second half of the twentieth century; he tells of the names we have given ourselves and the oppression we have had to fight in order to keep those names; he tells of heroism in all its hues and is even a hero himself.

But the hero of the world that Easy inhabits is Mouse.

Easy tells you how black men have suffered in America. How we've been beaten, turned away at the door, segregated, and humiliated. In the world that Easy came from, black men have had to learn to do without or to beg. That was his reality. That was everyone's reality. Everyone except Mouse.

You didn't fuck with Mouse. Mouse would kill you. He didn't care if you were white, black, or polka-dotted. He didn't care if you had the muzzle of your gun jammed up against his eyeball. If you went up against Mouse you would wind up dead.

For a group of oppressed people a man like Mouse is the greatest kind of hero. He's a man who will stand up against bone-cracking odds with absolute confidence. He's a man who won't accept even the smallest insult. And for a people for whom insult is as common as air, that's a man who will bring joy.

*I know freedom is possible as long as there's a man like Mouse on the streets.* That's what someone might say about Mouse. And if you asked that person, *But isn't all that violence wrong?* he would answer, *Sure it's wrong! It's been wrong all these years when they been doin' it to us but that didn't stop it.* And then you say, *But he kills black people as well as whites.* But you probably know the answer before it comes—*I know it, and I hate it. But this is a kind of war. We're fightin' in ourselves and against our great enemy. Mouse got the cops scared. They don't come around him all arrogant and sure of themselves. They don't come around for no reason an' they check their guns twice if they do. They respect Mouse because of the violence he's willing to do. And I tell you, man, respect is worth it at any price.*

•

It isn't only Mouse who is a hero of this kind. When Adam Clayton Powell was giving the white man hell down in Washington, his Harlem constituency backed him all the way. Malcolm X exhorted his followers to use violence when violence was used against them.

Often black men have to cross the white man's rules because we know that those rules never applied to us anyway. The laws and the lawmen were there to protect the property of dominant whites—there was no door for us to make our petitions.

5.

I suppose that it's not much of a coincidence that the first words in Easy's long tale and the first words in this article are both concerned with mice. The irony probably isn't lost either: just because we're small or outnumbered doesn't mean that we can't be great.

This is not a polemic or a call to violence. I'm not saying here what actions I think people should, or shouldn't, take. What I'm trying to do is to let the concept of Black Male Heroes breathe a little bit. Men who suffer violence also study it. If you think there's a man waiting out in the street for you with a club, you have three choices: you can go out there and take your beating, you can run out the back door, or you can try to stand up under the hail of blows—you can try to wrest the club from the hand of your foe, you can turn the tide of force, or you can die trying.

Which is the action of a hero?

That answer is for you, and those who depend on you, to come to.

# Pain and Glory:
# Some Thoughts on My Father

## Quincy Troupe

I grew up in a community of exiles and outcasts, a family of people who were systematically denied the full rights of citizenry in this country with the exception that we had to pay the same amount of taxes as our white American counterparts. This is nothing new. Everybody and his mama knows it by now—the evidence is everywhere, is irrefutable and undeniable.

My father, Quincy Trouppe, Sr., was forced to play baseball in the all-Negro leagues almost all of his career. He made the major leagues for only six months, when he was thirty-nine years of age, because he came along "20 Years Too Soon." My father came along before integration allowed players like Jackie Robinson, Willie Mays, Don Newcombe, Roy Campanella, Monte Irvin, Larry Doby, and Henry Aaron—all products of the old Negro leagues—to show their great gifts to a sometimes appreciative and other times unappreciative nation, by playing in the then almost all-white major leagues. The glory and the pain of his life and how that impacted my life and the lives of others around me is a great story, one filled with anguish, pathos, sadness, and pain. At the same time, it is filled with unbelievable achievements, incredible joy and happiness. It is a complex story of an extremely complex man who, had he been born later, would probably have lived to see his name become instantly recognizable throughout American households, like the names of Willie Mays, Jackie Robinson, Henry Aaron, and Roy Campenella. This is mere speculation on my part, because people are shaped by their times, and who can say with certainty what might have happened had my father been born later, during the generation of those great African-American baseball players—giants!—that I have mentioned above? Maybe he would have been more interested in medicine, or the law, or perhaps even basketball or football, or boxing, another sport at which he excelled. What we *do* know is that my father *was* born twenty years too soon, that he *did* come along before a lot of opportunities were there for African-American men and women. These are the facts, and while he *did* achieve great, even extraordinary things—many say he was the second or third greatest catcher of all time in the old Negro League, after the immortal Josh Gibson—in his lifetime his lack of opportunity to display his vast skills in the major leagues caused him extreme pain that lasted until the day he died.

But my father was more than a baseball player, more than merely a great athlete. He was also a manager of baseball teams and a historian as well, not only of the Negro leagues but of the Puerto Rican, Cuban, Venezuelan, and Mexican baseball leagues; my father played baseball ten or eleven months every year during his career, dividing his time equally between the Negro leagues and Latin America and the Caribbean. My father played on and managed the Kansas City Monarchs and the Cleveland Buckeyes to championships. He was a player and manager in Mexico and in Puerto Rico. He lead Ponce, Puerto Rico to five straight championships as a player and manager. He wrote his thoughts down about many things outside of baseball—about the politics of the day, about the great musicians and entertainers he liked and knew, like Lionel Hampton, Charlie Parker, and others. He loved music and fashion, and he spoke Spanish fluently and a passable French. He was also the first African-American baseball scout for the St. Louis Cardinals, after he finished his playing and managing career. He recommended that the Cardinals sign Roberto Clemente, Juan Marichial, Vic Powers, Willie McCovey, Orlando Cepeda, and other great players of color, but the Cardinals refused to sign these gifted players because of their own rampant organizational racism.

My father was a tall man, six-foot-three, strong and handsome. He was brown-skinned, a very dapper dresser, and wore the latest and best of fashions—wide-lapel suits and sports coats, oversized, with two buttons; loosely draped pants and "bad to the bone," two-toned Foot Joy shoes; wide-brimmed Panama hats and gold Rolex watches. He always drove a new Cadillac or Chrysler. Only the best was good enough for my father. And his smile was so radiant that it stripped the clothes right off the bodies of many a fine lady who loved him dearly and whom he loved too—which probably had something to do with why my father and mother divorced in 1948. That and the arguments they had over whether my mother's mother should live with them or not. My father didn't want her to and my mother did, so my grandmother—"Mama," we called her—stayed. But my father left or was thrown out (according to whose side of the story you believe) when I was nine, an event that traumatized my brother and me for years to come.

My father was a catcher whom some (as I already said) called the second or third greatest catcher of all time in the old Negro Baseball League. The greatest, without a doubt, was Josh Gibson, whom many believed was the greatest catcher that ever lived, regardless of race. My father agreed that Josh was a more powerful hitter than he was, but not a better hitter in terms of average. And he downright disagreed about Josh being a better catcher than he was defensively, or in the way that they both handled pitchers behind the plate. On this, my father—and, I might add, others like Satchel Paige and Monte Irvin—felt he had a decisive upper hand and was better. But baseball legends aren't made by the way a catcher might have handled a bunch of pitchers, or thrown out a score of runners trying to steal second or third, or the style and grace in which they might have caught a bushel load of towering pop flies behind the plate or along the first and third base foul lines. Baseball legends are made in the way that someone swings a bat, and in this area Josh Gibson was head and shoulders above the rest, numero uno, bar none, just as Satchel Paige was as a pitcher and Cool Papa Bell as a base runner. According to eyewitness accounts, Gibson was a colossus, hitting baseballs further than anyone else ever hit them in the history of the game. The only films of those days are the ones my father made, and he never caught Josh on any of them swinging his bat.

Even so, it is as a historian, a recorder of events with his camera (both 8-millimeter home motion pictures and still photographs) and his words—through his memoir, *20 Years Too Soon*—that I feel my father will leave his lasting mark on baseball history. The motion pictures taken of the old Negro leagues are the films of my father, the only true historian of his kind during those long-gone days. My father's pictures are the definitive records that we have of those incredible African-American players and their days in the sun! For this alone I am absolutely proud of him.

Once, in the middle to late 1980s, my wife, Margaret, and I were returning from a vacation in Guadeloupe, in the French West Indies. Our American Airlines flight brought us through customs in San Juan, Puerto Rico. Now, I wear my hair in the Jamaican dreadlock style and in many places in the West Indies this is perceived as a sign of a potential drug dealer, or at least of someone who might use drugs. So when the Puerto Rican customs officer saw me coming I sensed him watching me closely.

"Passports and open up all your bags," he demanded of Margaret and me.

I handed over my passport, lifted our bags into his work area and opened all of them. Meantime, the customs officer, an older man perhaps in his late fifties or early sixties, looked at my passport. Suddenly he lifted his eyes, fixing me with an intense gaze.

"Quincy Troupe. Is that your name?"

"Yes," I said, preparing myself for the worst.

"Are you any relations to the baseball catcher named Quincy Trouppe?" he asked. My father added a *p* to his last name because of the way they pronounced it in Latin America: *Troup-pe*!

"Yes," I said. "He is my father."

"Really!" the man said joyously, his eyes widening in great surprise. "He was a great, great player and a very fine man. A gentleman," he said, "I saw him play many, many times. He played on the team in Ponce, Puerto Rico, my hometown, and led them to five straight Puerto Rican championships." The he gave me back my passport, and without even looking through them, told me to close our bags (we didn't have any contraband anyway). Then he called out to all other customs officers: "Hey, this is the son of Quincy Trouppe!" and many of them turned around and saluted me with big smiles.

"Is he still alive?" the man asked.

"Yes," I told him, clear in that moment I was speaking what was most deeply true. "He's still alive."

"Well, when you see your father, you tell him for me that the people of Ponce, Puerto Rico, still remember him and love him for what he did for us while he was here. And you tell him also that if he wants to he can come back to Ponce to live, because there will always be a place for him there. Tell him to come and visit. Will you tell him that for me?"

"Yes, I will tell him," I said, proud as all get-out.

Then he shook my hand and smiled a beautiful smile at me and Margaret as we left his area.

( ( speak my name ) )

"Don't forget to tell him that we remember him, Okay?" the man said again as we began moving past customs.

"I won't," I yelled back as we cleared security with the eyes of most of the American passengers who'd heard the conversation on my back. They were probably wondering who in the hell I was, without even a clue of who my father was. This is what I mean when I say most African Americans are outcasts and exiles. If these same passengers had heard the names of Mickey Mantle or Babe Ruth, most of them would have known who was being spoken of.

My father was the only athlete in Missouri's history to make All State in baseball, basketball, and football and win the Open Division Golden Glove Heavyweight Boxing Championship. Had he been a White American with the same talents, accomplishments, and charisma, his sports history and athletic achievements would not be obscure. Even until his death, the state of Missouri never acknowledged his great contributions. But my father is not the only African American with great achievements to suffer this fate in this country. There are countless others whose accomplishments during this nation's history must be, in time, brought out into the light of day for all to see—and they must be celebrated—if we are to ever know our *true* selves as a people and the *real* history of this complex land.

# Race, Rage, and Intellectual Development: A Personal Journey

## Haki R. Madhubuti

This is not fiction, nor is it complete autobiography. I share this slice of my life only to make a connection to readers that may indeed be impossible to make in any other way. I do not believe in victimology, even though I am a victim. As an intelligent, productive black man, husband, father, poet, teacher, publisher, editor, community cultural worker, political entrepreneur, and "brother," my story, with all its horror and unforgettable heartbreaking insights, is not unusual in the context of growing up in urban America. However, in the final (and hopefully most revealing) analysis, self-examination, self-realization, and self-definition in the context of a known and understood history are the first steps toward enlightened empowerment.

If I extend my hand as a willing victim of American racism (white supremacy) and leave it at that, I do you—the reader—no good and ultimately fail myself. It is easy, yet debilitating and weakening, to be a victim. Being a victim, living as the object of victimization, is the denial of the possibility to become more than others (others who don't like you or your family) think you can become. A victim is not a contributor; rather, he or she is but a childlike participant, looking for the easy and less difficult or responsible way to survive. Victimhood is modern enslavement, with invisible reinforced steel chains firmly placed around one's legs, arms, and mind. Anytime you capture a person's mind, nine times out of ten you have his or her body as well. Victimhood is the prerequisite to self-hatred and dependency, political and economic neutralization, and joyless living. I ask myself two questions every day: (1) What good can I do for myself, my family, my extended family, black people, and others today? (2) How can I continue to rise above the limiting expectations of others, especially my enemies?

I now share these factual slices from my life only to place myself in a cultural and historical context.

I grew up on the Lower East Side of Detroit and the West Side of Chicago, in a family that lived too often from week to week. My mother, sister, and I represented the nucleus of our family. In 1943, my mother migrated from Little Rock, Arkansas, moving, as John O. Killens would say, 'up-South' to Michigan. She came with my father, who stayed long enough to father my sister, who is a year and a half younger than I. I was born in 1942.

Those years, the 1940s and 1950s, were not kind to us, and my father wandered in and out of our lives from the day we hit Detroit. My mother, alone with two children and no skills, ended up working as a janitor in an apartment building owned by a Negro preacher/undertaker. My earliest memory is of her cleaning that three-story, sixteen-unit building each day, carrying garbage cans on her back to the alley once a week. Seldom did I see her without a broom, mop, or washcloth in her hands. By this time I was eight years old, and my sister was seven. We helped as much as possible because we knew that staying in our basement apartment depended upon our keeping the building clean. I did not know then that our housing also depended upon my mother's sexual involvement with the Negro building owner. These encounters took place when we were at school or while we were asleep. My mother began to trade her body quite early in order for us to live. In the 1950s there were few "safety nets" for single women with children. Consequently, my mother became a victim in a white supremacist, monied system which allowed some black men to become surrogate oppressors.

With no family in Detroit, and left to her own limited resources, my mother sought to survive with her children in a way that would have the least possible negative impact on us. However, due to the violent nature of her relationship with the landlord, we stayed in our Lower East Side apartment only until she was able to find work less threatening and taxing on her, physically and psychologically. At least that is what my sister and

I thought. What I've failed to tell you about my mother is that she was probably one of the most beautiful women in the world. I've seen her beauty not only stop traffic but compel men to literally get out of their cars to introduce themselves to her. Her beauty, which was both physical and internal, was something that only the few women she associated with could handle. Women would stare at her with dropped mouths. Her beauty would ultimately place her in an environment that would destroy her.

My mother's next job was that of a barmaid. She started serving drinks at one of the newest and classiest locations in Detroit, Sonny Wilson's. Along with this job came the slow but destructive habit of alcohol consumption. Also, she began to run in very fast company. She was named Miss Barmaid of 1951, carrying with that title all of the superficiality and glitter of the Negro entertainment world of that time. To cut to the bone of all of this is to note rather emphatically that my family's condition of poverty drove my mother into a culture that dictated both her destruction and great misery for my sister and me. By the time I was thirteen, my mother was a confirmed alcoholic and was fast losing her health. When I turned fifteen, she had moved to hard drugs and was not functional most of the time.

My sister, who had just turned fourteen, announced to us that she was pregnant. This was in the late 1950s, and pregnancy out of wedlock was not a common or acceptable occurrence. I went looking for the man who had impregnated her. He was a local gang leader, twenty-one years old, who had as much potential as a husband or father as I did at fifteen. After briefly talking to him about my sister's condition and getting virtually nowhere, I did what most "men" did in similar situations at that time—I hit him. And he, in a rather surgical fashion, responded by literally "kicking my ass." After I reported this to my mother, she, in a drunken stupor, gave me another whipping for getting whipped.

Shortly after that incident, my mother's need for alcohol and drugs increased. She prostituted herself to feed her habit. Many nights I searched Detroit's transient hotels looking for her. Needless to say, I had grown up rather quickly and felt that there was no hope for me or my sister. Just before I turned sixteen, my mother overdosed on drugs and died. She had been physically and sexually abused by someone so badly that we were not able to view her body at her funeral. My sister was pregnant again. By the time she was twenty she had three children; before she was thirty she had six children and had never been married. She has endured a life of pain and difficulty that has often been the exact duplicate of our mother's. To this day she lives in great pain.

I could not cry at my mother's funeral. My heart was cold and my mind was psychologically tired. I felt a quiet feeling of relief and release at her death, but also an underlying tone of guilt. At sixteen, I felt that I had not done enough to save my mother. It was clear to me that her final days had been filled with long hours of tragic suffering over which she had no control. All I could do was watch in confused pain, hostility, anger, resentment, and rage.

At first I could not understand my anger. Why did she have to die so young and so viciously? Why were my sister, her baby, and I alone without help or hope? Why were we so poor? It seemed that my life was one big fight. There was no escape from problems and very little peace. And I guess my mother's death brought a moment of peace. The fight to survive remained uppermost in my mind. Yet it seemed I was being torn apart from the inside. A part of my own fear was connected to how my sister and I were going to survive. I had seen and been a part of too much destruction and death in my young life. I knew that the only person who really cared about our future was me, and that was not enough.

I had few friends, partially because of my economic condition; I had little time to play because I had to work. Also, my social skills were not the best and the path of the loner best suited me at that time. I did not realize then that my solitary existence was to eventually save my life.

### Color in America

A part of the problem that my mother, sister, and I faced in America was that our skin color was neither black nor white, but yellow! The unusual beauty that centered in my mother was not only due to the distinctive bone structure of her face and her small, well-connected body. It also had to do with the fact that all of her physical beauty was wrapped in yellow. Yes, we were Arkansas blacks, but my mother could easily have passed for Puerto Rican or dark Italian if she did not have to open her mouth. Her language was Southern Black English, and it carried in it the rural slowness that urban America does not have pity on.

However, it was her beauty, illuminated by very light skin color that attracted the darkest of black men and, of those I remember, the most abusive of black men. They seemed to be steaming in anger, hatred, and internal rage. It seems as though by being with her they were as close to white women as was allowed at that time. And their often intense love/hate relationship with her was only a mirror of the fight they were having daily with themselves and the white world. They could not touch or physically retaliate against white people, but my mother was there for many of them to play out their deepest hurt in their "loving" and abusive treatment of her. I was not to understand, until much later, the deep color-rage that plagued them and that lay at the surface of my own reality.

Being a "yellow nigger" in urban America was like walking on roasted toothpicks hanging from the mouths of brothers who did not like the taste of wood or understand themselves. Many of the black men who populated my early life used self-defacing language twenty-four hours a day. The two operative words used constantly were "nigger" and "mothafucka." We had not only been seasoned to dislike or hate the "us" in us, but also had adopted the language of self-abuse and self-hatred. I learned early to walk the fine line between black and white. I began to understand the anger, hatred, and rage in me by studying black literature and black music.

## What Saved Me?

At thirteen, my mother asked me to go to the Detroit Public Library to check out a book for her. The title of the book was *Black Boy*, by Richard Wright. I refused to go because I didn't want to go anywhere asking for anything "black." The self-hatred that occupied my mind, body, and soul simply prohibited me from going to a white library in 1955 to request from a white librarian a book by a black author, especially one with "Black" in the title.

I and millions of other young blacks were products of a white educational system that at best taught us to read and respect the literary, creative, scientific, technological, and commercial development of others. No one actually told me, "You should hate yourself," however, the images, symbols, products, creations, promotions, and authorities of white America all very subtly and often quite openly taught me white supremacy, taught me to hate myself.

This white supremacist philosophy of life was unconsciously reinforced in black homes, churches, clubs, schools, and communities throughout the nation. Therefore, my refusal to go check out *Black Boy* was only in keeping with a culture that twenty-four hours a day not only denied me and my people fundamental rights and privileges as citizens, but refused to admit that we were whole human beings. Few articulated it in popular culture at that time, but we lived in Apartheid, U.S.A.

However, *Black Boy* had somehow attached itself to my mother's mind and would not let go. I went to the library, found the book on the shelf myself, put it to my chest, found an unpeopled spot, and began to read the book that would profoundly alter my life.

For the first time in my life I was reading words developed into ideas that were not insulting to my own personhood. Richard Wright's experiences were mine, even though we were separated by geography. I read close to half of the book before the library closed. I checked *Black Boy* out, hurried home, went into the room I shared with my sister, and read for the rest of the night. Upon completing *Black Boy* the next morning, I was somehow a different type of questioner in school and at home. I had not totally changed, but the foundation had been planted. Deeply. I became more concerned about the shape of things around me. I also read Wright's *Native Son*, *Uncle Tom's Children*, and *12 Million Black Voices*. Richard Wright painted pictures with words that connected to the real me. I could relate to Bigger Thomas because his fears, doubts, and internal rage were the same that I experienced. Layers of ignorance were being removed by just opening my mind to a world that included me as a whole person. Wright entered my life at the right time.

After my mother's death, I took the Greyhound to Chicago, where I stayed with an aunt for a while, then I rented a room at the Southside YMCA. I completed high school in Chicago and ended up in St. Louis, Missouri, where I joined the United States Army.

The military was the poor boy's employment. On the way to basic training at Fort Leonard Wood, Missouri, I was reading Paul Robeson's *Here I Stand*. When we arrived at boot camp, the white, middle-thirtyish drill sergeant ordered us off the bus. We were about two hundred men. Three black men, including myself, and one hundred ninety-seven white men. The black men had all joined voluntarily, but most of the white men had been drafted. This was 1960, and the Army was practicing "integration."

As I stepped off the bus, the white drill sergeant sighted Paul Robeson's face on my book and snatched it from my hand. He pulled me out of line and barked into my face, "What's your Negro mind doing reading this black communist?" Of course, many thoughts ran through my head as potential responses to his question. This was the first time I had heard a double negative used so creatively. The drill sergeant ordered all of us up against the bus and commenced to tear the pages from the book, giving a page to each recruit, and telling the recruits to use the pages for toilet paper. By this time I was questioning my own sanity about joining the military, and examining my options.

Luckily, I was also reading John O. Killens's *And Then We Heard the Thunder*, a powerful and telling book about black men in Europe's War on the World Number Two (commonly referred to as World War II). What I learned from Killens was the importance of using one's time wisely and never to speak from the top of one's head in anger when outnumbered. As I stood, lips closed, cold and shaking with fear, anger, and loneliness—while the sergeant destroyed my copy of Robeson's work—I decided four things that would stay with me for the rest of my life:

1. I would never, never again apologize for being black. I am who I am, I realized then, and if black literature has taught me anything, it clarified for me that I was a man of African descent in America serving time in the United States Army rather than the United States prison system.

2. I would never again put myself in a cultural or intellectual setting where people outside of my culture or race would know more about me than I knew about myself. This meant that I had to go on the offense and put myself on a reeducation program that prepared me internally as an African in America, as a black man.

3. I was in the United States Army because I was black, poor, and ignorant of the forces that controlled my life and the lives of other men— black and white—with whom I was to train. These forces were racial, economic, and political, and I needed accurate information on all of them. While many of the other brothers in my platoon searched for fun, I visited the libraries. Few could understand why I chose to be alone with books. The reason was that I found new friends, uncritical friends, in the literature. I was a sponge. Reading became as important as water and food.

4. If *ideas* were that powerful and could cause such a reaction, then I was going to get into the *idea* business. For that drill sergeant to act so violently against a book that contained ideas that he probably did not even understand was frightening. He was reacting to the image and idea of Paul Robeson that had been created by monied, political, and mass-media white power brokers.

From that day on I have been on a mission to understand the world and to be among the progressive men who want to change it for the benefit of the majority who occupy it.

My two years and ten months in the military were essentially my undergraduate education. I read close to a book a day, concentrating in history, political science, black literature, and (of course) black poetry—the written/oral music of our people. I read and reread, studied the history and culture of black people, and extended my study into the areas of political economy. One of the most influential writers to impact my thinking was W. E. B. Du Bois.

Du Bois had already articulated that the problem of the twentieth century would be color. As I studied his work, I began to see possibilities for myself for two reasons: (1) Du Bois was a high-yellow black man who had devoted his life to the uncompromising development and liberation of black people, and (2) his writing represented liberating medicine for my mind. All of Du Bois's work, whether in sociology, politics, fiction, or poetry, led to the reconstruction of the black mind. The passage that both freed me intellectually and gave meaning to the rage that continued to tear me apart came from *The Souls of Black Folk*:

> After the Egyptian and the Indian, the Greek and Roman, the Teuton and Mongolian, the Negro is a sort of seventh son, born with a veil and gifted with second sight in this American world—a world which yields him no true self-consciousness, but only lets him see himself through the revelation of the other world. It is a peculiar sensation, this double consciousness, this sense of always looking at one's self through the eyes of others, of measuring one's soul by the tape of a world that looks on in amused contempt and pity.
>
> One ever feels his twoness—an American, a Negro; two souls, two thoughts, two unreconciled strivings; two warring ideals in one dark body, whose dogged strength alone keeps it from being torn asunder. The history of the American Negro is the history of this strife—this longing to attain self-conscious manhood to merge his double self into a better and truer self.

Yes, I knew that I was different and black. However, it was Du Bois's analysis that brought me to where I could appreciate and begin to reconcile the different "selves" in me. Color and psychology, color and history, color and enslavement, color and politics, color and economics, color and rage, took on new meanings for me. I came to understand that the white images and symbols that assigned me to certain roles in life had nothing to do with the quality and content of my history or my mind.

My search for authenticity was being led by the literature of W. E. B. Du Bois and others.

However, Du Bois's *Black Reconstruction* and *The World and Africa* were the two books that ultimately unlockéd my brain and liberated my own thought. Dr. Du Bois was a black intellectual who remained true to his calling in that he not only wrote and documented history, he, by his actions, via the NAACP (National Association for the Advancement of Colored People) and other progressive organizations, tried to change the world for the best. He went to his grave in Ghana in 1963 at the age of ninety-five, never giving in to the "long and comfortable compromises." Du Bois was a political activist for life.

I left the military in August 1963. In September of that same year, four little girls were murdered in Birmingham, Alabama. They were bombed in their church while praying to a God who did not even look like them. This violent act against our children confirmed for me the course of my life. For two years and ten months, I had been trained to be a killer in the U.S. Army. Later I realized that all the targets I shot at were either black or colored, however, I knew even then the color of the people who were blowing up our children. To this day, they, and the millions of brain-mismanaged Negroes that they control, continue to tapdance on the dreams of our children.

I am against dancing to and entertaining the enemies of the world. As a young man, I reeducated myself. The poet-writer that I've become is directly connected to my education and political involvement over the last thirty-four years. Each day I also realize that I too am an activist for life, and that serious struggle and organizing will only bear fruit if it is on-going, institutionalized, rethought, updated, involves the young, remains honest, and is open-minded and combative. Struggle must be renewing and productive if it is to grow. Additionally, one must struggle with like-minded people.

The rage that I and most sane people feel toward the death and human damage inflicted upon the weak by this society and others must be chan-neled and released in a healthy manner. Otherwise we internalize it or let it loose on those persons closest to us.

Often our lives may seem like pieces of slave fiction; however, by se-riously studying history and political economy, we can come to under-stand that one way we can have an impact on the nightmare that covers the lives of most people is through organized struggle at every level of hu-man involvement. If such cultural work is to be fruitful, we must concentrate on that which we are *for* as opposed to only fighting and articulating that which we are *against*.

This is not rhetoric or playground boasting. If the condition of our people and that of the majority of the world's people is not recognized as proof enough of the destructive path we are on, we are truly lost. Our greatest tasks remain (1) discovering a way to neutralize racism and oppression without becoming racists and oppressors ourselves, (2) destroying an abusive economic system while trying to create something better, (3) reversing destructive habits with the knowledge of that which is best and better. We cannot build on the "anti" only. I am African, I am black (a political, cultural, and color designation in the U.S.), even though my skin complexion is what is loosely described as high yellow. Yet, to look at me any time of the day or night few would conclude that I am any person other than one of African descent. I am clear about this fact just as I am certain that all black people descended from the continent of Africa. That this is still debatable in some quarters speaks highly of the global effects of white world supremacy propaganda (see Frances Cress Welsing's *The Isis Papers: The Keys to the Colors*, John Henrik Clarke's *Notes for an African World Revolution*, Marimba Ani's *Yurugu: An African-centered Critique of European Cultural Thought and Behavior* and Chancellor Williams's *The Destruction of Black Civilization*).

I have traveled to Africa at least eight times. I am not sure of the number because I stopped counting after I realized that my journeys were about me centering myself, rather than going to give papers, participate in international gatherings, or to read my poetry. Africa had become the source, a connecting spirit that revitalized me, a place where I could gather new knowledge and the best cure for Africa romanticism.

Again, it was the literature that pointed me to Africa—Du Bois, yes, but also Carter G. Woodson, Alaine Locke, Langston Hughes, Marcus Garvey, and Richard Wright (especially his 1954 book on Ghana and Kwame Nkrumah, *Black Power*). My life changed as the knowledge I absorbed lifted me into the African world community of builders, creators, inventors, and producers. Reading and studying, reflecting and internalizing the words and works of black (African) authors represented a type of cultural food that would shape me into the culturally conscious man that I am today. Ideas about the African (black) reality became liberating food. I consumed black (African) ideas and literature like a desert taking to raindrops. I learned to stop making excuses for black people as well as for whites. It should be a given fact that everything black is not right. There are many good white people in the world—the problem is that they are in the minority and do not hold power.

There is no separation between my cultural self and my political, professional, business, familial, and writer selves. I am one, and I am clear—always open for new knowledge, ideas, and revelations, but firmly anchored and connected to the millions of African (black) women and men that led the way for my enlightenment and normalcy. Those of us that understand this heritage must be at the forefront of creating, producing, and building that which we are for and of sharing such development with our families, extended families, community, and world. It is easy to be against any number of ideas and institutions. The larger task is to fight that which we consider evil by building that which we consider good, just, and correct.

The role of the black intellectual is not only to understand the text but to write his/her version of the story, not only to teach the young the positive objectives of life but to be involved at a community level—where theory is often untested—in making real and substantive, long-term changes in the lives of those who are truly suffering.

This is transforming work. It is moral and ethical work. The monetary rewards are few, if any. However, the love generated by the hope in the eyes of our children as a result of such work is for me the best payment. We must give our children a fighting chance in a world that long ago counted them out, diminished their chances of success to below zero. To see the yes in their eyes is also to hear the yes in our own heartbeats. This is why the drum is our magical instrument: you cannot kill the beat of hungry hearts.

# Rickydoc: The Black Man as Hero

## Arthur Flowers

I am Flowers of the delta clan Flowers and the line of O Killens. I wanna be a hero. I wanna be a hero bad.

In fact, I think everyman is potentially a hero. I think that deep down inside, where he really lives and rarely shows, any man worth his keep considers himself a hero, a champion of the tribe, in shield and spear, with his finger plugged into the dike that was assigned to him.

•

How I got to this questionable and possibly foolish state of mind is traceable. First off it's personal. It's in me to be a hero. Too many marvel comics, delta myths, legends and tall tales when I was a kid.

Furthermore, I come from a heroic line, the delta clan Flowers. My mama and my daddy were heroes, and so too are a great many of my relatives. My mama was the flashy type, she never accepted the status quo of the old south. A race woman, Im proud to say, who never left a battle un- done. My daddy was a quieter model, a classic crusty old general practitioner who felt a distinct responsibility for the health of all the colored folks of south Memphis. It's said in old Memphis that half the kids on the southside still belong to Doc Flowers cause they were never paid for. (I love that line.) And my mama and daddy passed that sense of social responsibility on to me.

An equally significant part of my state of mind is that Im a child of the 60s. Flower Power. Civil Rights. Black Power. The whole bit. I remember the day the King was killed, my senior year at Hamilton High School in Memphis. I remember pitched battles with the police the next day. We would charge them with sticks and stones and they would drive us back with batons and tear gas but they couldnt come on the school grounds. We'd retreat, regroup, and charge again. I had just been elected Mr. Brain of the senior class and Ms. Martha P. Flowers, a notoriously demanding english teacher and another one of the delta clan Flowers heroes, told us that anybody who walked out of her class to join the street battle outside wouldnt graduate. The whole class looked at me as if to say, She's your aunt, what you gon' do, Mr. Brain? What could I do? I upped and walked (what kind of graduation would it be without Mr. Brain?) and the rest of the honors class followed me. Standing at the crossroads. One of my first steps in the Struggle. The Almighty Movement. A luta continua.

And, understand, the 60s were more than street battles or sex, drugs, and rock 'n' roll, the 60s were about "commitment." We cared. We tried. It was important (and doable) for us to "make a better world." It was important to "save the race." And it still is.

For all our excesses, we felt a responsibility to be forces for good and drummajors for righteousness. And still do.

And then there was Nam. In the middle of my black power thing, along came Nam. I brought back from Nam a sense of racial solidarity that can never be broken. Never. My commitment is absolute. I was already a black militant when I got there, all afro and attitude. And Nam was, shall we say, a hostile environment. Not just the war, but blackfolks was still being dumped upon. Being dumped upon in Nam was potentially lethal. Blackmen in Nam responded with a sense of racial solidarity that was phenomenal. Any blackman of my generation who experienced what we called blackinization will testify. I tried to in my first novel and didnt touch it. We survived—brotherme, brotherblood, brotherblack. I been a warrior ever since. I have been at times a chief and at times a spear-carrier. I've often stumbled and tacticswise I've zigged and zagged, but by Ogun's beard I'ma live and die a warrior.

The next jewel in my shield was John O Killens and the Guild literary movement. One day I will have to sit down and tell the tale of John O Killens, cause he dont get nowhere near the respect he deserves. I tell you the half aint never been told. John O Killens and the Guild school taught me not only how to be a writer but how to be a historical force. An ideological orchestrator. A master player. Even more, John O filled me with the "divine responsibility" of a master of the word.

John O's luminous love for blackfolk and all humanity gathered unto him a cadre of young writers whose destinical influence has not yet begun to be felt. John O taught us how to be "longdistance runners." John O gave us vision.

•

So by the time I come to the hoodoo way, Im ready to play. Learned my early hoodoo licks from Ishmael. Mumbo Jumbo & Conjure. Literary hoodoo I call it. Efforts of mystically inclined black writers such as Zora Neale, Ishmael, and myself to manifest hoodoo, the indigenous African-American spiritual tradition, through our works. To operate as contemporary shamans & medicine-workers. Cultural custodians. Archetypic guides and guardians of the tribe. Its destiny and its generations. Conjurors & Rootdoctors.

Using longgame vision to peer as far into the future as possible. Determine what challenges the tribe will have to face. Prepare the tribal soul to meet them.

The hoodoo way. The most westernized of the family of African religious retentions in the Newworld. Voodoo, Santería, Macumba, Ocha, Obeah, et al. The hoodoo way had degenerated into a primarily magical system. Until Ishmael made it a functional 20th-century Afrocentric ideology.

An African Way of God. Neither hoodoo nor African religion in general are respected in the world spiritual tradition. There are those, even righteous blackfolk, who would passionately declare there is no such thing as an African Way of God. We disagree. Antiquated perhaps, outdated perhaps. Contemporary hoodoo consequently striving to update the hoodoo way. Update the entire multitudinous African religious tradition. Synergize and refine it. Illuminate it. Make it a contemporary instrument of spiritual and political redemption. Compatible with the 21st-century mind. And soul.

Ase.

•

We of the Hoodoo Way understand. The way of the spirit is a more profound instrument of redemption than that of politics. Jesus has turned more heads than Marx ever thought of.

The test of a good healthy spiritual tradition: its adherents lead good healthy lives. Brimming with strength and meaning, beauty and grace. They build good healthy communities.

Look at the condition of blackfolks worldwide. Everywhere blackfolks on the bottom of their respective societies. Cant blame Everywhere on nobody else. Aint nobody's fault but ours. A race that must look deep inside. Find and finesse the weaknesses that have crippled us in global competition. Transform them into strengths.

Each person, each generation, has its own tasks. Its own mission to be found.

Increasingly clear, is it not? Ongoing struggles against competitive and / or hostile groups must always be subordinate to the struggle within. A strong, illuminated people cope with and adapt to any assault. Human or natural. KKK or AIDS. A strong people cope, a weak people fold. We generally fold. Genocidally weak. Mere survival no longer sufficient. If it ever was.

For this is. A time of testing. Gods instrument. Forged. Tempered upon the anvil of adversity.
For life is Trial. & Tribulation. And it is only through adversity. That we are truly challenged.

Do what you do. With style and grace. Maintain serenity of purpose. Savor life's fleeting joys.

For we must. Ennoble ourselves. Find again the high ground. Heal thyself. Be the great and mighty people we were meant to be—the Children of the Sun.

•

Look at the tribal soul. Manifested as a given culture's spiritual tradition. The primary instrument through which perceived survival knowledge passed from generation to generation. All other efforts incremental. Swallowed by the sheer immensity. And comprehensiveness. Of our problems. Of life. A strong spiritual tradition will permeate every aspect of our lives. All our efforts. Enhanced. Work dem roots, chi'dren. Rootdoctors all.

Not a couple of months, years, or even a lifetime. Orchestrating the tribal soul, you thinking in generations. Longgame.

What we know in our heads, our children will know in their hearts, our generations in their souls.

Rootwork. The thought becomes the act—the act becomes the reality.

•

Shalabongo: Gods-Will be done.

Longgame. Geas by rickydoc: not only responsibility for shaping our own destiny but also responsibility for all the peoples of the planet. Enhancement of the human condition. And even further. The orchestration of cosmic harmony. Spiritual responsibility equals spiritual power. Y'all listen up now. Stay with me. Dis here de old rootdoctor. And he talking big truth: to lead you must serve.

Firstborn. Living ancestors of humanity. Some of the most spiritual people on the planet. But the essence has been warped. Witness dysfunctional cultures and lifestyles.

We must reclaim our legacy as Gods Instrument. Strive to become the most illuminated peoples on the planet. In the cosmos. Humanity's spiritual guides.

The chosen people syndrome.

A greater destiny for all.

Strive, then, o ye firstborn. To be the most righteous peoples on the planet. Gods true chosen. Be ye of the righteous and God shall watch over you with a special care. For God doth love a righteous people.

Oluddumare Mojuba: Gods Blessings on us all.

•

Im from the oldschool. If a race is conquered and oppressed their men were weak. Say what? Thats right. Weak men. Including me.
So just what does it mean to be a strong black man?

Rickydoc's Generic ShortList: *commitment and responsibility. love. compassion. power. quiet composed game. hard, strategic work. right thought, right words, right deeds. magnanimity in abundance. honor. discipline. service. humility. dignity. righteousness. tolerance, tolerance.* I could go on, etc., & on. Basically the old boy scout oath. Basically saying, Carry yourself well, brother.

But in the final analysis I keep getting back to a personal thing. Each man has to decide for himself. In his own context. Just what it means. To be a strong black man.

Heroship in front of the multitudes is easy pickings. The real work of heroship is often done in the quiet spaces. Drudgery. Often alone, unsung, unappreciated, and without pay. Simply because it is the right and righteous thing to do.

History sees everything, God sees all.

·

Flashy myself, I admire the quiet ones. The dependable brothers who. Quietly take care of business. Fathers who stay, love, honor & obey, raise families, man block associations, vote, build institutions. Stable secure types who *do*. The real work.

Me as hero? Well. More joke than not. Artist and mystic. Delta Griot. Bluesman. Hoodooman. Sorcerer & Wouldbe Prophet. Being strong for me just aint the same as for other folk. It aint. I got unique struggles. So I got to assume there is no one way. To be a strong blackman.

Just do it.

·

*Irie. All tings.*

Most folk dont understand good longgame. Cant let that concern you. Got to play for real and not to the gallery. As de High Hoodoo once wrote, "Just cause you cant see the stones dont mean I aint building."

Kinda embarrassing. To be out here. Selling these wolf tickets like this. But thats I job. Both conjuration and ideological orchestration. I got to prepare the ground for my seed, I got to make my trip real in the world, I got to publicly validate the hoodoo way in the world spiritual tradition.

I am. Not only a writer and a spokesperson of my culture and my age. I am. The Voice of Oluddumare.

·

Dont care if you understand it. Dont care if you believe it. Magic and prophecy work both best in the shadows of mystery. Im just a ole regulation delta hoodooman doing my job best I know how. An ideological orchestrator strategically placing my destinic vision into the historical record and leaving a message for future generations:

I am Rickydoc
when you need me
call me
I will come.

# Contributors

HOUSTON A. BAKER, JR., is a professor of English and the Albert M. Greenfield Professor of Human Relations at the University of Pennsylvania, where he also directs the Center for the Study of Black Literature and Culture. Among his many publications are *The Journey Back: Blues, Ideology, and Afro-American Literature*; *Modernism and the Harlem Renaissance*; *Black Studies, Rap and the Academy*; and *Workings of the Spirit*.

AMIRI BARAKA has written twelve volumes of poetry and eight works of nonfiction. His novels are *The System of Dante's Hell* and *Tales*. His many plays have been produced internationally for more than twenty-five years. He has edited a number of anthologies, most notably *Black Fire* and *Confirmation*. He lives in Newark, New Jersey.

DERRICK BELL, author of *Confronting Authority*, *And We Are Not Saved*, and *Faces at the Bottom of the Well*, is currently a visiting professor at New York University Law School.

DON BELTON, author of *Almost Midnight*, teaches at Macalester College. A former reporter for *Newsweek*, he has been a fellow at MacDowell, Yaddo, and the Rockefeller Center in Bellagio, Italy.

CECIL BROWN was born in North Carolina and educated at Columbia University and the University of Chicago. He is the author of three books, including his critically acclaimed novel *The Life and Loves of Mr. Jiveass Nigger*. He recently received his Ph.D. in English and is currently teaching at the University of California at Berkeley.

LOUIS EDWARDS is the author of the novel *Ten Seconds*. He has won both a Guggenheim Fellowship and the Whiting Writer's Award. NAL/Dutton will publish his novel *N* in 1996. He lives in New Orleans, Louisiana.

QUINN ELI, a native of the Bronx, New York, has written about books for *Emerge*, *Black Warrior Review*, and other publications. He is a regular contributor to the *Philadelphia Inquirer* and has recently completed a collection of short stories. He lives in Philadelphia.

TREY ELLIS, the author of *Home Repairs* and *Platitudes*, lives in Santa Monica, California.

ARTHUR FLOWERS is the author of *DeMojo Blues* and *Another Loving Blues*. He teaches writing at Medgar Evers College in Brooklyn, New York.

HENRY LOUIS GATES, JR., is the author of *Colored People* and *The Signifying Monkey*, for which he received an American Book Award. He has edited several works, including *Our Nig* by Harriet Wilson, the thirty-volume *Schomburg Library of Nineteenth Century Black Women's Writings*, and *The Works of Zora Neale Hurston*. He is the W. E. B. DuBois Professor of the Humanities and Chair of the Department of Afro-American Studies at Harvard University.

ESSEX HEMPHILL is the editor of *Brother to Brother: New Writings by Black Gay Men*. He is the author of *Ceremonies: Prose and Poetry*, winner of a 1992 ALA literature award.

ISAAC JULIEN is a critic and filmmaker whose work addresses issues of race and gay sexuality. Among his most recent productions are *Looking for Langston*, *Young Soul Rebels*, *Black and White in Color*, *The Attendant*, and *Darker Side of Black*.

ROBIN D. G. KELLEY is a professor of history and Africana at New York University and the author of *Hammer and Hoe: Alabama Communists During the Great Depression* (1990) and *Race Rebels: Culture, Politics, and the Black Working Class* (1994).

RANDALL KENAN's first novel, *A Visitation of Spirits*, was published in 1989. His collection of stories, *Let the Dead Bury Their Dead*, was nominated for the 1993 National Book Critics Award and won the Whiting Award.

JERROLD LADD is a single parent living in Dallas, Texas. He has written for the *Dallas Morning News*, the *Philadelphia Inquirer*, *Texas Monthly*, and North Carolina's *Sun Magazine*. A commentator for National Public Radio and a recipient of the Robert F. Kennedy Journalism Award, Ladd is the author of *Out of the Madness: From the Projects to a Life of Hope*.

DANY LAFERRIERE was born in Port-au-Prince, Haiti, where he practiced journalism under Duvalier. He went into exile in Canada in 1978. In 1985 he published his first novel, *How to Make Love to a Negro (Without Getting Tired)*, which was a bestseller both in the original French and in English (1987) and was made into a feature film. His other books are *Eroshima* (1991); *An Aroma of Coffee* (1993); and *Dining with the Dictator* (1994). Laferriere now divides his time between Montreal and Miami.

WILLIAM HENRY LEWIS is the author of *In the Arms of Our Elders*, a short story collection. He teaches writing at Mary Washington College in Fredericksburg, Virginia.

REGINALD MCKNIGHT won the O. Henry and the Kenyon Review Award for Literary Excellence for the story "The Kind of Light that Shines on Texas." The author of the novel *I Get on the Bus*, he is also the recipient of a National Endowment for the Arts Grant for Literature. His first collection of short stories, *Moustapha's Eclipse*, was awarded the 1988 Drue Heinz Literary Prize.

HAKI R. MADHUBUTI, writer, poet, and lecturer, is the author of *Black Men: Obsolete, Single, and Dangerous* and the founder of the Third World Press. He is professor of English and director of the Gwendolyn Brooks Center at Chicago State University. Madhubuti lives in Chicago with his wife and children.

CLARENCE MAJOR is the author of five novels, most recently *My Amputations* and *Such Was the Season*, and several volumes of poetry. He is the editor of *Calling the Wind: Twentieth-Century African-American Short Stories*.

BRUCE MORROW is an associate director of the Teachers &Writers Collaborative in New York and an advisory editor of *Callaloo*. Currently, he is coediting an anthology of black gay men's short fiction, to be published by Avon Books in 1996.

WALTER MOSLEY, a native of Los Angeles, now lives in New York City. His first Easy Rawlins mystery, *Devil in a Blue Dress*, was an immediate international success, nominated for an Edgar Award, selected by two book clubs, and published in seven languages. The equally acclaimed *A Red Death*, *White Butterfly*, and *Black Betty* followed. Heralded by President Bill Clinton as his favorite mystery author, Mr. Mosley's next novel is *RL's Dream*. *Devil in a Blue Dress* will soon be a major motion picture starring Denzel Washington.

ALBERT MURRAY is the author of several collections of essays, including *The Omni-Americans* and *Stomping the Blues*, as well as an autobiographical work, *South to a Very Old Place*. He lives in New York City.

DAVID NICHOLSON is an assistant editor of the *Washington Post Book World* and the founding editor of the magazine *Black Film Review*.

RICHARD PERRY is the author of the novels *No Other Tale to Tell* and *Montgomery's Children*. He lives in Englewood, New Jersey.

QUINCY TROUPE is a poet, journalist, and professor of creative writing at the University of California, San Diego, in La Jolla. His essays and articles have appeared in the *Village Voice*, *Spin*, *Musician*, and many other publications. He is the editor of *James Baldwin: The Legacy* and coauthor of the bestselling and award-winning *Miles: The Autobiography*. Troupe is currently at work on a Hollywood film adaptation of the Miles Davis biography.

JOHN EDGAR WIDEMAN is the author of ten highly acclaimed works of fiction, including *Fever*, *Damballah*, *Hiding Place*, *Sent for You Yesterday*, and *Philadelphia Fire*, the last two of which won the prestigious PEN/

Faulkner Award. He is also the author of two works of nonfiction, *Brothers and Keepers* and *Fatheralong* (both National Book Critics Award finalists). He lives in Amherst, Massachusetts.

DENNIS A. WILLIAMS is the author of *Crossover*, a novel, and coauthor with John A. Williams of *If I Stop I'll Die: The Comedy and Tragedy of Richard Pryor*. He teaches writing at Cornell University in Ithaca, New York.

AUGUST WILSON is at work on a series of plays about the black experience in America. He is the recipient of many awards, including Pulitzer Prizes for *Fences* and *The Piano Lesson*. He lives in Seattle, Washington.

JOE WOOD is a writer living in Brooklyn, New York. He writes a column for the *Village Voice* and is the editor of *Malcolm X: In Our Own Image*.

BAKER "On the Distinction of 'Jr.'" by Houston A. Baker, used by permission of the author.

BARAKA "The Black Family" by Amiri Baraka, used by permission of the author.

BELL "The Sexual Diversion: The Black Man/Black Woman Debate in Context" by Derrick Bell, used by permission of the author.

BROWN "Go Home to Your Wife" by Cecil Brown, used by permission of the author.

EDWARDS "Albert Murray on Stage: An Interview" by Louis Edwards, used by permission of the author.

ELI "A Liar In Love" by Quinn Eli, from *Testimony*, edited by Natasha Tarpley. Copyright © 1994 by Natasha Tarpley. Reprinted by permission of Beacon Press.

ELLIS "How Does It Feel to Be a Problem?" by Trey Ellis, reprinted by permission of the author.

FLOWERS "Rickydoc: The Black Man as Hero" by Arthur Flowers, used by permission of the author.

GATES Excerpt from *Colored People* by Henry Louis Gates, Jr. Copyright © 1994 by Henry Louis Gates, Jr. Reprinted by permission of Alfred A. Knopf, Inc.

HEMPHILL & JULIEN Interview with Essex Hemphill by Isaac Julien with Don Belton, used by permission of Essex Hemphill and Isaac Julien.

KELLEY "Confessions of a Nice Negro, or Why I Shaved My Head" by Robin D. G. Kelley, used by permission of the author.

KENAN "Mr. Brown and the Sweet Science" by Randall Kenan, used by permission of the author.

LADD "Cool Brother," excerpt from *Out of the Madness: From the Projects to a Life of Hope*, reprinted by permission of Warner Books/New York. Copyright © 1994 by Jerrold Ladd.